Rescued by...
UNIX

Augie Hansen

JAMSA
P·R·E·S·S
...a computer user's best friend

a division of Kris Jamsa Software, Inc.

Published by
Jamsa Press
2821 High Sail Ct.
Las Vegas, NV 89117
U.S.A.

For information about the translation or distribution of any Jamsa Press book, please write to Jamsa Press at the address listed above.

Rescued by UNIX

Printed in the United States of America.
98765432

ISBN 1-884133-00-2

Publisher
   Debbie Jamsa

Technical Editor
   Kris Jamsa

Copy Editor
   Paul Medoff

Illustrator
   Augie Hansen

Composition
   Kevin Hutchinson

Indexer
   Ken Cope

Cover Design
   Jeff Wolfley & Associates

Cover Photograph
   O'Gara/Bissell

Layout Design
   Discovery Computing, Inc.

Technical Advisor
   Phil Schmauder

Table of Contents

GETTING STARTED
WITH UNIX

Several million computers worldwide run some version of the UNIX System. When you read this, you might reasonably assume that the size of the UNIX user community is dwarfed by that of MS-DOS and its siblings. After all, DOS runs on more that 100 million personal computers. But such numbers can be deceiving.

Taking into account the fact that most UNIX systems serve multiple users, the picture changes dramatically. PC-class microcomputer UNIX systems typically serve from one to 16 simultaneous users via directly connected or dial-up terminals. Larger supermicro- and minicomputer systems can handle scores of users at one time. Mainframes running maxi-UNIX versions easily support hundreds of simultaneous users.

In this section you learn about the UNIX System and how to begin putting it to work for you:

Section One

Lesson 1

What is the UNIX System?

Before you become immersed in the details of using the UNIX System, you should gain some understanding of what the system is. Most UNIX users need to have a basic understanding of the system's external interfaces (how UNIX presents itself to the user). Users who spend the bulk of their time running a single application program (accounting package or spreadsheet, for example) or in a small number of applications can be shielded from the UNIX command line. At the opposite extreme, UNIX system administrators and programmers need extensive knowledge of the user interfaces and varying degrees of knowledge of the inner workings of the system. In this lesson, you take the first steps of your journey to UNIX mastery. You will learn

- What an operating system is
- The benefits and importance of operating systems in general
- The unique position the UNIX System holds in this arena compared to other popular operating systems
- What a user interface is and how UNIX presents itself to the user
- What the two most common interfaces are
- What personal UNIX is

WHAT IS AN OPERATING SYSTEM?

UNIX is an *operating system*, a program (or a collection of programs) that harnesses the power and manages the complexity of computer hardware. The operating system facilitates the construction and execution of other programs, called *applications*, on behalf of the user. It does so by controlling these system resources:

- Central processing unit (CPU)
- Primary memory (random-access memory, RAM)
- Secondary memory (disk, tape, or read-only memory, ROM)
- Other peripheral devices (such as printer, serial communication hardware, or CD-ROM reader)

An operating system provides a set of basic services that handle the messy details of scheduling tasks, loading programs into memory and running them, reading and writing data, providing security, tracking resource usage, and communicating with other systems and remote devices. The *user interface* is the component of an operating system that is seen by users of the computer system. UNIX is primarily known for its aging but effective *command-line interface*. It prompts the user for input in the form of commands, reads the user's commands, and attempts to carry them out.

UNIX also maintains data that defines each user's operating *environment*. The environment is a list of preferences and data values that specify such items as default program behaviors, how often the user's mailbox is checked, the type of terminal being used, and so on. Security is an important aspect of operating system design. However, it is literally missing in some operating systems, such as MS-DOS, the popular single-user system. Multiuser systems provide various security mechanisms that protect each user from all others on the system, and most importantly, protect the system itself from accidental or deliberate attack.

User accounting, another optional feature, tracks each user's use of system resources (CPU time, disk space, and others). It also tracks what commands are run and how often. The accounting data is most often used as a diagnostic tool by system administrators. In some settings it is used to determine cost allocations for billing purposes. Systems that provide user accounting usually give an administrator a way to disable it because the feature can generate reams of data in a very short time.

UNDERSTANDING THE OPERATING SYSTEM

An operating system is one or more programs that oversees the use of your computer's hardware. Specifically, an operating system lets you run programs, store information in files on your disk, print information, and so on. When the computer's power is first turned on, the operating system is the first program that runs. After the operating system is running, it allows you to use your computer. MS-DOS and UNIX are the two most widely used operating systems. MS-DOS is a PC-based operating system that lets one person use the computer at any given time. UNIX, on the other hand, runs on large, medium, and even personal computers. UNIX is a multiuser user operating system which means two or more (up to hundreds) of users can use the same computer at the same time!

THE UNIX SYSTEM

First, let's deal with the name. UNIX is not an acronym, but rather a weak pun on the name Multics, an earlier operating system effort from which important design concepts and system features of UNIX were derived. In effect, UNIX was originally thought of as an emasculated version of Multics (called Unics), but, in time, it has superseded Multics in the marketplace. UNIX could therefore be written as Unix, and sometimes is. The name is usually presented in all capital letters, as it is in this book, following the tradition established in the documentation provided by AT&T and by most current vendors of the system software.

The current implementations of the UNIX System—and there are far too many differing ones—are considerably larger and more comprehensive than the original UNIX developed in the early 1970s at Bell Telephone Laboratories (BTL). However, the underlying elegance and versatility of

UNIX persists. Like wildflowers poking through high mountain tundra, good ideas survive all attempts to "kill" them.

THE DESIGN OF THE UNIX SYSTEM

What most dramatically distinguishes UNIX from its many competitors is its nonproprietary status. Most current operating systems are tied to a specific software vendor. They are usually wedded to a particular processor family as well; DOS on Intel processors is a prime example. When I first encountered UNIX in the late 1970s, while working at BTL, it was already running on a wide range of *hardware platforms* (computers). Its developers had coded most of the system in C, a high-level language that had been developed primarily to make UNIX *portable* (easily implemented on different hardware platforms). Moving to a new platform is possible, although not trivial by any means. UNIX *ports*, as they are called, have been done for almost every computer hardware platform. It even runs on top of other operating systems in some settings.

The essential core of the UNIX operating system is called the *kernel*. It is depicted in Figure 1.1. This is the software layer that interacts most closely with the computer hardware.

The next layer of UNIX software is a collection of user programs, such as the command interpreter, programming tools, utilities, and application programs. Notice that the command interpreter, which implements the user interface and is usually called the *shell*, is simply a user program. It can be replaced by other shells that have different behaviors and present different screen appearances.

This book presents UNIX in its standard command-line interface form because most users still access a UNIX system via remote terminals or from terminal-emulation programs running on personal computers. Even if you have a system that provides a graphical user interface on a directly attached console, it is important that you know how to use the command line and how to create and edit files using traditional tools.

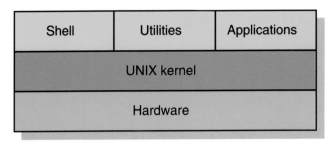

Figure 1.1 The UNIX System is comprised of the kernel system layer atop the hardware, and the application layer, which consists of a command interpreter (shell), system utilities, and other user programs.

UNIX VARIANTS AND WORK-ALIKES

UNIX has been modified and added to by thousands of programmers within what used to be the Bell System and at universities and research organizations around the world. More recently, it has been the subject of intense scrutiny and standardization efforts by various commercial consortia, user groups, and government entities. This has been both a blessing and a curse.

The constant modification of UNIX greatly added to its value for many end-user communities and has kept it fresh over the years. But it also produced a system that lacks a pure identity, leading to confusion in the marketplace. The confusion has been successfully exploited by several purveyors of arguably inferior operating systems that have taken on dominant roles in the desktop operating systems arena. However, UNIX continues to expand its market share well beyond its traditional technical workstation and large system markets as business computer users discover its power and versatility and as UNIX is adapted to serve the needs of the business world.

Many operating systems sold under names other than UNIX are, in fact, its direct descendants. Berkeley UNIX (BSD), Xenix, Sun OS and Interactive UNIX, which Sun now owns, and numerous others are based on the AT&T UNIX source code. That code is now controlled by Novell. Other operating systems are UNIX-like in that they are written from scratch to emulate the behavior of some version of UNIX. Such systems include Coherent, and QNX, among others. You can also get the look and feel of command-line UNIX by using the Hamilton C Shell or the MKS Toolkit on OS/2 and Windows-based systems.

WHAT YOU NEED TO KNOW

This lesson has presented an overview of the UNIX System, its basic design, and its place in the computer operating system market. Lesson 2 describes and compares the newer graphical user interface (GUI) versions of UNIX, which I call "personal UNIX," that can run on personal computers, to the more traditional command-line versions. Before you continue with Lesson 2, make sure that you have learned the following:

- ☑ An operating system is one or more programs that harness the computer's power, letting you run programs, store information in files, and use the computer's hardware such as a printer, keyboard, or terminal.

- ☑ The user interface defines how UNIX presents itself to the user. The two most common interfaces are a text-based command line and a picture-based graphical user interface.

- ☑ In the past, UNIX was used only on large mainframe or minicomputers. With the speed of today's personal computers, UNIX now runs on desktop systems. Such PC-based UNIX versions are often called *personal UNIX*.

Lesson 2

Personal UNIX Systems

Since the arrival on the scene of microcomputers in the mid-1970s, the trend in business was first to ignore them and later to embrace them, supplementing mainframe and minicomputer systems with desktop or deskside computer systems. Nearly two decades after their introduction, micro-computer systems threaten the very existence of big systems in a typical business setting.

The situation in engineering and scientific circles is similar. Batch processing on "big iron" (or large mainframe computers) gave way to high-powered graphics workstations on networks. The UNIX System has held a dominant position in the technical workstation market for many years, handling tasks such as engineering design, drafting, plant management, and scientific analysis.

Although it has been a great success in technical settings, UNIX has had a difficult time compet-ing against DOS- and Windows-based systems in the business office and in the home. Fortunately, this situation is changing. UNIX sales are increasing rapidly as the system continues to evolve into a standard platform that supports popular application programs. In addition to a wealth of pro-gram-development tools, always a strong suit for UNIX, it now supports multiuser versions of word processors, spreadsheets, databases, financial-analysis tools, and many other programs.

In this lesson you will learn

- What hardware you need to run UNIX on a personal computer
- What the command-line interface is
- What a graphical interface, X Window System, client, and server are
- What a window manager is
- How you can run UNIX and DOS-based programs at the same time

The Ubiquitous Command Line

The character-mode command-line interface is the most visible part of the system to most UNIX users. The standard system prompt issued by the shell is a dollar sign followed by a space. (Ken Thompson, the primary creator of UNIX, must have suspected that someone would make some money from his invention.) If you are using a different shell or have modified your prompt string, you might see a different prompt.

You type commands to tell UNIX what you want done. Each command line consists of a program name, which must be the first entry on the line, followed by optional arguments and filenames. The following sample screen shows the appearance of a typical command-line session. The screen uses the symbol ↵ to represent the ENTER or RETURN key being pressed. When you see the symbol within example screens, press ENTER or RETURN depending on your keyboard:

```
           Command prompt
                                         Command name (in lowercase)
  $ pwd ↵                                ENTER key pressed
  /home/arh                              Command result
  $ ls -al ↵                                    Command name (in lowercase)
                                                ENTER key pressed
  total 956                                     Command result
  drwxr-xr-x    6 arh       other        1024 Dec 16 09:44 .
  drwxrwxr-x    5 root      sys            96 Dec 12 09:05 ..
  -rw-r--r--    1 arh       other         681 Dec 14 04:56 .profile
  -rw-------    1 arh       other        1590 Dec 16 17:01 .sh_history
  -rw-r--r--    1 arh       other          64 Dec 10 15:08 .vtlrc
  -rw-r--r--    1 arh       other         531 Dec 10 15:08 .vtlrc.els
  drwxr-xr-x    2 arh       other          96 Dec 14 16:40 admin
  drwxr-xr-x    2 arh       other          96 Dec 14 16:40 bin
  drwxr-xr-x    2 arh       other          96 Dec 14 16:40 letters
  -rw-r--r--    1 arh       other      483179 Dec 16 09:44 rootwin.xwd
  drwxr-xr-x    2 arh       other          96 Dec 14 16:40 src
  $ date ↵                                      Command name (in lowercase)
                                                ENTER key pressed
  Thu Dec 16 17:01:59 MST 1993                  Command result
  $ ▢                                           Flashing cursor
```

*Note: UNIX is sensitive to letter case. Most commands and responses are presented in lowercase letters. Unlike DOS and many other systems, you cannot use uppercase letters when lowercase letters are expected. Thus, typing **LS** to list a directory instead of **ls** will result in an error (the command won't be found).*

To many would-be UNIX users, this kind of interface is simply too cryptic. For them, relief is spelled *G-U-I* (graphical user interface).

PUTTING ON A FRIENDLY FACE

Efforts to make UNIX more friendly have been going on for a number of years. Visual shells were developed to obviate the need to memorize commands. Users point to commands with a light bar controlled by arrow keys or special key codes. Pressing the RETURN (or ENTER key) executes the highlighted command. A virtue of these visual shells is that they can be used on standard character terminals.

The widespread availability of graphics-equipped computer systems has led to other ways for humans to interact with computers. The UNIX System running on workstations and PCs permits direct, speedy access to the console display, making the use of a graphical user interface a practical alternative to the command line.

A graphical user interface for UNIX (and other operating systems) consists of two major components: the *X Window System* (often simply called X), which is a popular network-transparent window system, and a *window manager*. An X *server* on a computer system manages the screen, keyboard, and mouse and their interactions with *client* applications that reside either on the same system or on another computer on a network. Figure 2.1 shows examples of typical UNIX system arrangements.

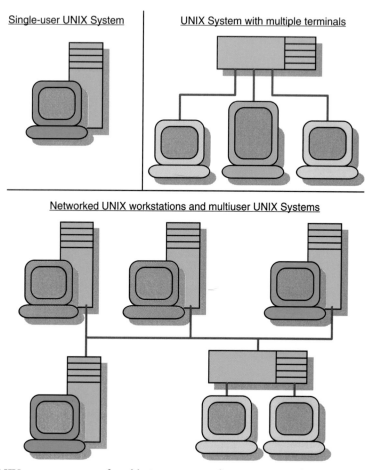

Single-user UNIX System   **UNIX System with multiple terminals**

Networked UNIX workstations and multiuser UNIX Systems

Figure 2.1 UNIX *systems run comfortably in a variety of situations: single-user systems, host systems with users on local or remote terminals, and networked arrangements of workstations and multiuser systems.*

The window manager, a client application, controls the window decorations and behaviors, such as resizing, moving, stacking order of multiple windows. Motif and Open Look are the window managers most often provided with UNIX for graphical environments. Many UNIX system providers deliver more than one window manager, setting one as the system default, and letting the user easily select another.

OSF/Motif

Motif is the most popular window manager. It has gained wide acceptance among users and UNIX vendors other than Sun. Motif is based on work done by members of the Open Software Foundation (OSF). Figure 2.2 is an example of the Motif window manager as implemented on Novell's UnixWare product. Motif is also the interface for Open Desktop (ODT) from the Santa Cruz Operations (SCO).

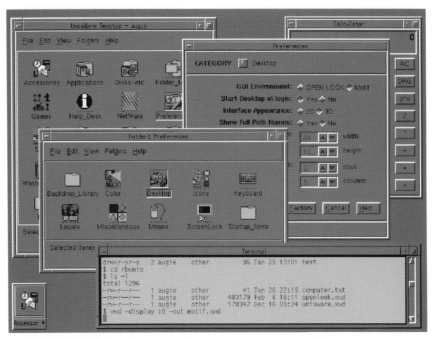

Figure 2.2 The Motif window manager is the most popular with UNIX users. This figure shows the appearance of default Motif interface. Notice the Preferences window that permits selection of the desktop configuration.

The desktop manager imparts what has become known as the "look and feel" of the interface. The screen appearance of Motif varies a bit from one system to another because the desktop manager component is not specified.

OPEN LOOK

Designed by Sun Microsystems and AT&T, Open Look is a comprehensive window manager that incorporates the desktop management component, providing greater consistency from one platform to the next. Figure 2.3 shows the appearance of an Open Look display from the UnixWare product.

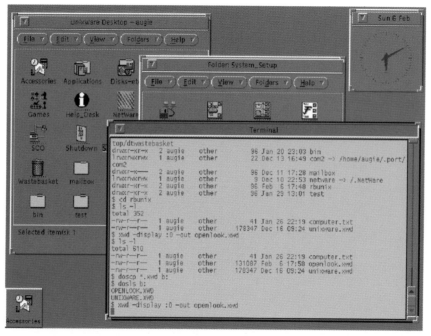

***Figure 2.3** The Open Look window manager is used primarily on Sun workstations and PCs running Solaris. Other vendors supply it as an option. Novell UnixWare is shown here with Open Look as the selected interface.*

The Novell UnixWare product has a split personality. It provides a Motif mode, which is its default graphical user interface mode, and an Open Look mode, which can be selected by the user with a few simple mouse clicks. The selected interface starts the next time the user logs in.

APPLICATION COMPATIBILITY

One of the more attractive features of the personal UNIX systems is their ability to run programs designed for other operating systems. The versions of UNIX designed for the 386- and 486-based systems let you load DOS and Windows applications and run them in windows along side UNIX-specific programs. Some UNIX versions designed for other processor environments provide a DOS-emulation capability for this purpose.

Figure 2.4 depicts a personal UNIX system running DOS-specific and UNIX-specific applications simultaneously. You can copy and cut and paste between applications just as you would under Windows. What is not so apparent is that the system might also be handling electronic mail and printing tasks in the background while serving other users on direct or dial-up lines.

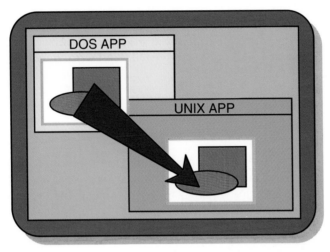

Figure 2.4 DOS application programs can run simultaneously with UNIX programs on personal UNIX systems. You can even cut and paste and copy between applications of the two environments by using the clipboard.

Understanding the Graphical User Interface

With the power of today's graphics workstations, many systems run UNIX using a graphical user interface, which presents UNIX programs within windows on your screen. To work with a specific window, you simply select the desired window with your mouse or keyboard commands. As you work, you may have several programs running simultaneously within different windows. Displaying UNIX programs within multiple windows in this way is much like have several different terminals or computers on your desk.

The UNIX graphical interfaces are noticeably different than those of Microsoft Windows or the Macintosh. The trend is toward a common interface that presents to the user a consistent, predictable, and comfortable operating environment. Someday soon, you may neither know nor care which operating system lurks behind that pretty face—as long as it helps you get your work done, it shouldn't matter.

PAYING THE PIPER

Friendlier UNIX is certainly a boon to many computer users who were intimidated by the operating system in its earlier incarnations. But what's the cost? Is it worth paying?

The hardware requirement for a DOS-plus-Windows system, if it is to run reasonably well, is currently 4Mb of RAM or more and an 80386 or better microprocessor running at 25 MHz or faster.

Current versions of OS/2 and UNIX run acceptably in 8MB of RAM. For multiuser UNIX systems, you should add about 2MB per additional user to maintain reasonable performance. Windows NT, positioned by Microsoft primarily as an application server, needs 12Mb minimum (16Mb or more recommended). All things considered, UNIX makes rather efficient use of system resources.

WHAT YOU NEED TO KNOW

The UNIX operating system runs on large, medium, and as your learned in this lesson, even personal computers. Before you can use a UNIX-based system, you must have a user account. In Lesson 3 you will learn how to log into UNIX using your account name. Before you continue with Lesson 3, make sure you understand the following topics:

☑ Due to the power of today's PCs, UNIX can now run well on small desktop computers. Such PC-based implementations of UNIX are often called personal UNIX.

☑ The user interface defines how UNIX presents itself to the user. Many UNIX systems offer both command-line interfaces, where you type commands at a prompt, and picture-based graphical user interfaces.

☑ Virtually all personal UNIX systems let you run DOS, Windows, and UNIX programs simultaneously.

☑ A graphical user interface for UNIX (and other operating systems) consists of two major components: the X Window System (often simply called X), which is a popular network-transparent window system, and a window manager.

☑ Don't let names such as OS/F, Motif, or X confuse you. For most user purposes, UNIX is UNIX. Your primary concern should be whether your system is using a command-line or graphical user interface.

Lesson 3

User Accounts and Security

A multiuser operating system must afford each user protection from all other users. In addition, the operating system must protect itself by keeping would-be intruders at bay. In this lesson you will learn:

- How UNIX protects itself
- What a user account is and how to get one
- What a good account name (or username) is
- What a system account is and how it differs from a user account
- Who the superuser is and the operations the superuser performs
- What a password is and what makes good and bad passwords
- Who is responsible for system security

As a first step, UNIX controls access by using unique *user accounts*. Before you can use a UNIX system, you will need to obtain your own user account. To get an account, see your system administrator. If you run a personal UNIX system and are your own administrator, you can use administration tools during installation or at any later time to add user accounts for yourself and others.

UNIX USER ACCOUNTS

UNIX is a *multiuser* operating system, which means two or more users can use UNIX at the same time. Each user on a UNIX system has an account that is identified by a unique *account name*. Associated with the name is a password entry that should be known only by the user. If additional security is needed, additional passwords can be put in place by a system administrator to control external access.

ACCOUNT NAMES

An account name, also known as a *username*, is usually personalized. This is the name by which the system and any users will know you. You can tell all your friends and associates your user account name—they can use it to send you electronic mail or to correspond with you in other ways. The system administrator will be able to track your use of the system resources through this name. Typical account names are formed from:

- The user's first name or nickname (such as augie).

- The user's initials (such as arh).

- The user's first name and last initial (such as augieh).

- The user's first initial and last name (such as ahansen).

The naming scheme used is often specified by some institutional policy that is implemented by a system administrator. Of course, variances must be allowed to avoid duplicate account names.

PASSWORDS

A *password* is a sequence of characters that must contain at least two alphabetic characters (mixed cases allowed) and at least one digit or other nonalphabetic character. A password must be at least three characters long, and only the first eight characters are significant. You cannot use your account name as a password, nor any rotation of it. The purpose of the password is to allow you *and only you* to access the system through your terminal, thus ensuring the safety of your files.

In choosing a password, keep the following guidelines in mind:

- Avoid obvious words (spouse's name, pet's name, your phone number or birthday, and so on).

- Choose a sequence that is memorable so that you won't feel compelled to write it anywhere.

To ensure that another user has not learned your password and can access the system, you should change your password at least once a month. In some cases, your system administrator will activate *password aging*. The aging mechanism forces you to change your password periodically. The aging period is set by a system administrator. In addition, after you install or change your password, you are prevented from changing it again for some time, typically two weeks. You will learn more about user accounts and passwords in Lesson 5.

SYSTEM ACCOUNTS

Every UNIX system has reserved accounts that are used for various system administration tasks. The reserved accounts are generally called *superuser* accounts because of the power their users obtain. They are needed because tasks associated with system installation, maintenance, and repair require the ability to "go anywhere and do anything". Because of security restrictions placed on them, ordinary users can neither roam freely around the system nor change system files and directories.

The most powerful of the reserved accounts is **root**. Anyone logged in as **root** has the authority to view and modify files anywhere on the system. It is important that the root account not fall into the wrong hands. Other superuser accounts include **adm**, **bin**, **uucp**, and **sysadm**. If you are going to be responsible for system administration, consult your system documentation.

UNDERSTANDING USERNAMES AND PASSWORDS

To access a UNIX system, you must have a user account name and a password. You can tell all your friends and associates your user account name—they will use the account name to send you electronic mail or to correspond with you in other ways. Do not give another your user your password, ever, period. If a user knows your account name and password, they can access the system as you. They can send electronic mail on your behalf, read your existing mail, and even remove all of your disk files from the system.

Warning: Do not give your password to another user for any reason—ever. If another user requests your password, notify your system administrator. Do not share your account with another user.

A USER'S SECURITY RESPONSIBILITIES

The security of a computer system must be maintained at two levels: *physical security* and *logical security*. Physical security is a management and administration responsibility. It is obtained by using equipment and facilities that prevent intrusion. Locked and guarded facilities are commonly employed in big business, government, and military settings.

Logical security is a shared responsibility among all system users. It involves the use of password-controlled accounts as described in this lesson and various other mechanisms, such as file permissions, periodic system audits, and others.

As a user, you can do several things to help maintain a secure system:

- Choose a good password and keep it private.

- If you believe that someone has obtained your password, change it and notify your system administrator.

- Don't leave your terminal or workstation unattended without either locking it or logging off.

- Use file permissions to control access to your files and directories (see Lesson 12).

System security considerations are summarized graphically in Figure 3.1. No system can be made perfectly secure, but by using the tools available and by applying common sense and diligence, you can keep your system safe.

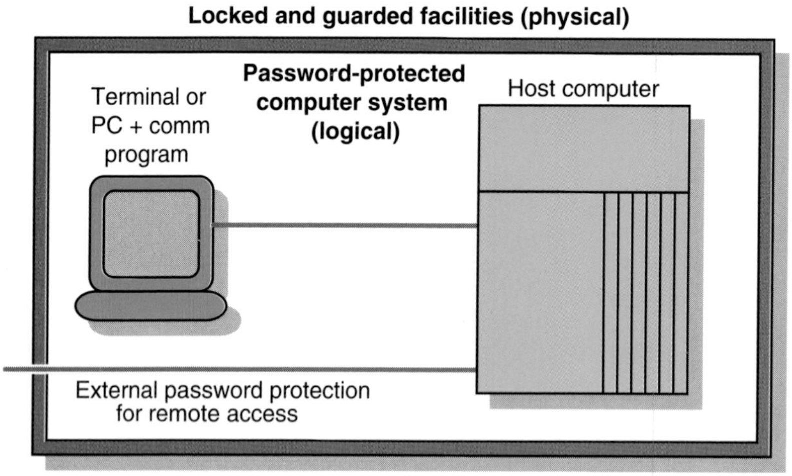

Locked and guarded facilities (physical)

Terminal or
PC + comm
program

**Password-protected
computer system
(logical)**

Host computer

External password protection
for remote access

Figure 3.1 System security has both physical and logical components.

What You Need to Know

If you are using a workstation or a personal UNIX system, you can probably just log in. If you are accessing a UNIX system from a terminal or from a communication program on a different system there is the matter of establishing communications with the UNIX host. That is the subject of the next lesson.

Before attempting to log in, you should understand the following:

- ☑ Each UNIX user must have his or her own unique account name. Account naming is the responsibility of the system administrator.

- ☑ Every user account has its own name, by which its user is known to the system and other users. Your friends can use this name as an address for electronic mail. This name should be easy to remember and similar to your name.

- ☑ Every user account should be protected by a password. Use care in choosing passwords to be sure they are not obvious or otherwise easily cracked. *Keep passwords private.*

- ☑ System security is everybody's responsibility. Follow suggested practices to maintain both physical and logical security.

Lesson 4

Making Connections

A computer running UNIX provides several ways to access the system. You either access the computer system hardware directly or via an external connection (dial-up or hardwired). If you can already successfully access your UNIX system by simply typing at your keyboard, you might want to continue your reading with Lesson 5. If you are trying to connect to UNIX over telephone lines, read this lesson carefully—it contains the secrets you need! In this lesson you will learn

* What the system console is and how it is used

* What is required to make dial-up connections for remote access

* Which communication parameters local and remote systems must match

* The requirements for a hardwired terminal

THE SYSTEM CONSOLE

If you are fortunate enough to be using a workstation or a personal computer running UNIX, you probably have access to the *system console*. The system console consists of directly connected display and keyboard devices, offering the speediest response possible. On graphical systems, a *pointing device* (mouse or trackball) is used for selecting and executing programs and controlling the appearances of displayed windows, as shown in Figure 4.1.

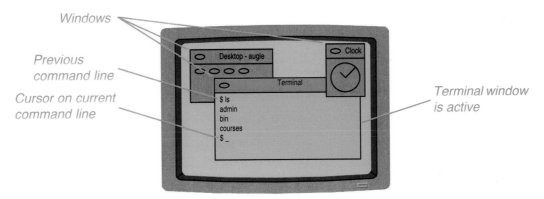

Figure 4.1 *The best situation for a UNIX user is access to the system console (display, keyboard, and pointing device) because this arrangement provides the speediest and most natural interaction with the computer.*

Even if you are using the system console in the graphical mode, you might find it necessary or desirable to use an alphanumeric terminal (uses the command line) for some tasks. One of the items available on the desktop is a terminal window. For all intents and purposes, it looks and acts like an alphanumeric terminal.

If your computer is connected to a network and is running X Window System support, you can run application programs that reside on other machines as if they were on your own machine— and, of course, other users can access programs on your machine. Users can also choose whether to share data on the network or block access to it. Whether you choose to share files or not, data access is controlled by *file permissions*, described in detail in Lesson 12.

Figure 4.2 depicts a portion of a network on which users at workstations share resources. A *process* is a running program. In the figure, one system is running a window manager, such as Motif or Open Look, and an application program, say a word processor. Another user on the network is able to run the program because his or her system is running an X *server*, which provides the screen, keyboard, and mouse services needed by the application program, the *client*.

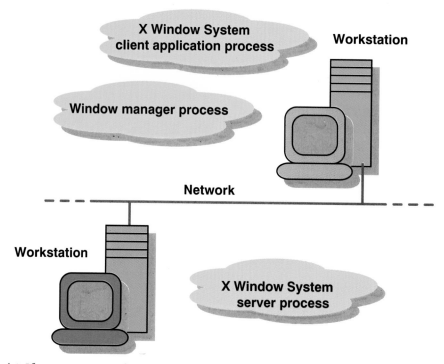

Figure 4.2 If you are connected to a network running the X Window System, you can easily share programs with other users. Each system runs a server, which manages the keyboard, mouse, and screen. The applications are clients on the network.

DIAL-UP CONNECTIONS

A large number of UNIX users access their systems via public and private telephone networks. Many are telecommuters who happily substitute "connect time" for "drive time." Others keep in touch with the home office while traveling to trade shows, meetings, or other events. Figure 4.3 depicts an alphanumeric terminal display that is typical of the millions in current use with UNIX systems around the world.

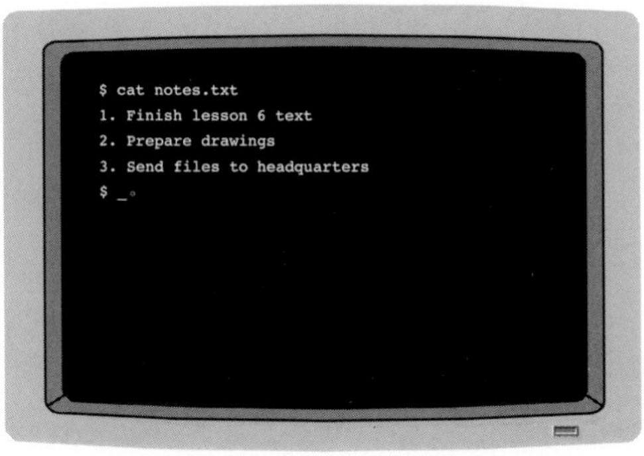

```
$ cat notes.txt
1. Finish lesson 6 text
2. Prepare drawings
3. Send files to headquarters
$ _
```

Figure 4.3 *Alphanumeric terminals, although they produce a rather stark-looking display, continue to provide the primary means of access to UNIX systems for the majority of users.*

This technology is certainly one of the most efficient and cost-effective computing solutions available. Contrast a UNIX system that serves, say, eight users on a PC-class machine with the alternative of eight separate PCs, one for each user. Most of the time, the single-user systems are doing nothing very fast, waiting for the users to type something.

Connecting a terminal to a remote computer over a telephone network is a bit more difficult than tying your shoes, but anyone can do it. The process of connecting involves the use of *data terminal equipment* (DTE), which is at the end of the line, *data communication equipment* (DCE), which is in the middle doing the communicating, and some cables. A typical connection is shown in Figure 4.4. Don't let the terms scare you off. Learn them and you'll knock the socks off the sales rep at your local hardware emporium.

To communicate over phone lines, your terminal must be cabled, through a serial port, to a *modem* (**mo**dulator/**dem**odulator), which *modulates* a computer's digital data into the analog signals suitable for transmission over a telephone network. At the other end, the other computer uses a modem to *demodulate* the analog signal back into the digital signals that computers understand. As a user, you need be concerned only with the hardware on the left side of the figure and which number to call to access the host computer system. Unless you are your own administrator, someone else enjoys the many pleasures of setting up the host system.

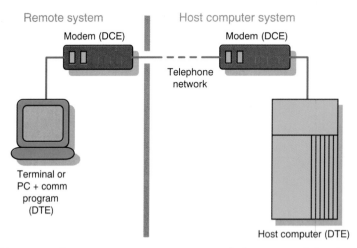

Figure 4.4 *Making connections to a computer system over a telephone network involves the use of signal converters called modems (modulator/demodulator). One is needed at each end of the connection.*

The cable that connects a terminal to a modem contains wires for data in and out, several control signals, and a ground return lead. This is called a *serial data cable* or a *modem cable*, and is readily available at computer and electronic stores (soon to be in grocery stores everywhere!). There is some variation among systems, so you need to consult the documentation for your terminal (or computer) and modem to determine which cable to use or find out how to wire one yourself.

Serial devices differ from parallel devices in that, instead of sending bytes of data over eight separate wires (one wire for each bit) simultaneously, they send all the data in a *series* over one wire. This creates a traffic problem that requires the sending and receiving machines to agree on certain communication parameters, such as how to tell when one byte stops and the next one starts. Therefore, you might also need to configure your modem, either by adjusting switches (or jumpers) or by using software to control settings. Here again, there is no hard and fast rule. UNIX systems originally required the following settings:

- Full duplex
- One stop bit
- 7-bit data
- XON/XOFF flow control
- No parity

This combination of data bits, parity, and stop bits is usually abbreviated to read 7-N-1. A commonly used combination today is 8-N-1, which means eight-bit data, no parity, and one stop bit. The important thing is that the values you set on your end of the connection match those used at the other end.

DIRECT CONNECTIONS

If your terminal is within a short distance (up to a thousand feet or so) of the host computer, you can use a direct, hardwired connection, which is much faster than communication through a modem. In this setting you have terminal equipment on both ends. No modems are needed, but you do need to obtain the correct wire connection. The output lead (data transmit) from one device must be connected to the input (data receive) lead of the other and vice versa. The signal ground lead must also be connected. It is not usually necessary to connect the control signals, but some systems might require it.

A handy way to achieve the needed swapping of signal leads is to use a straight-through cable together with a *null-modem block*. The null-modem block obviates the need to buy a special cable or modify a perfectly good standard cable. It puts the changeover in a convenient, small package that can be easily inserted or removed as dictated by a particular installation. This type of connection is illustrated in Figure 4.5.

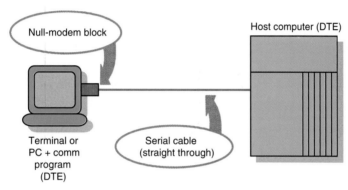

Figure 4.5 *Use a null-modem block in series with a standard (straight-through) serial cable when connecting two DTE devices.*

WHAT YOU NEED TO KNOW

This lesson has shown you how to make connections. Before trying to log in, which is described in the next lesson, be sure you understand the following points:

☑ The system console is directly connected to the computer (PC or workstation) and provides the best response.

☑ Dial-up connections for remote access require the use of modems. The local and remotes systems must have matching communication parameters (data bits, parity, stop bits, and speed). Use full duplex and XON/XOFF flow control.

☑ A hardwired terminal does not require modems, but it needs either special crossover wiring or a straight-through cable with a null-modem block.

Lesson 5

Logging In and Logging Out

As soon as you have obtained a user account (see Lesson 3) and established connections (see Lesson 4), you can log in and begin using UNIX. This lesson shows you how to

- Perform the steps to log in to the system

- Try a few simple commands to explore your surroundings

- Log out from the system when you are done working

- Understand differences in login and logout procedures between users on the system console, workstation or hardwired terminals, and dial-up modems

In the material that follows, and throughout the rest of this book, samples of the terminal screens show user inputs and program responses. User input at the command line is always terminated by pressing RETURN (called ENTER on PC keyboards and some terminals). In the screen samples, the symbol ↵ stands for the RETURN key.

To show you as accurately as possible what appears on screen, the samples also show the prompt line that returns after a program completes its work. The line includes the cursor, shown by the ❏ symbol (visualize it as a blinking block).

LOGGING IN

Logging in is the process of starting a UNIX session. To log in, you must provide information that lets UNIX verify that you have a valid account on the system. You are prompted, in turn, for your account name and your password. If either one of your responses is incorrect, your attempt to log in is rejected. You are not told which entry was wrong; only that the login attempt failed. The system then prompts you again for a login name.

If you fail five times in a row, the system delays for a while before restarting the login sequence. This delay mechanism is designed to thwart those who would try to access a UNIX system by "cracking" a password (repeated login attempts with a computer-generated set of passwords).

There are some differences between logging into a computer from directly connected devices and logging in remotely. Let's examine each separately.

FROM THE CONSOLE, WORKSTATION, OR A HARDWIRED TERMINAL

When you begin working at the system console, or at a workstation or a hardwired terminal, you probably see a login prompt already displayed. If you don't, press the RETURN key one or more times until you do. Then key in your account name and press RETURN.

The system then prompts for a password. As you type your password, nothing is echoed to the display (what you type is not printed on your screen). This prevents someone from seeing the number of characters in the password, information that could help them crack it. (Some systems echo dots or asterisks as you key in the password—not a good design.)

This is the appearance of the screen as user **arh** logs onto a UNIX system called **mars** (some vendor-specific notices have been edited out to make these sessions as generic as possible):

```
login: arh ↵ ─────────────────────────────────── Account name
Password: ↵ ─────────────── Password does not appear as you type it
UNIX System V/386 Release 4.2 │                   System information and
mars                          │                   system name (mars)


Welcome to the Omniware computer network. │
Your system administrator is Augie Hansen. │ ──── Welcome message
$ ☐ ──────────────────────────────────────────── System prompt
```

If both of your responses are correct, as in the example, you are greeted by some startup messages and the system prompt. In Lesson 8 you will learn how to organize the files you store on disk using directories. A directory is best viewed as a drawer within a filing cabinet, within which you store files. To keep your files separate from other users, each user is given his or her own directory (called the home directory). When you log into UNIX, you are placed in your home directory—your starting point and primary operating location when you access UNIX.

*Note to System Administrators: The two-line welcome message comes from a file named **motd**, which stands for "message of the day." The system administrator creates this message by editing the file, which starts out as a zero-length (empty) file. This is the electronic equivalent of the Welcome Wagon. The administrator can change the message as often as necessary to give users up-to-date system information each time they log in.*

FROM A DIAL-UP TERMINAL

The process of logging in from a remote terminal or computer over a dial-up line is largely the same as described for direct connections. However, you need to establish a connection first. The UNIX host may be set to communicate at, say, 9600 bps, as a default, but most systems will cycle through a range of transmission rates to match the speed of a caller's system.

If you don't get a login prompt right away, try pressing the BREAK key a time or two. The BREAK key produces an attention-getting signal that should wake up a device that is stuck or inattentive. It is a physical key on most terminals. Terminal-emulator programs usually assign the break signal to the CONTROL-BREAK key combination on a PC (or they let you specify a key to use for this purpose).

Note: On many keyboards, the CONTROL key appears as simply CTRL, which is used in this book.

If you still get no response, or if you see garbled characters on your display, you may have incorrectly set some communication parameters in the modem or in your terminal device. Correct the problem and try to log in again.

External access is one of the potential holes in a system's security, so many administrators set up an external password to be used by anyone calling from a remote location. The password is usually changed at least once a month. If the system you are calling requires it, you will see a third prompt:

```
External Password:□
```

If you don't know the external password, contact the administrator (or just give up and read a good book).

LOGGING OUT

In the lessons that follow you will spend time cruising around the system and learning about UNIX files and commands. For now, though, you will terminate the current session by *logging out*.

To log out, you can use the **exit** command. This is a command that is built into the UNIX shell. It causes an immediate termination of the currently running program, which in this case is your login shell.

```
$ exit ↵
```

An alternative that works on most systems is to press CTRL-D (press CTRL and the d key simultaneously; then release both). This key combination sends a code that stops a running program, such as your shell. The display of control codes on screen often shows the letter as a capital, such as CTRL-D, but you can press the key either SHIFTed or unSHIFTed.

A NOTE TO SYSTEM CONSOLE USERS

Logging out terminates your session, but it does not stop the operating system. Don't turn off the power to the computer unless you go through a formal shutdown sequence. There are several reasons for doing this:

- The system might still be serving other users. Killing the system while they are still logged in is antisocial behavior.

- The system could lose data if you don't give it a chance to save buffered data to disk.

- Some activities run as background tasks. They must be terminated in an orderly manner.

To perform a shutdown, you must be logged in either as **root** or (starting with System V, Release 4) as the system owner. In the following example, the prompt is a crosshatch (#), which is the standard **root** prompt. Type the command:

```
# shutdown ↵
# ❏
```

A system-dependent grace period, usually in the range of 5–10 minutes, is allowed for logged-in users to save their work and log out. They receive periodic broadcast messages on the screen that inform them of impending doom.

If you are the only active user, you can skip the grace period by entering the command option of **–g0** (that's dash-g-zero):

```
# shutdown -g0 ↵
# ❏
```

This form of the command effectively shortens the grace period to 0, invoking an immediate shutdown. When the shutdown sequence completes, you receive a message that tells you it is safe to turn off the power or reboot.

A Note to Workstation and Hardwired Terminal Users

Depending on how the system is configured, a directly-connected terminal device exhibits one of the following behaviors:

- It reissues the log-in prompt. The device is ready to be used again, either by you or another user.

- It appears to stop dead. If you (or another user) want to log in, press the BREAK key a few times until you see a login prompt.

In either case, if no one plans to use the terminal, you can simply turn it off.

A Note to Dial-up Terminal Users

If you were logged in over a dial-up connection, you are apt to see a status message, a sign that the connection has been broken:

```
NO CARRIER
```

At this point you can turn off your terminal or terminate your communication program. When you want to log in again, you'll have to redial.

Understanding a UNIX Session

As you have learned, to access a UNIX system you must first log in by typing your account name and password at the UNIX login prompts. After you successfully log on, you can issue a command by typing the command name at the system prompt and pressing Return or Enter.

When you are done using the system, you need to log out by typing the **exit** command or by pressing the CTRL-D keyboard combination.

Warning: Never walk away from a system that you are currently logged into. In the few moments that you are away from your desk, another user can read all of your electronic mail or even remove all the files from your disk. If you are going to be away from your keyboard, log out or lock your terminal.

What You Need to Know

To issue commands, you normally type the command name at the UNIX command prompt. Lesson 6 examines such operations in detail. Before moving on to the next lesson, be sure that you have learned the following:

- ☑ You need a login name and a matching password to gain access to a UNIX system.

- ☑ Some system administrators require an additional password for external access of any kind (direct wire or remote dial-up).

- ☑ Remote access via modem might require that you press the BREAK key a few times to force the modems to synchronize.

- ☑ Type **exit** or press CTRL-D to log out.

- ☑ If you are using the system console, don't shut off the power without first doing a controlled shutdown.

Lesson 6

The UNIX System Command Line

The primary purpose of this book is to show you how to use command-line UNIX. Even if you use a graphical system and spend most of your time pointing and clicking, there are going to be times when you need to operate from a remote terminal or use a terminal window on your desktop system. Under these circumstances, you work with a command-line oriented shell, which is a traditional UNIX user-interface program. In this lesson you will learn

- What the command line is

- How to enter commands in UNIX

- The proper syntax for UNIX commands, including options, parameters, and arguments

- How to edit your command-line entries

USING THE COMMAND LINE

You use the command line to tell the UNIX system what you want it to do. The command line is where the system displays a *prompt string* (the default is "$ " for users and "# " for administrators, although these can be changed). It is also where you type your commands. Given that the system is not always able to oblige, some users are inclined to call their inputs *requests*.

COMMAND-LINE SYNTAX

When you log in, UNIX runs a program called the *shell*, which is a *command interpreter*. It displays the command prompt on your screen and then waits for you to type commands. The form of the command you type must match the pattern expected by the command interpreter (the shell). Figure 6.1 shows the general form of a command.

Only the program name component is required in most cases. Most programs accept *options* to alter or refine their behaviors, and many expect the name of a file or a list of files upon which to perform their actions. Italics are used to identify *placeholder variables*. These are generic names that you replace with actual values when you type your commands. The square brackets are called *delimiters*. They identify optional components of the command. You don't type the square brackets in your commands.

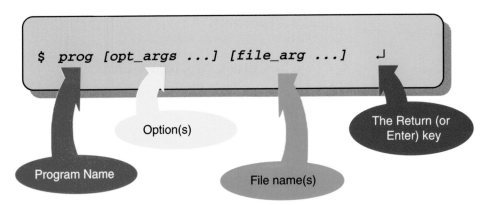

Figure 6.1 A command fits this general form. The program name is a required component of all commands. Options, when used, alter the basic program operation. Filename arguments specify the items to be created, read, or modified.

The shell doesn't see any part of your command until you type the whole command and press the RETURN key (on PCs and some terminals, this key is labeled ENTER). To emphasize the fact that this string is a label on a keycap and is therefore, a single keypress, the label is usually presented with surrounding angle brackets or in SMALL CAPS. As Lesson 5 noted, this book uses the ↵ symbol to mean "press the RETURN key." Let's begin by working with programs that do their basic jobs when summoned by name only. Then we'll use more complex commands by adding options and filename arguments.

PROGRAM NAME

The design of the UNIX shell adheres to a basic tenet: The default behavior of a program (no options specified) should satisfy the needs of most users most of the time. When you key in a command, the shell attempts to find the program specified by the command, loads it into memory, and runs it. For example, the **date** command displays both the current date and time.

```
$ date ↵ ———— Command name
Thu Dec 16 15:17:09 MST 1993 ———— Command output
$ ▢
```

If the program cannot be found, as would be the case if you mistyped its name, the shell displays an error message:

```
$ datr ↵ ———— Misspelled command
sh: datr:  not found ———— Error message
$ ▢
```

The error message contains useful information: the name of the program sending the message (**sh**, the shell), the command you typed (**datr**), and a description of the problem. The "not found" message could be due to other reasons, such as a correctly spelled name for a program that is not installed on your system.

Note: Keep in mind that UNIX considers upper- and lowercase letters to be distinct. Thus, if you issue the **date** command as **DATE**, UNIX will display the "not found" error message.

The **who** command, sans arguments, tells you who is logged in to the system. The output shows for each users the login name, how the user is logged in, and the starting date and time of the current login session, as in this example:

```
$ who ↵
augie          console        Dec 18 21:36
arh            tp/12          Dec 18 16:26
$ ▢
```

Here, I am logged in at the system console using one login name and into a hardwired terminal using another.

If you want information only about your current login session, you can provide some optional arguments. The **who** command was written to understand the arguments "**am i**" (or "**am I**"), which restricts output to information about the user making the request.

```
                     ┌────────── Command name
                   ┌─┴──────── Optional arguments
$ who  am  i ↵
arh            tp/12              Dec 18 16:26
$ ▢
```

Most UNIX commands follow a convention that optional arguments begin with a dash (or minus sign, if you prefer) to distinguish such arguments from filenames, but the **who** command and several others vary from the convention to permit this kind of silliness. The **who** command also accepts certain options with the leading dash. For example, the –H option causes the command to print headers over each of the output columns:

```
                 ┌──────── Precede a command option with a dash
$ who  -H ↵
NAME           LINE           TIME
augie          console        Dec 18 21:36
arh            tp/12          Dec 18 16:26
$ ▢
```

Most command options are specified by the use of single digits or letters, such as the one just described. Like the English language, UNIX has almost as many exceptions as rules, so there are commands that have full-text options (for example, `find / -name filename -print`), some that use a plus sign as a lead character for options (`chmod +x filename`), and so on. Don't fret about this situation and don't worry about what these commands mean. Most of these exceptions make sense in context, as you will see in later lessons.

Most commands deal with files in some way. Filename arguments identify files or directories that are to be used or manipulated in some way by a command. For example **ed books.lst** is a command that edits a file called **books.lst**. This command is not modified by any options, so it runs with its default behavior. If given the option –s option, the **ed** editor, known for being rather terse

29

in its default configuration, becomes virtually silent because the option means "suppress messages" about file size and other status information. The command with the option looks like this: **ed —s books.txt**. (See Section 4 for instructions on the use of the **ed** editor.)

CORRECTING TYPING ERRORS

As you type commands, you will probably make typing mistakes. If you detect the error before pressing RETURN, you can back up, fix it, and continue typing your command. If you press RE-TURN before noticing the error, the shell will try to execute the badly formed command. If you mistype a character or a sequence of characters, use the *erase key*, which is usually the BACKSPACE key (symbolized by the sequence ^h, ^H, CTRL-H, or CTRL-h, but this is a single keypress combination, not two). If your terminal has no separate BACKSPACE key, press the **h** key while holding down the CTRL key and then release both. If you press the erase key repeatedly (or hold it down continuously to engage the autorepeat feature of the terminal), you can erase character sequences.

Another key, called the *kill key* or the *line kill key*, is used to erase the entire current line of input. The default value for the kill key is the @ key (usually a SHIFT- **2**), but some systems use CTRL-U (symbolized as ^u or ^U). You can use the **stty** command to find out what your settings are.

```
$ stty -a ↵
speed 9600 baud;
intr = DEL; quit = ^|; erase = ^h; kill = @;
...
$ ☐
```

The ellipsis replaces a lot of output that would serve only to confuse you at this point. Notice the values shown for the erase and kill keys. If you prefer other values, you can set them by using **stty**, but we'll deal with configuration in Lesson 18.

WHAT YOU NEED TO KNOW

This lesson presents vital information about the command line. In Lesson 7 you will learn ways to troubleshoot errors that can occur when you connect to and use a UNIX system. Before you continue with Lesson 7, make sure you have learned the following:

☑ The command line's prompt-and-reply mechanism is your means of interacting with the standard UNIX shells. Even when there are friendly graphical interfaces available, you might still find that some tasks are best done from the command line because the power and flexibility of the shell language give you great leverage.

☑ The format of a command line is rigid, with the program name as the first component, followed by option arguments and then filename arguments.

☑ The erase and kill keys provide minimal editing capabilities during command-line input.

Lesson 7

Troubleshooting

For any activity, getting started is usually the hard part. Once you're on the move, you can establish momentum, gain ground rapidly, and feel like you're making progress. So it is with learning to use a computer operating system.

This lesson is designed to help you resolve the common problems that occur when you attempt to connect, log in, and use a UNIX system. By the time you finish this lesson you will know how to resolve errors such as the following:

- Your screen displays garbled or meaningless letter combinations

- Your screen double-spaces output

- Your screen displays all output in uppercase

- You cannot log into the system or you don't remember your password

CONNECTION PROBLEMS

One of the stumbling blocks for new UNIX users occurs before they type their first characters. Lesson 4 describes the basic access situations and methods of connecting. Review that material to be sure you have done the required setup and cabling.

If you are connecting from a hardwired or dial-up terminal, you might experience garbled displays, double-spaced output, or double characters in displays. These problems are all due to incorrect settings of your terminal device and are easily corrected. If you experience the ALL CAPS NIGHTMARE, there is really nothing wrong; it just doesn't look right and makes keying a bit difficult. There is a simple cause and an equally simple solution.

GARBLED DISPLAY

If you see garbage like this on your display when you attempt to log in, you have a *transmission rate mismatch*:

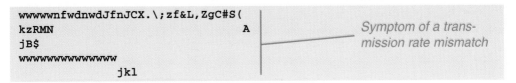

```
wwwwwnfwdnwdJfnJCX.\;zf&L,ZgC#S(
kzRMN                          A
jB$
wwwwwwwwwwwww
          jkl
```

Symptom of a transmission rate mismatch

Although most systems are set up to adjust their transmission speed to match that of an incoming caller's signal, some are set to a single speed and will not try to synchronize.

If this happens, disconnect (turn off and restart the terminal or modem), find out which speed you should be using, and retry.

Another source of garbled displays is an incorrect word size (data bits) or parity setting. The ASCII character set is a 7-bit encoding of symbols. If you are using a terminal or a terminal-emulation program that uses an extended (8-bit) character set, you could see weirdness like this:

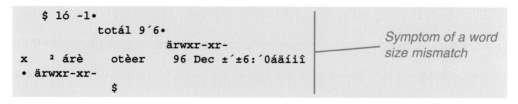

Displays like this mean that your terminal is displaying the extended character set. Change your terminal settings to 7-E-1 (7 data bits, even parity, 1 stop bit), or turn on a feature that filters out the high bit, and the display should become readable.

DOUBLE-SPACED OUTPUT

If your display is double-spaced (one clear line separating each pair of displayed lines), your terminal device is inserting extra linefeeds (<LF>):

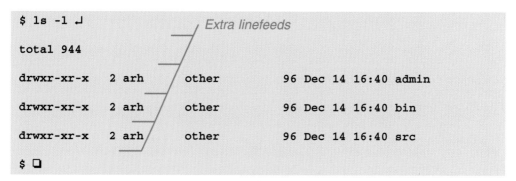

Check your terminal or emulator to see if incoming carriage returns (<CR>) are being expanded to <CR><LF>. If so, disable this feature.

DOUBLE CHARACTERS

If the commands you type have you seeing double, you have *local echo* enabled on your terminal or emulation program. The system responses look right, but your keystrokes are doubled:

```
$ ppwwdd ↵              ───── Double character display on input
/home/arh
$ ☐
```

With local echo on, your terminal displays what you type as you type it; then UNIX receives the character and echoes it to your display, effectively doubling your input, but not your fun.

Set the terminal device to local echo off to clear this problem.

EVERYTHING DISPLAYS IN UPPERCASE

Here's one that might surprise you the first time it occurs. You get logged in all right, but all text is displayed in uppercase letters and you see a lot of backslashes:

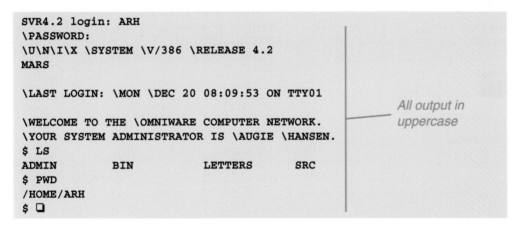

```
SVR4.2 login: ARH
\PASSWORD:
\U\N\I\X \SYSTEM \V/386 \RELEASE 4.2
MARS

\LAST LOGIN: \MON \DEC 20 08:09:53 ON TTY01
                                                    All output in
                                                    uppercase
\WELCOME TO THE \OMNIWARE COMPUTER NETWORK.
\YOUR SYSTEM ADMINISTRATOR IS \AUGIE \HANSEN.
$ LS
ADMIN          BIN          LETTERS          SRC
$ PWD
/HOME/ARH
$ ☐
```

This is actually a feature, not a problem. UNIX was designed to work with any terminal, including those that could only send capital letters (back in the Stone Age). If you log in with your keyboard CAPS LOCK engaged, UNIX assumes you have one of those terminals. Lowercase letters are displayed as capitals. Capital letters are displayed with a preceding backslash.

The solution is to log off (type **EXIT**), disable CAPS LOCK, and start over.

USER ACCOUNT PROBLEMS

You might have problems with your account if your short-term memory fails you. Seek the assistance of your system administrator if you can't resolve these problems any other way.

FORGOTTEN PASSWORD

If you forget your password, you will not be able to log in. That's why I suggest you try to think of memorable passwords. If you wrote your password on paper as a backup (secured properly, of course), use it to recover.

If you have no backup and you try but can't crack the password, have your administrator install a new temporary password. This is usually a one-time-only password that lets you get logged in. You are then immediately prompted for a new password, which you will use until the next time you change it of your own volition or are forced to by the password-aging feature.

LOCKED ACCOUNT

Some UNIX systems are set up to lock accounts if too many failed attempts are made to log into an account. This is a good security measure, but it could leave you out in the cold until you get an administrator to reactivate your account. The recovery process is the same as the one just described.

WHAT YOU NEED TO KNOW

This lesson presents solutions to several problems you might encounter when you try to connect to a UNIX system. In Lesson 8 you will learn about files, directories, and file systems. Before you continue with Lesson 8, make sure that you have learned the following:

- ☑ If your screen displays garbled or meaningless characters, you have a data communication error. Correct your modem and terminal settings or the values used by your data communication software.

- ☑ If your screen double-spaces all output, set your terminal to LOCAL ECHO OFF.

- ☑ If your system displays all output in uppercase, log out of the system, turn Caps Lock off and try again. If the error persists, contact your system administrator.

- ☑ If you cannot log into your account or if you forget your password, contact your system administrator.

Section Two

WORKING WITH FILES AND DIRECTORIES

When you use your computer for any purpose, you work with files. The programs you run are stored in files. The text you create with an editor or word processor is stored in files. The values and labels in a spreadsheet are stored in files.

The UNIX system itself consists of thousands of files, many of which are programs that you run as commands. Other UNIX files support the efforts of programmers (development tools and header files), administrators (system setup and maintenance tools), and so on.

Given the pervasiveness and importance of files, the next seven lessons are devoted to defining what a file is, describing how files are named and how collections of files are organized in directories and file systems, and showing you how to control access to your files.

Lesson 8

Files, Directories, and File Systems

This lesson presents an overview of files, directories, and file systems. The background information presented here will help you to understand what you are doing when you create, edit, copy, move, remove, and view files; make, list, and remove directories; or change from one directory to another.

As you work through this lesson, you will learn about a number of important concepts and practices related to the storage and retrieval of data in UNIX:

- What a file in UNIX is

- What an inode is

- What a directory is

- What a file system is and which types there are

- Which type of file system UNIX uses

- Which directories users do work in

UNDERSTANDING FILES

Our primary concern in this lesson is understanding the mechanisms used to store data and retrieve it at a later time. The focus is on disk storage (hard disk and floppy disk). The mechanisms apply to other storage media (such as optical disk or CD-ROMs), as well, although the implementation details may differ.

The UNIX system treats a *file* as a named sequence of *bytes*. A byte is a collection of *bits*, the fundamental unit of digital storage. A byte, typically composed of eight bits (although other sizes are used in some environments), is large enough to hold a *character*. According to the American Standard Code for Information Interchange (ASCII), a 7-bit encoding scheme, a character code represents one of the following items:

- An uppercase or lowercase letter

- A digit

- A punctuation mark or other special character

- A control code.

Various extensions to ASCII use the eighth bit or even collections of bytes to represent a greater range of characters, permitting the use of international characters sets, some of which contain thousands of symbols.

As a rule, the UNIX operating system places no restrictions on the format of a file. A file is viewed by the system as an unformatted byte stream, where one byte in the file follows the previous until the end of the file is encountered. However, application programs impose formats on byte streams. For example, a text editor marks the end of each line of text with a newline character. A database program organizes data into records, with each record having a set of defined fields.

UNDERSTANDING UNIX FILES

No matter how you use UNIX, you will use files to store information such as letters, memos, reports, of even the programs you run. Files provide a way for UNIX to store related information on the computer's disk. When users discuss file sizes, they normally use the term *byte*, saying, for example that a certain file is 1000 bytes long. In a text file, a byte is a character of information. Experienced UNIX users may refer to files as a stream of bytes, where one byte follows the next until the end of the file is encountered.

DISK STORAGE AND DATA BLOCKS

A disk is organized as a *block-storage device*. A *block* is the smallest allocatable collection of storage locations. When you save data to disk, a minimum of one block is used. More blocks are allocated as needed to store data that doesn't fit in the first block. In other words, a file is a collection of one or more data blocks on disk. The operating system finds suitable locations for the data of a file and handles all the details associated with the storage process (writing, checking for and responding to errors, keeping track of where the pieces are, and so on).

Figure 8.1 presents a simplified view of how a couple of files might be stored on a disk. Notice that the blocks of a file are not necessarily together on the disk—space allocations become *fragmented* as files are removed and added over time. Block sizes vary from one system to another, but 1024 bytes is a common block size, and the one used for discussion purposes in this book. Other common block sizes are 512, 2048, 4096, and even 8192 bytes per block.

MAPPING DATA BLOCKS WITH INODES

As you just read, a file can contain one or more blocks that are dispersed across your disk. The operating system, in this case UNIX, is responsible for tracking which blocks correspond to each file. The system uses a set of *inodes* (information nodes) in a table to manage files. Each file has a unique inode. The inode table is stored on disk, and when the system is running, a copy of the table resides in memory. Figure 8.2 depicts the general content of an inode. The inode does not contain a file's data. It stores information *about* a file: ownership, file type, file permissions, access times, file size, and the locations of the data blocks that comprise the file.

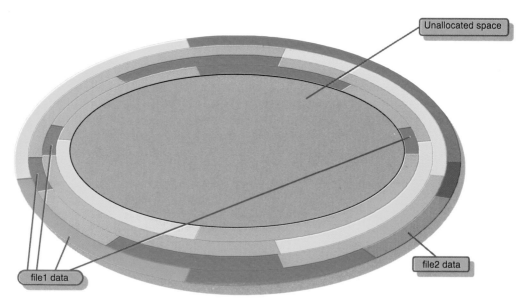

Figure 8.1 *Disks are organized as concentric tracks, which are further divided into blocks. When files are stored on disk, their contents are stored in one or more data blocks (identically colored blocks in the figure belong to the same file). The data for file1 is fragmented, while the file2 allocation is contiguous.*

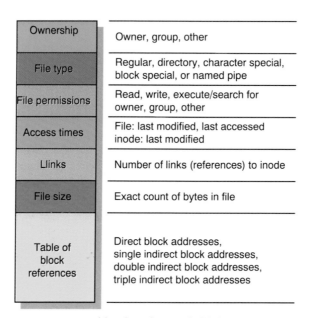

Figure 8.2 *An inode is an entry in a table of inodes. Each file has a unique inode that contains vital information about the file.*

Notice that an inode does not contain a filename. Names of files are stored in directories (see "Understanding Directories" later in this lesson). A file can be referred to from more than one directory entry. Each reference is called a *link*. The inode keeps a count of the number of links to the file. UNIX uses this flexible linking scheme to great advantage, as you will see in other lessons.

Having multiple links to a file is analogous to a person having a formal name and a nickname or two.

For example, my given first name is August, my family and friends call me Augie (you can, too), and my ham radio buddies know me as Gus. Each of those names is effectively a link, or reference, to me. Each of the names is used in a different context, but they all "point" to the same person.

The content of a file, be it plain text or the binary data of a program, is stored in disk blocks identified by the table of block references in the inode. The storage mechanism is designed to make access to small files, which most are, as efficient as possible while allowing for very large files.

The file size field in the inode is a 32-bit integer (four bytes), which limits files to four gigabytes, but your system administrator may choose to set other file size limits on users as a way of managing disk space.

UNDERSTANDING DIRECTORIES

A *directory* is a file that contains the names of other files and directories, and the inode numbers associated with them. As you have learned, each file has a unique inode. A directory is effectively a table of contents. Each directory entry identifies items by name and number, the number being the offset of the inode in the inode table. Figure 8.3 shows a partial directory and its relationship to the inode table, which maps the files on disk.

This design permits a file to be referred to by more than one name. Most files have only one name, but some situations require access to a file by aliases. In the figure, the filenames **file1.txt** and **file2.txt** are associated with the same inode number. Therefore, they both refer to the same file. Note, however, that a single directory entry cannot refer to more than one file.

UNDERSTANDING FILE SYSTEMS

One of the major components of an operating system is its *file system*. A file system describes the type and arrangement of data stored on a disk or other storage device. One form of file system is called a *flat file system*, in which every file exists at the same level. This design was used by CP/M and early versions on DOS. It is a marginally acceptable design if the amount of storage is small, such as on a low-density floppy disk, but it is not suited to mass-storage devices.

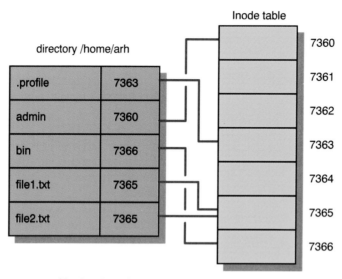

Figure 8.3 *A directory is a file that lists the names and associated inode numbers of other files and directories (the inode numbers used in this figure are arbitrary).*

Another design is called a *hierarchical file system*. It uses an arrangement of directories and files that is analogous to a file cabinet, with drawers and folders (directories) and collections of data on paper (files) stored in labeled folders. This design is used with minor variations by UNIX and many other modern operating systems.

UNIX FILE SYSTEMS

Figure 8.4 shows a portion of a directory hierarchy. This is a highly simplified view; only a few directories are shown. The top level is called the *root directory*, symbolized by a forward slash (/).

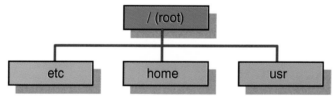

Figure 8.4 *The topmost levels of a directory hierarchy show the location of the **home** directory for users.*

Just below root you can see several directories. The **etc** directory, identified fully as **/etc**, contains commands for the system administrator. The **/usr** directory contains numerous directories, all of which contain files, mostly commands, that are of direct or indirect value to all users. Most of the commands you use are located in directories below the **/usr** directory.

The directory called **/home** is the one in which most users' login directories are placed. On pre-System V, Release 4 UNIX systems, users are similarly collected under a common directory, but the name is different. Directory names such as **/usr**, just plain **/u**, and **/users** are prevalent. If the directories get too large (more that 320 entries), a second directory with the digit 2 appended to the same base name is used to split the directory for speedier access. Thus, **/home** would get a companion directory called **/home2**, and about half the files from **/home** would be relocated to **/home2**.

WHAT YOU NEED TO KNOW

In the rest of the lessons of this section, you will learn how to use files and directories to your advantage. You next learn about the file and directory naming conventions. Before moving on, check your knowledge. You should understand the following topics:

- ☑ A file is a named sequence of bytes (characters). UNIX imposes no specific format on ordinary files, but application programs are free to do so.

- ☑ An inode (information node) is a storage location in a table that contains information about files and directories (size, times, permissions, data locations, and so on).

- ☑ A directory is a file that has a predefined format. It contains the names of files and directories and their associate inode numbers.

- ☑ A file system is an arrangement of files for convenient access. The UNIX file system is implemented as a hierarchy of files and directories.

- ☑ The UNIX file system contains a **/home** directory (or its equivalent), which is the repository for users' login directories.

Lesson 9

File and Directory Names

As you learned in the previous lesson, every file has at least one filename—possibly more than one if other directory entries are linked to the file's inode. This lesson shows you how to form valid names for files and directories, and how to construct *pathnames* (a series of directories you or UNIX must traverse to locate a file). You will also learn:

- UNIX filename requirements—how many characters a UNIX filename can have, which characters can be used, and that letter case is significant

- Which characters to use to avoid problems with the shell

- What your current directory is and how you can change it

- What full pathnames are and how to use them

- What wildcard characters can do for you in UNIX

General Naming Conventions

The first thing to know about UNIX filenames is that letter case matters. Therefore, the names **result**, **Result**, and **RESULT** refer to three distinct files. Most filenames are typed in lowercase letters, possibly mixed with digits and non-alphanumeric characters. For example, you might name a file **ch05-rev01** to indicate that it contains Revision 1 (rev01) of Chapter 5 (ch05). The second fact to remember is that filenames can be up to 14 characters long (255 for UNIX System V, Release 4 and later). Long names can be more descriptive than short ones, but compatibility with earlier systems is assured only if the names are unique in the first 14 characters.

Allowed Characters in Filenames

The list of characters you can use in filenames is extensive. Only the / is not allowed in a filename because it is the pathname separator (see "Fully Qualified Pathnames" in this lesson). However, you should avoid using some characters because they have special meaning to the shell:

```
?  @  #  $  ^  *  (  )  `
                                ——— Characters to avoid in filenames
[  ]  \  |  ;  '  "  <  >
```

You can use spaces and tabs in filenames if you enclose the names in quotation marks on the command line. Although such names are legal, they are hard to work with. Use underscores or dots (.) to get visual separation of name components. For example, use **data_file** or **data.file** instead of **"data file"** (the quotes cause the shell to see the two words as a single name). Another possibility is to use mixed case, for example, **DataFile**.

Don't use a – or + as the first character of a filename. These characters are used with many commands to introduce options. Also, avoid starting filenames with a dot (.). Names that start with a dot are used by the system to make the names invisible to normal directory listings. However, you can use one or more dots within filenames, as shown in the data file example, to obtain visual separation of name components. Although names like **...File...**, **a...z**, and even **.....** are legal, they are a bit short on aesthetics and definitely lacking in mnemonic value. Avoid being cute—choose meaningful names.

The UNIX system does not require filename extensions. In fact, the standard commands and application programs have none. Some application programs and development tools, by convention, look for certain filename extensions, such as **.c** for C program source files, but these are application-specific requirements that have nothing to do with the operating system.

FULLY QUALIFIED PATHNAMES

A pathname is a mechanism for specifying the location of a file or directory in a file-system hierarchy. Building on the hierarchy from the previous lesson, three user-level directories are shown in Figure 9-1. The directories **arh**, **rocky**, and **bratcat** have been added into the **/home** directory by the system administrator.

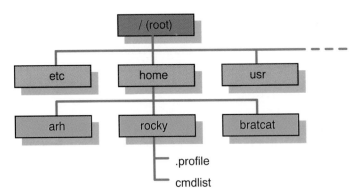

Figure 9.1 *In addition to directories, shown as boxed items, this hierarchy includes ordinary files* (**.profile** *and* **cmdlist**).

Let's use the login directory of a user named Rocky to explore pathnames. The *fully-qualified pathname*, sometimes called an *absolute pathname*, to the user's login directory is **/home/rocky**. It is described as fully qualified because the name starts at the root of the file system (**/**) and includes the names of all directories (**home**) up to the terminal filename or directory name (**rocky**).

Figure 9-2 shows you how to interpret pathnames. The **/** character at the beginning of the pathname is the name of the root directory. The other **/** characters are pathname *separators* or *delimiters*. The names **home** and **rocky** identify directories. In the terminology of UNIX, **home** is the *parent directory* of **rocky**, and conversely, **rocky** is a *child directory* of **home**.

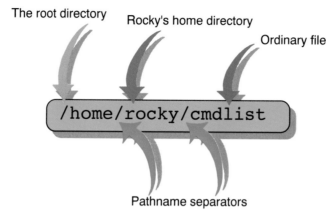

*Figure 9.2 The file **cmdlist** is identified by the fully qualified pathname /home/rocky/cmdlist.*

HOME AND CURRENT DIRECTORIES

When Rocky logs in, the system places him in the **/home/rocky** directory. This is the *home directory* for this user. Each user has a home directory that is assigned by the system administrator when the login account is set up.

Note: When you work at a desk or table, you might well have lots of documents (books, files, notepad, tax forms, and so on) scattered around the work area (if you're like me) or arranged in neat little stacks (if you're not). At any time you are focusing *on one of those documents. (If you can focus on two or more at a time, I can sign you up as the subject of some nifty research projects.) The object of your attention at any time is said to be your* focus.

On a UNIX system, the user's focus (you can also think of this as your current "location"—where you "are") is identified as the *current directory*. The user's home directory is the initial focus of his or her work at the time of logging in. Therefore, the current directory is initially the home directory. By using the **cd** (change directory) command, the user can change focus to a different directory. For example, **cd /home** changes focus to the directory **/home**.

NAMING FOR COMPATIBILITY WITH OTHER SYSTEMS

File and directory names for DOS (all versions), Windows (through version 3.1), and OS/2 are very restricted. The "8.3 rule," as it is known, means that filenames consist of one or two parts: a filename part of up to eight characters, and an optional extension part of up to three characters. If an extension is used, it is preceded by a dot (.).

If you are going to be working both with UNIX and a system with a more limited naming policy, it might be to your advantage to use the more restrictive rules. This practice makes it easier to exchange files among systems without having to remember or track different names for the same file.

AMBIGUOUS NAMES

At times it can be to your advantage to use names that are deliberately ambiguous. Instead of having to type the full name of a file, you can use a shorthand expression that matches a portion of the name. By extension, you can use an expression that matches more than one filename. The shell interprets filenames that consist of literal characters (such as **abc**) and *metacharacters*. Metacharacters have meanings that transcend their normal interpretations as symbols. In filenames and directory names, the characters * and ? have special meanings, as shown in Table 9.1:

Metacharacter	Matches
?	Any single character (except an initial .)
*	Any sequence of characters, including none
[*s*]	One character from the class *s* (see lesson 22)

Table 9.1 *Metacharacters match characters in filenames and extensions like wildcards match suits or values in some card games.*

Thus the filename expression **?at** matches any three-character name that ends in "at," such as **bat**, **cat**, **fat**, and **hat**. The name **data*** matches **data**, **data1**, **data_store**, **data.old**, and any other filename starting with **data**, and **b*.txt** matches every filename that starts with the letter **b** has a **.txt** extension.

Due to the similarity to the way certain cards in a deck of playing cards are used to take on values other than those indicated on their faces, these characters are often called *wildcard characters*. Ambiguous names will be of considerable value to you as you learn about file- and directory-oriented commands in the lessons that follow.

WHAT YOU NEED TO KNOW

In this lesson you learned the rules for naming files and directories and various ways of referring to them. The next two lessons introduce you to a set of frequently used programs that interact with files and directories. Before continuing, be sure you understand these points:

- ☑ Use only letters, digits, underscores, and dots within your filenames to avoid problems with the shell.

- ☑ Your current directory identifies your working focus (where you "are"). It is initially set to your home directory, but you can change it by using the **cd** command.

- ☑ A full pathname starts at the root directory (*/*). A relative pathname starts at the current directory.

- ☑ Use filenames that are acceptable on all systems you access regularly.

- ☑ Wildcard characters give you a convenient shorthand for specifying file and directory names in commands.

Lesson 10

Directory-Oriented Programs and Commands

The UNIX System uses several files to control each user's operating environment. This lesson describes these files, the default values stored in them, and how they affect your login sessions. More detailed coverage is provided in Lesson 18, "Customizing Your Operating Environment."

A relatively small percentage of the available UNIX *utility programs*, or simply *utilities*, do most of the work. This lesson introduces you to a set of UNIX utilities that you use frequently in issuing directory-oriented commands. When you finish reading this lesson, you will have learned:

- How to find out the name of the current (working) directory
- How to list the contents of directories
- What hidden files are and how to reveal them
- What a relative pathname is
- What the PATH variable does for you
- What the **echo** command does
- How to use **mkdir** and **rmdir**

GETTING INFORMATION ABOUT DIRECTORIES AND FILES

Several utilities and built-in shell commands provide information about your directories and files. The commands described here help you to find out where you are in the file system and to examine the contents of directories.

FINDING OUT WHERE YOU ARE

As you learned in the previous lesson, the current directory is the one in which the user is said to be "working" (hence the alternative term *working directory*). In other words, the working directory is the directory within which UNIX automatically stores or searches for files unless you specifically tell it to look elsewhere. If you need to know the name of the current directory, use the **pwd** (print working directory) command. The term "print" is rooted in the origins of UNIX when hardcopy terminals were the order of the day. Virtually all user output was printed on paper instead of to screen. Today, "display" would be a more appropriate term for most users.

When Rocky first logs in, his working directory is his home directory. Checking it, he sees the following:

```
$ pwd ↵
/home/rocky
$ ❑
```

UNDERSTANDING YOUR WORKING DIRECTORY

When you work within UNIX, you must tell it where to store or locate files. To simplify such operations, UNIX defines a working directory. As you have learned, a directory is very much like a filing-cabinet drawer. Think of your working directory as the open file drawer. To view the name of your working directory, you can use the **pwd** command. Later in this lesson you will learn how to change working directories (close one drawer of file cabinet and open another) using the **cd** (change directory) command.

LISTING A DIRECTORY

When you are positioned in a directory, you might want to know the names of files and directories in that directory. Use **ls** (list directory) to obtain this information. (Most UNIX program names are two- or three-letter abbreviations, designed to minimize typing.) The **ls** program, without options, produces a listing of filenames and directory names in the current directory. Given filename and directory arguments, **ls** attempts to list information about each named file and directory. The format under SVR4 systems is a columnar listing, the number of columns being determined by the length of the longest name in the list. Earlier versions of UNIX produce a listing of one file or directory name per line.

When Rocky tries to use **ls**, he gets a surprise:

```
$ ls ↵
$ ❑
```

Nothing. No files or directories are listed—but the system administrator told Rocky there would be a few files in his home directory. Where are they?

For ordinary users, **ls** does not list files whose names begin with a dot. (Privileged users, such as root or other administrative users see all files when using **ls**.) The system uses such names to hide configuration files from normal directory searches. Ordinary users can see the names of hidden files by using the **–a** option, which instructs **ls** to print the names of all files:

```
$ ls -a ↵
.            ..            .profile
$ ❑
```

This listing shows three files. On your system, the number of files you have in your home directory upon first logging in will differ from this. One of the filenames listed in this example, **.profile**, is a text file that contains user configuration data.

The other two files listed are shorthand names of directories. The first is a single dot (.) that refers to the current directory. The second is a pair of dots (..) that is a reference to the directory above the current directory in the file system hierarchy; that is, the parent of the current directory. Every directory has a parent except root (/). Both the . and .. directory entries in the **root** directory refer to **root** itself.

LISTING THE CONTENTS IN A DIRECTORY

As you have learned, a directory can contain the names of one or more files or even other directories. To list the contents of a directory, use the **ls** command. If you suspect the directory may contain hidden files whose names begin with a dot, invoke **ls** using the -a option (**ls -a**).

RELATIVE PATHNAMES

Pathnames don't have to start at the root directory. In fact, it is downright inconvenient to use fully qualified pathnames most of the time. The further down in a directory hierarchy you go, the more troublesome it is to type full pathnames, so UNIX permits the use of *relative pathnames*. A relative pathname names a file or directory starting from a directory other than **root**, typically your current directory.

The file **.profile** is an ordinary file in Rocky's home directory. Its full pathname is **/home/rocky/.profile**. If the current directory is **/home/rocky**, the relative pathname to the file is simply **.profile**. A pathname that is not fully qualified is assumed to be relative to the user's current directory, unless some other starting point is specified. Any file or directory that is immediately subordinate can be specified by its name only; no path information is needed.

If the current directory is **/home**, the relative pathname to the file is **rocky/.profile** because **rocky** is a directory immediately below **home**, and **.profile** is just below **rocky**. The intermediate directory (**rocky**) must be specified here to fill in the gap between the starting point (**/home**) and the ending point (**.profile**).

Figure 10.1 shows how the . and .. names point to the current and parent directories. It also shows the relative pathnames you can use to identify .profile from various locations.

You can use **ls** to list a directory other than the one you're in. For example, the following command lists the names of files and directories in the **/home** directory. Because this is a full pathname, it doesn't matter what your current directory is when you issue the list directory command.

```
$ ls /home ↵
arh        augie     bratcat  config   doris    rocky
$ □
```

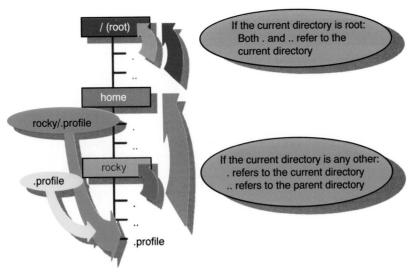

Figure 10.1 The . and .. directory names are shorthand notations for the current directory and parent directory, respectively. These names are used extensively in forming relative pathnames.

If your current directory is any one of the directories under **/home**, you can get the same result by typing the command **ls ..** because the directory .. relative to your current directory means **/home**. However, if your current directory is **/home**, then **ls ..** lists the contents of the root directory instead. As Einstein would have said, "It's all relative!"

UNDERSTANDING . AND ..

To help you simplify directory and file commands, each directory contains two special directory name symbols (.) and (..). These directories are abbreviations for the current (or working) directory (.) and the parent directory (..) which is immediately above the current directory. In later lessons you will learn how to use these symbols within your commands. For now, however, remember that these two symbols are simply abbreviations.

PROGRAM DIRECTORIES AND YOUR PATH VARIABLE

When you type a command, the UNIX shell first must find its location (UNIX stores most commands in files on your disk), load the command into memory (if it's not already loaded), then execute it on your behalf. The shell looks in directories identified by your PATH variable, one of the many environment variables associated with each active user's session. Each user can specify a different PATH value, but the basis of every user's PATH is a set of directories specified by the system administrator.

The simplest way to find out the value of PATH, or any other environment variable, is to use the **echo** command. The following command shows you the value of PATH:

```
$ echo $PATH ↵
/usr/bin:/usr/dbin:/usr/ldbin
$ ☐
```

The **echo** command simply prints (or displays) its arguments. The command **echo baseball** simply prints the word "baseball". In the PATH example above, the name PATH is preceded by a dollar sign, which is a way of getting at the value stored in the PATH variable. The command **echo PATH** (no dollar sign) simply prints the literal text "PATH"; **echo $PATH** prints the value of the PATH variable, as shown in the example.

The example PATH contains three directory names separated by colons. The **/usr/bin** directory contains most of the standard UNIX user utility programs. The **/usr/dbin** and **/usr/ldbin** directories are found on systems that support DOS capabilities, such as UnixWare and SCO Open Desktop. Figure 10.2 illustrates this arrangement of program directories.

Most UNIX systems prior to SVR4 have a directory named **/bin** (connected by the dashed line in the figure) in addition to the **/usr/bin** directory. In fact, **/bin** was originally the primary high-use command directory, and **/usr/bin** was an auxiliary directory. Recent UNIX offerings based on SVR4 and later releases put all user-related command directories into **/usr**.

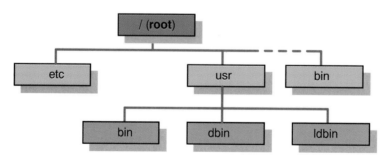

Figure 10.2 *The PATH variable specifies the locations of standard UNIX utility programs. The system initializes a default PATH, but you can modify it to suit your needs by using interactive commands or by editing your* **.profile***.*

ALTERING THE DIRECTORY HIERARCHY

As you have seen, the UNIX file system consists of system-related directories and user-related directories. You can alter the portion of the file system that effectively belongs to you, but you can alter neither portions owned by the system account nor those portions owned by other users, unless they give you permission.

CREATING NEW DIRECTORIES

To create a new directory or a set of directories, use **mkdir** (an abbreviation for **make dir**ectory). This utility takes a list of names and attempts to create a directory for each name. In the following example, our intrepid user, Rocky, uses **mkdir** to create the **admin** and **letters** directories under his home directory:

```
$ mkdir admin letters ↵
$ ▢
```

As Figure 10.3 shows, the command creates two new entries in the **rocky** directory. Not shown in the figure are the . and .. directory entries that **mkdir** creates automatically when it creates a new directory. To simplify the figures, the two hidden directories are omitted, but they exist in every directory of the hierarchy.

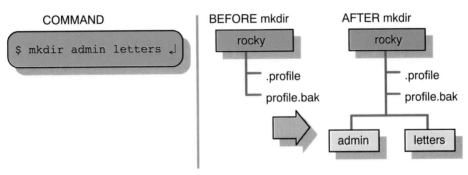

*Figure 10.3 The **mkdir** program creates new directories.*

The two new directories are subordinate to **/home/rocky** in the file system hierarchy. Subordinate directories are often referred to as *subdirectories* when describing the relationships among various levels of the hierarchy.

Error messages tell you of any problems encountered by **mkdir**. Typical errors are attempting to create a directory that already exists and not having permission to write in a directory. In this example, Rocky tries to create a directory that already exists:

```
$ mkdir admin ↵
mkdir: Cannot make directory "admin"; File exists (error 17)
$ ▢
```

The error message identifies the program that sent it, describes the transgression, and shows the error code that refers to detailed descriptions of error messages. These descriptions are provided in the user documentation delivered with most UNIX systems.

REMOVING DIRECTORIES

To remove a directory, use **rmdir** (an abbreviation for **remove directory**). The program accepts a list of directory names. It attempts to remove each one, but fails to remove a directory if it is not empty (except for . and .. entries) or if access is denied for any reason. To remove a directory that has files in it, first remove or relocate the files (see **rm** in Lesson 11); then remove the directory.

CREATING AND REMOVING DIRECTORIES

To help you organize files on you create on disk, UNIX lets you create directories, much as you might create additional folders or file drawers within a file cabinet. To create a directory, you use the **mkdir** command. The following command, for example, creates a directory named **notes**:

```
$ mkdir notes ↵
$ □
```

When you no longer need a directory, remove the files the directory contains (using **rm**, as described in Lesson 11) and then remove the directory itself using **rmdir**. The following command, for example, removes the directory **reports**, assuming the directory is empty:

```
$ rmdir reports ↵
$ □
```

WHAT YOU NEED TO KNOW

You now have the tools you need to set up and organize your directory hierarchy, which is your personal electronic file cabinet. Before moving on to Lesson 11 to learn about file-oriented programs, verify your knowledge of these points:

- ☑ To find out the name of the current (working) directory, use **pwd**.
- ☑ Use the **ls** program to list the contents of directories. The **–a** option reveals hidden files (files with names that start with a .).
- ☑ The PATH variable tells you what directories are searched for program files when you issue commands.
- ☑ The **echo** command prints whatever arguments it is given, including in this case, the contents of the PATH variable, to the screen.
- ☑ You use the **mkdir** and **rmdir** programs to organize and maintain your directory hierarchy by making and removing directories.

Lesson 11

File-Oriented Programs and Commands

So far you have been introduced to utility programs that tell you about files and let you organize your files into directories. This lesson presents information about some important programs that let you manipulate files in various ways and give you access to the contents of files.

The lesson begins with a description of text and binary files. Then it describes programs that let you do the following tasks:

- Examine the contents of files
- Copy and move files
- Remove files when you no longer need them

UNDERSTANDING TEXT AND BINARY FILES

A *text file* is one that contains only letters, digits, punctuation marks and a limited set of control codes. The codes are from the 7-bit ASCII character set described in Lesson 8.

The control codes used in text files are called *format effectors*. Format effectors provide basic text formatting, such as newline (or carriage return + linefeed) to mark the end of a line, and horizontal tab. Most other control codes are not allowed in text files.

Another type of file is a *binary file*, in which 8-bit codes are used. Binary files are used primarily to store the instructions and data of programs. However, application programs such as word processors, drawing programs, and many others use binary codes to incorporate special formatting into their data files. For example, a word processor program might use 8-bit binary codes to store text along with character and paragraph formatting information.

The programs described in this lesson that display the contents of files work correctly only with text files. Don't use the programs to look at binary files. If you attempt to display the contents of a binary file with text-oriented programs, you will see some rather strange-looking symbols mixed in with plain text, and the terminal bell will probably ring a lot. If you accidentally try to view a binary file, press the DEL key to stop the command.

Attempting to view a binary file with **cat**, described next, or some other text-oriented utilities can put your terminal into an unstable mode because some of the binary codes effectively reprogram its settings. If your terminal seems to be acting strangely, you can obtain a stable condition by typing the following command:

```
$ stty sane ↵
$ ☐
```

You may have to type the command without seeing it if your terminal is not echoing properly. Once back in a stable state, log off and then log in again to be sure everything is reinitialized properly before continuing with your work.

VIEWING AND CONCATENATING TEXT FILES

The **cat** program, which is a short name for *concatenate* (to append one item on to the end of another), effectively combines the contents a set of named input files into a continuous output stream. If only a single filename is given as an argument to **cat**, the effect is to print (display) its contents to the output device. In the following example, you use **cat** to view the contents of **.profile**:

```
$ cat .profile ↵
# Default .profile
... # lots of lines omitted
MAIL=/var/mail/${LOGNAME:?}
$ ☐
```

Be more concerned at this time with the means of viewing the contents of a file than with the actual contents.

If you want to combine a set of files into a continuous output display, use a command of the form **cat** *file ...* . The ellipsis represents names of files not explicitly shown. The contents of each named file, if the file exists, are displayed. The **cat** program emits an error message if a file can not be found or if it is not accessible by you for any reason.

If you want to collect the contents of multiple files into a single disk file, use a feature of the shell called *redirection*, symbolized by the > character. Program-output redirection takes the output that would normally go to your terminal and sends it to the named file or device. The original files are neither removed nor modified.

The previous command with redirection becomes **cat** *file ... > outfile*. If the file *outfile* does not exist, it is created.

Note: *Be very careful. If **outfile** does exist, its contents are overwritten by the command output, which causes the file's previous contents to be lost. This statement also implies that you should not use one of the source filenames as the output filename:* **cat x y z > x**. *In this case, the previous contents of file* **x** *would be lost.*

The following example shows how to use **cat** to combine the contents of two files, **text1** and **text2**, into a new file called **document**.

```
$ cat text1 text2 > document ↵
$ □
```

DISPLAYING A TEXT FILE'S CONTENTS

A text file is a file that contains only standard 7-bit ASCII characters (letters, numbers, punctuation marks, and a few text-formatting control codes, such as newline and tab). When you work with UNIX, you use text files for memos, electronic mail messages, script files, and many other purposes. To display or print the contents of a file called **mail.list** on your terminal, you can use the UNIX **cat** command, as shown here:

```
$ cat mail.list ↵
```

To display two or more files using one command, place each filename in **cat**'s command line, as shown here (the command assumes that three files, **front.txt**, **middle.txt**, and **back.txt**, contain text that you want to merge for viewing):

```
$ cat front.txt middle.txt back.txt ↵
```

COPYING FILES

You might need to copy a file's contents, perhaps to save the file's current contents before you change the file in some way. Use the **cp** utility to create a copy of a file (**cp** *sourcefile targetfile*) or to copy a set of files (one of more) to a different directory (**cp** *file ... directory*).

WITHIN THE SAME DIRECTORY

The first form of the command copies *sourcefile* to *targetfile*. The two files cannot be identically named because no two files can have exactly the same pathname. If the target file, *targetfile*, is in a different directory, it can have the same filename as the source file, *sourcefile*, because the pathnames are different.

To make a backup copy of your **.profile** configuration file, for example, use a **cp** command similar to the following:

```
$ cp .profile profile.bak ↵
$ □
```

The new file, **profile.bak**, is created in the current directory. Its contents are identical to the contents of **.profile**, and it is in the same directory, but it has a different name. Figure 11.1 shows the effect of this simple command.

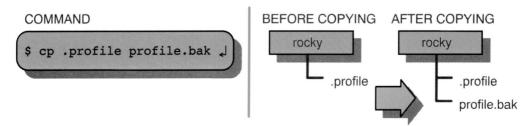

COMMAND

```
$ cp .profile profile.bak ↵
```

BEFORE COPYING

rocky
└── .profile

AFTER COPYING

rocky
├── .profile
└── profile.bak

Figure 11.1 Copying a file creates another file with the same contents as the original but a different name. This command creates a backup copy of Rocky's configuration file (.profile).

Note: By not using a dot as the first character of the target filename, you make the file visible to normal directory listings. If you want to produce a hidden file, use a dot for the first character of the name (.profile.bak). Recall that UNIX filenames can contain more than one dot, and the dots can be placed anywhere in the name.

To Another Directory

A situation that arises often is copying a file into different directory. Let's assume that Rocky prefers to place all his backup file copies in a directory called **preserve** under his home directory (**/home/rocky/preserve**). In this example, as in the previous example, the file gets a new name:

```
$ cp .profile preserve/profile.bak ↵
$ □
```

The second form of **cp** command copies a file or files to a target directory. The directory must exist before you run the command. If it doesn't exist, create it and then issue the **cp** command.

The target directory can be specified by a literal (specific name) or a symbolic reference (such as . or ..). To copy a file from some other directory into the current directory, use a command of the form **cp** *file* . where the current directory is represented by its shorthand name (dot).

The file **/etc/group** is available on virtually all UNIX systems. It is a readable text file that contains information about the various groups, group owners, and members. Rocky can make a copy of it in his current directory (.) by using this command:

```
$ cp /etc/group . ↵
$ □
```

Of course, Rocky must have permission to write in the target directory. Normally, as long as Rocky is in his home directory or one of its subdirectories, Rocky will have permission to write files in the directory. After this command completes, a new file called **group** is in the current directory.

If the target is the user's home directory, . is a suitable name only if the user's current directory is the home directory. If the user is in some other directory, he or she can use the literal pathname, such as **/home/rocky**.

A useful symbolic way of specifying the user's home directory is $HOME. HOME is another of the environment variables. It is set to the user's home directory path at login. Thus, the following command copies a file to the user's home directory, regardless of the user's current directory:

```
$ cp /etc/group $HOME ⏎
$ □
```

To view the contents of the HOME variable, use the **echo** command as previously discussed: **echo $HOME**.

COPYING ONE FILE'S CONTENTS TO ANOTHER

As you work with files, you might want make backup copies, copy the file for other uses, or even copy another user's file to your own directory. To copy one file's contents (often called the source file) to another file (called the target or destination file), you use the **cp** command. The following command, for example copies the contents of the file **memo** to the file **work_memo**:

```
$ cp memo work_memo ⏎
$ □
```

Keep in mind that if a file with the name **work_memo** already exists, the **cp** command will overwrite the file's current contents.

MOVING FILES

The UNIX utility program that renames and moves files is called **mv**. This program has two general forms that deal with files. The first form renames or moves a single file (**mv** *file1 file2*). The second form moves a set of files to a target directory (**mv** *file ... directory*).

TO A DIFFERENT NAME IN THE SAME DIRECTORY

To rename the file **profile.bak** to **prof.txt**, for example, use the following command line:

```
$ mv profile.bak prof.txt ⏎
$ □
```

Figure 11.2 illustrates the effect of this command. The file's content is not changed, nor is it relocated on the disk. Only the directory entry is changed to reflect the new name. Use caution, however. If a file by the name **prof.txt** already exists, its contents are lost when the renaming takes place.

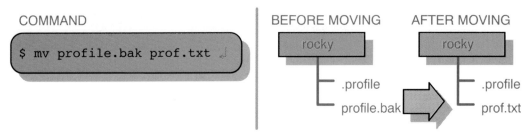

COMMAND

```
$ mv profile.bak prof.txt ↵
```

BEFORE MOVING   AFTER MOVING

rocky   rocky

.profile   .profile

profile.bak   prof.txt

Figure 11.2 *Moving a file to a different name in the same directory effectively renames the file.*

TO ANOTHER DIRECTORY

The second form of **mv** lets you move a single file or a group of files to a different directory. The target directory must exist and you must have permission to write in it. Assuming that a directory called **save** exists and the user may write to it, the following example moves two data files into the directory, presumably for safekeeping:

```
$ mv data1 data2 save ↵
$ □
```

If a named source file does not exist or is not accessible, **mv** emits a suitable error message, but completes the moves of other files. If the target directory is not found or not accessible, no files are moved, and **mv** emits an error message.

RENAMING AND MOVING FILES

If you need to rename a file, use the **mv** program to change the name of an existing file. For example, the following command changes the extension part of a filename:

```
$ mv dec93.exp dec93.sav ↵
$ □
```

You can also use **mv** to make wholesale revisions to a directory hierarchy. This command relocates all the expense files in a directory to a different directory:

```
$ mv *.exp lastyear ↵
$ □
```

REMOVING FILES

To remove a file or a set of files, use the **rm** program. When you no longer need a file, you should remove it to free disk space. For example, to get rid of the **prof.txt** file, use this command:

```
$ rm prof.txt ↵
$ ▢
```

You can provide a list of file names for **rm** to remove. If a named file does not exist or is not accessible, **rm** emits a suitable error message, but completes the removal of other files.

You can use wildcards to tell the shell to generate a list of filenames for the **rm** program. To get rid of a set of old data files, for example, you could use a command similar to this one:

```
$ rm *.dat ↵
$ ▢
```

Do be careful with commands like this. If you make a typing mistake, such as putting a space after the *, you could get a very unpleasant surprise:

```
$ rm * .dat ↵
rm: .dat non-existent
$ ▢
```

The message tells you that the **.dat** file can't be found, but that's the least of your worries. The **rm** program did what you told it to do. It removed *every* visible file from the current directory (**rm ***) and then tried to remove **.dat** from the empty directory. Ouch!

Maybe it's time to book that long overdue vacation you've been thinking about. At least check with your system administrator about recovering the lost files from the most recent daily backup. (If you haven't seen a need for daily backups yet, perhaps you do now.)

Note: Unless your system is running special programs designed to prevent accidental data loss, when you remove a file, it's gone forever. Multiuser systems typically don't afford you the luxury of easily recovering files. Be sure you really want to remove a file before you press the RETURN *key.*

REMOVING FILES

In the interest of good citizenship in a multiuser environment, you should remove files when you no longer need them. This frees disk space, which is invariably in short supply, for use by you and other users. The **rm** program removes a file or a list of files named on the command line.

You can use ambiguous filenames to generate the file list, but use caution. Once files are removed from a UNIX system, they are really gone. Frequent backups and the use of special software can minimize the pain of losing files, but some data loss is possible.

What You Need to Know

This lesson shows you how to use standard UNIX utility programs to perform a variety of tasks with files. Lesson 12 addresses file and directory permissions and the importance of controlling access to your resources. Before you leave this lesson, be sure you understand these points:

☑ Use the **cat** program to view the contents of files. Use with redirection to combine the contents of text files.

☑ You can copy files by using the **cp** program. Copied files must have different pathnames than the files from which they are copied.

☑ Use the **mv** utility to rename or to move files. Use caution to avoid overwriting existing files.

☑ Use **rm** to remove files. Beware, removed files cannot be recovered unless you have backups or special file-recovery software.

Lesson 12

Access and Permissions

Because UNIX systems allow multiple users to store and access information from disk at the same time, you need a way to protect your files from other users. Earlier lessons made references to file and directory permissions and to controlling access to your resources. This lesson describes the mechanism by which UNIX lets users and administrators grant or deny access to any file and directory that they own. You will learn

- Who the owner of a file is

- What controls access to a file for reading, writing, or executing

- How to get detailed information about your files and directories

- How to set permissions and control ownership of files and directories

- How to remove files you don't own

- How to share resources with some users while denying access to others

- How to set the default permissions for newly created files and directories

FILE OWNERSHIP AND ACCESS

With respect to file and directory access, the user community on a UNIX system is partitioned into three categories: user (or owner), group, and other. The *owner* of a file determines who can access the file and for what purposes. The same applies to directories. The categories are summarized in Table 12.1, which identifies the categories by name and briefly describes each.

NAME	DESCRIPTION
user (u)	The owner of the files and directories.
group (g)	Group members. Groups are users who agree to share certain files and directories. Groups are usually formed along project or business organizational lines.
other (o)	All other users of the system.

Table 12.1 The system user community is partitioned into three categories. Every file and directory is assigned permissions for each category.

The letter in parentheses after each category name is used to specify options in commands. The user category is often referred to as the owner category in UNIX documentation. Thus, you can treat the names *user* and *owner* as synonyms.

FILE PERMISSIONS

Each file has a set of values stored in its inode that specifies its *permissions* (also called its *protection mode*, or simply *mode*). The permissions indicate, for each category of user, the kind of access allowed. Table 12.2 identifies and describes the permission values and codes as they apply to files and directories.

Type	File Action	Directory Action
read (r)	Allows file to be viewed, copied, and printed	Allows directory to be listed
write (w)	Allows file to be moved, removed, and modified	Allows files to be created in directory
execute (x)	Allows file to be run as a command	Allows directory to be searched

Table 12.2 File permissions are specified by codes that grant or deny read, write, and execute access.

To facilitate the displaying and setting of file permissions, UNIX utilities use character string and numeric expressions of file modes. Figure 12.1 shows how the permission bit patterns relate to frequently used octal codes.

Figure 12.1 The file permission values can be expressed in various formats. The mode bit patterns (left) can also be expressed as octal numbers (right).

Octal codes are numbers from 0 to 7 (a range of eight values) that provide a single-digit code to specify the conditions of three bits. The bit patterns in the figure use a dash to indicate that a bit is *off* and a letter to indicate that it is *on*. You need to be familiar with the two forms shown in the figure because both forms are used by several important UNIX utilities.

UNDERSTANDING FILE OWNERSHIP AND PERMISSIONS

In a multiuser environment, users need access-control mechanisms that let them share resources with other users while protecting those same resources from harm.

The UNIX approach to access control is to provide read (r), write (w), and execute (x) permissions for all files and directories at three levels: user/owner (u), group (g), and other (o). Execute permission for directories means that users have permission to search or list them. File owners decide what level of access to grant to themselves and others on a file-by-file basis.

USING THE LONG LISTING FORMAT

If you need to obtain detailed information about the files in a directory, use the long listing format. You do this by invoking the -l option of ls, either by itself or with other options. In the following example, the long listing format is applied in combination with the all files option (-a):

```
$ ls -al ↵
total 8
drwxr-xr-x    2 rocky      other        96 Dec 26 23:16 .
drwxrwxr-x    7 root       sys          96 Dec 24 07:40 ..
-rw-r--r--    1 rocky      other       613 Nov  2  1992 .profile
$ □
```

Notice that the option letters **a** and **l** were combined after a single dash. The **ls** command also accepts them separately, as in **ls -a -l**. You can also combine options in any order, so **ls -la** and **ls -l -a** would work just as well as the sample command.

The first output line (**total 8**) indicates the number of disk blocks used by the directory being listed—in this case eight. Then each file and directory in the listed directory causes a line of output. The default order is sorted by name, but you can change this by using command-line options. The long list shows, for each file and directory, the following information:

- Mode bits (file mode and permissions)
- Number of links to the file
- Owner ID (the user)
- Group ID
- File size (exact count in bytes)
- Date/time of last modification
- Filename

The mode bits are organized to give you visually a detailed summary of file or directory accessibility to you and other users, as shown in Figure 12.2.

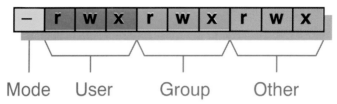

*Figure 12.2 The **ls** command displays file and directory permissions using this format when a long list is requested.*

The mode bit at the left indicates the type of file. A dash (-) indicates a normal file, and a **d** indicates a directory. Other codes indicate various kinds of device files and other special purpose files. Check your user manual page for **ls** if you need more information.

The remaining bits specify the permissions (read, write, execute/search) for each user category. The nine bits give you great flexibility in controlling access to your files and directories, as you will see later in this lesson. For example, a file owner in the accounting department can set a file permission on an expense summary of **rw-r-----** (640). He or she can read and write the file. Members of the accounting group can read it. No other user can do anything to the file.

The **ls** utility program accepts many options to alter its default behavior in various ways. After you have learned the forms shown in this book, you should read the detailed manual pages in your system's user's reference manual to find out about other options that may be of use to you in certain situations. Some UNIX systems make the manual pages available on line. The manuals take up a lot of disk space, so smaller systems usually don't provide extensive online documentation.

DEFAULT PERMISSIONS FOR FILES AND DIRECTORIES

When you create a file or a directory, the system is set up to give liberal access rights to all users. The default mode for a directory is 777 (**rwxrwxrwx**) and for a file, 666 (**rw-rw-rw-**). In most academic and commercial settings, this kind of free access invites disaster, so you should restrict access to yourself and possibly to a group of cooperating users.

You could set the mode to a more restrictive value each time you create a file or a directory, but you might forget or tire of doing it. To automate the process of protecting your files, set the *file-creation mode mask* to a value that imposes a more restrictive access policy than the default.

Use the **umask** program to check and set the mask value. Without arguments, **umask** tells you the current mask value:

```
$ umask ↵
000
$ □
```

If you see 000, it means that any files and directories you create will be wide open to every user, unless you change their modes after creation. I recommend that use **umask** to set a mask value of 027, which gives you essentially unrestricted access, members of your group, if any, read and execute/search access, and no access to anyone else:

```
$ umask 027 ↵
$ □
```

The mask value is applied to the default value to determine the permissions of new files and directories. It doesn't affect existing ones. For directories, 777 masked by 027 (the default mask) results in a mode of 750. For ordinary files, 666 masked by 027 results in a mode of 640. Figure 12.3 shows how this works.

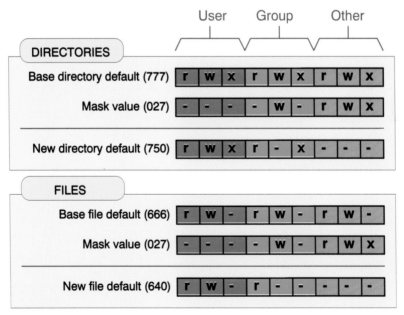

*Figure 12.3 The **umask** program sets a value that the shell uses to determine the permissions applied to newly created files and directories.*

If a bit in the mask value is on (a letter), it turns off the corresponding bit in the file or directory permission value. If the mask bit value is off (a dash), it has no effect on the default value. If a default bit is already off, it is unaffected by any mask value.

CHANGING PERMISSIONS

If you need to share a resource (such as a file or directory) that is restricted, use **chmod** to alter its permissions. The program takes options in various forms and names of files and directories. Let's say you have a data file that is currently set to mode 600 (only you can read and write it), but you now want to let anyone read it. The easiest way to make it readable by the world is to set the read permission bit on at all levels:

```
$ chmod +r data_file ↵
$ ▢
```

The **+r** option effectively turns on the read bit for the user, the group, and others. If the bit is already on (as for the user in this example), it stays on. Use a hyphen (-) as an option flag to turn a bit off. For example **-w** turns off write permission for all users. Of course, if the write bit is already off at a particular user level, it stays off.

You can also set the mode to an exact value by using another form of option:

```
$ chmod 755 data_file ↵
$ ▢
```

The octal mode value sets and clears mode bits to effect the requested mode. A mode of 755 is often used for directories to allow all users to search and list the directories. However, only the file owner can write the directories, so he or she is the only user who can add or remove files, rename or move files, and so on

CHANGING OWNERSHIP

You might need to give ownership of a file to another user, Perhaps you are moving to a new job or changing projects. Whatever the reason, you can change file ownership by using the **chown** (change owner) program. This command example shows a user giving a set of files to our friend Rocky:

```
$ chown rocky *.c ↵
$ ▢
```

The user running the command must be the current owner of the files (or the superuser). After the command completes, the original owner is on the outside looking in. The original owner's access to the files is determined by the group and other permissions, although the files remain in his or her directory until the new owner moves them.

Similarly, you can change the group identification of a file or files by running the **chgrp** (change group) program. You must be the owner of the files or a user who has group write privileges (or the superuser) to change the group ownership of files.

REMOVING FILES YOU DON'T OWN

You can remove a file that you don't own if it is in a directory in which you have write permission. This action may be necessary if you are cleaning up your directory hierarchy and you encounter a file that was copied to you by another user.

The situation is this: The file is owned by another user and you probably don't have write permission on the file. When you try to remove the file with **rm**, you are asked to confirm the removal of a file. Answer in the affirmative (anything that starts with a letter **y**) and, poof, the file is gone, as shown in the following example:

```
$ ls -l ↵
total 6
-r--r-----    1 doris      other         375 Jan 05 17:40 framus
-rw-r-----    1 augie      other         605 Jan 05 17:38 getbyte.c
-rw-r-----    1 augie      other         734 Jan 05 17:38 getint.c
$ rm framus ↵
framus: 440 mode ? yup ↵
$ ▯
```

If you don't want **rm** to bother you about such things, use the **-f** option, which forces the program to remove the files without warning you of file ownership mismatches (as long as you own the directory).

WHAT YOU NEED TO KNOW

In this lesson, the importance of controlling access to files and directories has been stressed, and mechanisms to achieve security have been described. The next lesson adds to your knowledge of directory hierarchies. Before leaving this lesson, be sure you have a good understanding of these topics:

☑ All files and directories on a UNIX system are owned by a user or by the system.

☑ Access to files for reading, writing, and executing (searching for directories) is controlled by permissions at the user, group, and other levels.

☑ The long-list (**-l**) format of **ls** gives you detailed information about your files and directories.

☑ The **umask**, **chmod**, **chown**, and **chgrp** programs let you set and change permissions, and control ownership of files and directories.

☑ You can remove files you don't own, as long as you own the directory they reside in.

Lesson 13

More About Directory Hierarchies

A file system is not a static entity, which means it is subject to change. If a computer system is being used at all, files and directories are probably being created, modified, and removed, altering the hierarchy in unpredictable ways. The UNIX file system has been designed to be very flexible so that it can grow and adapt to your changing needs. The adaptability of a UNIX system is achieved by mounting file systems onto existing hierarchies.

This lesson describes some features of the UNIX file system that can be important to you in certain situations. For example, you might work on a project that has its files stored on a different disk than the one your system runs on. How do you access those file? Or perhaps your system takes on more users and additional disks have to be added by your administrator to handle the load. Can you and the new users share files? How?

If this topic is of interest or importance to you now, continue reading. If you couldn't care less at this time, skip it and come back to it later when you discover that you need to know. Your first clue will be an inability to *link* to certain files that you know are there.

By the time you finish this lesson, you will have learned

- What makes the UNIX file hierarchy so adaptable
- How another entire file system gets connected to a root file system
- How to link files and why
- What hard links and symbolic links are
- How to remove an entire directory hierarchy (carefully!)

MOUNTED FILE SYSTEMS

You have probably noticed, especially if you are a DOS user, that there has been no mention of drive A or any other disk drive by name. The UNIX file system looks like a unified hierarchy, but on a system of even modest capacity, it is probably a collection of several file system components.

Figure 13.1 depicts a simplified root file system. It contains the required **root** directory and the usual set of system and user directories previously described. In addition it shows a **project** directory under **root** and a separate project file system. The project file system has its own root directory. It is a complete, self-contained file system that is stored on some device, such as a floppy disk, a CD-ROM (compact disk read-only memory), or even a different hard disk.

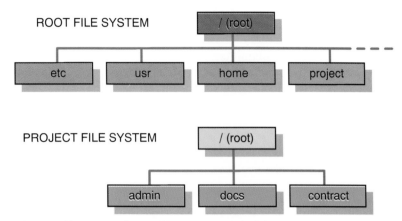

Figure 13.1 *The two file systems depicted here in simplified form are separate and unrelated. The project file system might be stored on a floppy disk, a CD-ROM, or some other device. Its files are not accessible to a user on the root file system.*

As you can see, these two file systems are not connected. Using administration tools, however, a privileged user (root or the system owner, for example) can *mount* the project file system onto the root file system. When this is done, the project hierarchy becomes a part of the root system hierarchy, as shown in Figure 13.2, and the files can be made available to authorized users.

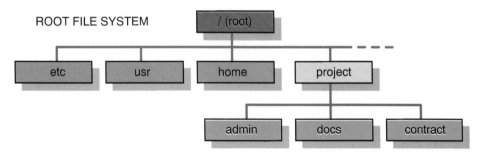

Figure 13.2 *When the project file system is mounted (by a privileged user) it becomes a part of the root system hierarchy. Given suitable permissions, the files and directories of the project hierarchy are available to authorized users.*

The process of mounting the project file system places its root directory onto the mount point (the **project** directory). Pathnames to files and directories on the mounted hierarchy follow the same rules that you have learned. Thus, the **admin** directory has a fully qualified pathname of **/project/admin**.

So why should you care about this stuff? It looks like one big file system. You can access files the same way whether they are part of the root file system or the mounted project file system. From a user's point of view nothing changes. Well, not quite.

LINKING FILES

A useful UNIX feature is the ability to link files. The **ln** program lets you establish a link to a file so that the file can be accessed by a different name. Review the description of directories and inodes presented in Lesson 8, if necessary. Note that a file can be referred to by more than a single directory entry, and the file's inode contains a count of the number of links to the file.

The **ln** program takes as arguments the name of the file you're linking to and the name you want to use to refer to the file. The following example shows how Rocky links to a file owned by another user, establishing what is sometimes called a *hard link*:

```
$ cd mydocs ↵
$ pwd ↵ ———————————————————— Display the current directory
/home/rocky/mydocs
$ ls -l ↵ ——————————————————— List files in the current directory
total 0
$ ls -l /home/doris ———————————— List files in directory doris
total 2
-rw-r-----   1 doris    other    605 Nov 16 10:35 basespec
$ ln /home/doris/basespec spec ↵ ———— Create the link spec
$ ▢                                    to the file basespec
```

The directory commands show how Rocky assures himself that the link is going to be in the right place. He lists the directory to be sure the name **spec** is not already being used. It isn't. In fact, the directory is empty. Then he checks the permissions on the file in Doris's directory. They look right. Finally he runs the **ln** command to establish the link.

Now the file is available to Rocky in his own directory. Figure 13.3 shows the link, which is a pointer from Rocky's directory to **/home/doris/basespec**. There is still only one copy of the file's data stored on disk, but two names refer to it from different directories.

Only Doris can modify the file (look at the permission values), but Rocky will have a file that is always up to date. If he had made a copy of it instead of linking to it, his file might get rancid if changes are made to the original and he doesn't update his copy.

UNDERSTANDING LINKS TO FILES

The UNIX system provides a file linking feature that lets you refer to a file by more than one name. This feature provides important benefits. A single program can use different names for its various behaviors. Disk space occupation is minimized (since only one copy of the file physically exists) and users don't have to remember lots of arcane options.

Users can use links to files owned by other users. This arrangement lets each user refer to the file by a name of his or her choosing. One user controls the contents of the file. All other linked users have access to the current contents using filenames in their own directories.

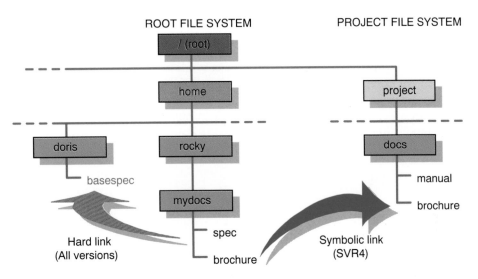

Figure 13.3 You can establish a hard link to a file in the same file system, but hard links across file system boundaries are not allowed. However, symbolic links to files across file system boundries and symbolic links to directories are allowed (as of SVR4).

SYMBOLIC LINKS

A problem with hard links is that they can not be made across file system boundaries. The reason is that each file system has its own control information in the form of inodes, and the probability of duplicate inode numbers is very high. The need to link across file systems has resulted in the addition of *symbolic links*, sometimes called *soft links*, starting with SVR4.

A symbolic link doesn't refer to a file by inode number. Instead it uses a pathname to identify the file that is the target of the link. The link across the boundary between the root and project file systems in Figure 13.3 shows how Rocky can use symbolic linking to advantage. He sets the link by using the **ln** program with the -s option:

```
$ ln -s /project/docs/brochure brochure ↵
$ ls -l
total 8
lrw-r--r--    1 randy     other       734 Nov 16 10:42 brochure ->
/project/docs/brochure
-rw-r-----    2 doris     other       605 Nov 16 10:35 basespec
$ ☐
```

The long listing that follows the creation of the link in this example shows the status of the two linked files. The symbolic link shows both the name of the link (**brochure**) and the name of the link target (**/project/docs/brochure**). The arrow shows the direction of the link. Also, the letter **l** is displayed in the file mode indicator to identify this as a symbolic link.

Because of the generality of this approach, you can also link to directories, forming aliases for directory names. An example of this is the **/bin** directory on the newer versions of UNIX. The directory is no longer used because all program files have been placed in directories under **/usr**, but a lot of older UNIX programs assume that needed utilities are located in **/bin**. Through the magic of a symbolic link, references to **/bin** are automatically translated to **/usr/bin**.

REMOVING A DIRECTORY TREE

One of the responsibilities of users (neglected by many, unfortunately) is removing old files to relieve the inevitable pressure for more disk space. This is particularly important on small business and personal systems, on which disk space is probably at a premium right from the start.

After you have saved files that need preserving by copying them to a backup store of some kind (such as tape or floppy disk), use the **rm** program to remove the files from the disk. If all the files reside in a single directory, **rm *** does the job easily. If your files are contained in a hierarchy, as would be the case if you organize your files along project lines, you may choose to remove the entire hierarchy. Options to the **rm** program make this job easy.

Assume that your project directory—let's call it **projectx**—is subordinate to your home directory and that your working directory is your home directory. (Type **cd** without any directory argument to return to your home directory, if you're not already there.) The following command quickly dispatches the **projectx** directory and everything beneath it:

```
$ rm -rf projectx ↵
$ ▢
```

The **-r** option tells **rm** to operate *recursively*, which causes it to descend the directory hierarchy from the named starting point. You can not remove a directory until it is empty, so **rm** must go to the bottom of each branch and then back its way out, removing files and directories as it retreats to the starting point.

The **-f** option was described in Lesson 12. In this use it prevents **rm** from issuing messages about ownership problems and file permissions and waiting for you to confirm removal. The fact is that the files are in your directory and you can remove them. This option makes it automatic.

Be careful with recursive removals. Once the files are removed, they can't be recovered unless you have a recent backup or your system is running special software that sends removed files to a temporary recovery directory.

Whacking Branches Off Directory Trees

The **rm -rf** command is the UNIX equivalent of a chainsaw in a forest. Use it with due caution to clean up portions of your directory hierarchy. The **-r** option to **rm** makes the command operate recursively, taking out everything from a specified starting point to the far reaches of every branch. The -f option tells **rm** to force the removal of files, regardless of ownership and mode (provided they're in a directory you own).

This is powerful stuff, but do yourself a favor. If you run a command of this type, look it over *carefully* before you press the RETURN key. If you're not absolutely sure what's going to happen, don't do it (press the @ key to kill the command line)—better safe than sorry.

What You Need to Know

☑ A file system can be extended by mounting other file systems into the hierarchy. Only a privileged user can mount file systems, but any user with needed access rights can use the mounted file systems.

☑ Files can be linked using the **ln** program. Hard links can not cross file-system boundaries.

☑ Symbolic (soft) links can span file system boundaries and can link to directories as well as files. Use **ln -s** to create symbolic links.

☑ You can use **rm -r** (recursive remove) to remove an entire directory hierarchy. Use caution to avoid the loss of data. Without special software support or frequent backup, removed files are gone forever.

Lesson 14

Additional UNIX Utilities

This lesson describes a collection of utility programs that you will find to be valuable as you work with text files. Read through once to get a feel for which programs to use in certain circumstances. By the time you finish with this lesson you will understand the following

- Determine file types using the **file** command

- Count lines, words, and characters in text files using **wc**

- Step through files in screen pages using **pg** (AT&T UNIX) or the **more** command (Berkeley)

- Format text into pages for printing using **pr**

- Spool print requests for background processing using the **lp** command

The material presented here will get you going quickly, but it is not meant to be rigorous. When you want to know more, read the detailed instructions in your system's command reference documents.

WHAT KIND OF FILE IS IT?

As you have read, UNIX doesn't use filename extensions to indicate the type of a file (although some application programs expect certain extensions). This lack of extensions means that you can't always tell what kind of file you're dealing with. Is it a program? A text file? Something else?

Use the **file** program to determine a file's type. You can check a single file or a group of files. In this example, all files that have names beginning with a dot (.*) in the current directory are checked:

```
$ file .* ↵
.:              directory
..:             directory
.profile:       English text
$ ▢
```

The **file** program attempts to determine the file type by examining portions of the file for clues. Certain program files have *magic numbers* that indicate their type. Some files contain UNIX shell commands. Others contain plain text or text in an identifiable human language. Programming language source files (Basic, Pascal, C, and so on) are usually, but not always, identified correctly.

COUNTING LINES, WORDS, AND CHARACTERS

A large part of your work on a UNIX system involves text files (files that contain only letters, digits, punctuation characters, and formatting codes, such as a memo or UNIX script file). You might want to know something about a file, such as how many lines or words it contains, or how many characters are stored in it.

Use **wc** to get a concise summary of this information. The program, named for its primary purpose of word counting, accepts a filename or a list of names. The following example shows **wc** counting a single file:

```
$ wc group ↵
      21       21     375 group
$ ▯        Lines   Words  Bytes
```

The analysis of the **group** file shows one of the failings of **wc**: it has a rather simplistic notion of what a *word* is. It counts long sequences of characters delimited by spaces, tabs, and newlines as a single word, which in this example means each line is one word.

When given a list of files, **wc** produces one line of output for each file and a summary for the list:

```
$ wc cqww help.txt ↵
     110     270    1790 cqww
      17      83     443 help.txt
     127     353    2233 total
$ ▯
```

PAGING THROUGH FILES

If the file is large and you are using a video display device, you might find that output scrolls off the top of the screen before you can read it. To solve this problem use one of the *pager* programs, **pg** and **more**.

The UNIX utility **pg**, introduced with System V, allows you to page through the contents of a file or a list of files. The page size is initially set to the number of lines on your screen (or window) minus one. You can change this value by using a command-line option (*-lines*, where *lines* is the page size you want specified in text lines or screen rows).

The **pg** program accepts a number of commands when it displays its prompt (the default is :) after displaying a page. Each command letter must be followed by a carriage return to take effect, unless you use the **-n** option when you start the program, which causes **pg** to react to commands immediately. Press the SPACEBAR to display the next page (or simply press RETURN by itself); press **h** to display a help screen; press **n** (**p**) to display the next (previous) file in a file list. To quit at any time, press **q**.

A similar utility called **more** has been available with Berkeley-derived versions of UNIX for many years. It was merged into System V as of Release 4. The **more** program processes commands immediately. Press the SPACEBAR to see the next screenful or RETURN to scroll the next line into view; press **b** to go back a page, and **h** to view the help screen. Commands for paging and scrolling accept a preceding multiplier. Typing **3b**, for example, moves back three pages in the file, if possible.

Both of these programs have text search capabilities and other features that you should explore when you have time. Try using either **pg** or **more** to view the **/etc/termcap** file, which on most UNIX systems contains more than a few screen pages of cryptic-looking text. Use one of these commands to start the paging process:

```
pg /etc/termcap          (commands require ↵)
pg -n /etc/termcap       (commands are immediate)
more /etc/termcap        (commands are immediate)
```

If these commands don't work right or you get a message about unknown terminal type, you may need to set the TERM variable and **export** it. The TERM variable stores a value in your environment, and **export** makes it available to programs that you run. If your terminal is relatively new or is actually the display of a PC system, you might be able to use the name **ansi**. Check with your administrator for the correct designation, and use one of these commands to set it (the second form is for Berkeley systems):

```
TERM=ansi; export TERM
setenv TERM ansi
```

You can also use a UNIX feature called a *pipe* to take the output of one program and feed it to another program as input. The pipe is symbolized by the vertical bar (|), and the resulting command is called a *pipeline*. Lesson 34, "Filters and Command Pipelines," provides detailed coverage of this important topic. Figure 14.1 illustrates the effect of a pipeline command consisting of two commands: **cmd1** generates data, and **cmd2** processes the data before delivering it to the user's terminal screen.

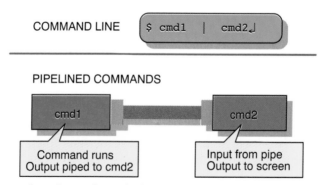

Figure 14.1 A command pipeline is formed when one program's output is sent to another program as input. The vertical bar (|) is the symbol used on the command line to specify a pipe.

The following example command line lists a large directory and pages the output to your screen by piping the lister output to the pager program:

```
$ ls /usr/bin | more ↵
STTY
X11
acctcom
adminrole
adminuser
ar
...
cat
charconv
--More--
```

Many lines of output have been left out, but this example should give you an idea of what to expect. The last line of the display contains the prompt for which the **more** program gets its name (the **pg** program uses a colon for a prompt unless you specify a different prompt). The pager program waits until you issue a command before displaying the next page or performing other requested actions.

PRINTING FILES

Use the **pr** program to format text files into printable pages. Each page is printed (displayed) on your terminal unless you direct the output to a different device. Figure 14.2 shows the default page layout produced by the **pr** program. You can use various command-line options to adjust the page layout to match your needs.

DEFAULT 66-LINE PAGE LAYOUT

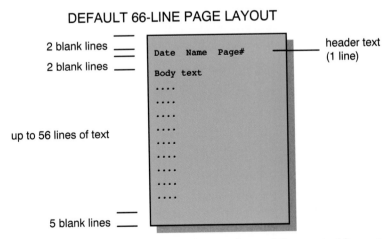

*Figure 14.2 The **pr** program uses a default page layout designed for a typical line printer. You can use command-line options to alter the layout to match your requirements and preferences.*

A page consists of a header, a body of text, and a footer for a total of 66 lines. Left and right margins are created, and long lines are *wrapped*. This means that a line of text that is longer than a physical line, accounting for margins and page width, is printed as two or more output lines. The header consists of a line containing the date and time. Filename, and page number embedded within a field of blank lines (two above, two below). The footer is a group of five blank lines.

Because the output goes to your terminal, it might scroll off your screen before you can read it. If your purpose is to preview the output before actually printing hard copy, use one of the pager programs to step through the output. If your purpose is to get hard copy, pipe the output of **pr** to a print spooler program, such **lp** (your system might have a different spooler program, such as **lpr** or **opr**—check local customs), as shown here:

```
$ pr .profile | lp ↵
request id is ps-534 (standard input)
$ □
```

The message about the print request is a response from **lp** telling you that the request has been queued as job number 534 on the laser printer named ps. The input to **lp** came from its standard input rather than from a named file or other source. Jot down the number in case you decide to cancel the job, request a higher priority, or ask an administrator for help if your printout never sees the light of day.

These uses of **pr** and **lp** barely scratch the surface of their features and capabilities, but most of the time it's all you need to know. When you need to know more, look it up in your command reference documents.

WHAT YOU NEED TO KNOW

The programs described in this lesson give you some useful tools that you will use again and again as you work with the UNIX system. Before starting Lesson 15, which begins the detailed coverage of the UNIX shells, check your knowledge of these topics:

- ☑ You can find out the type of a file (executable, plain text, source code, and so on) by using the **file** program.

- ☑ Use **wc** to count the number of lines, words, and characters in text files.

- ☑ To send output to your terminal in screen-sized chunks, use **pg** or **more**, either as a stand-alone program or as a component of a pipeline command.

- ☑ Use **pr** to format text files into printable pages. The output should be piped to a suitable print-spooler program or pager for viewing.

- ☑ A program for print spooling, typically named **lp**, **lpr**, **opr**, or something similar, provides a way of getting your print jobs done while you work on other tasks.

Section Three

UNIX User Interfaces

When you work with UNIX, your interactions are mediated by the shell, which is the primary user interface. This section describes the standard shell and a couple of popular alternatives.

The topics include an introduction to the standard UNIX shell (**sh**), a description of how the user environment works and how it can be modified, and an introduction to the standard input and output files, which provide so much of the renowned versatility of the UNIX system.

You might prefer one of the two major alternatives to the standard shell. This section describes the features and benefits of both the C shell (**csh**) and the KornShell (**ksh**) command languages. In addition, all of the shells support background processing and each provides a form of job control that allows the management of foreground and background tasks. These important features are described and demonstrated in a separate lesson.

Lesson 15

The Standard Shell

This lesson describes the standard UNIX shell. Along the way, it introduces you to some important concepts and terminology that will help you understand how the UNIX system works from a user's point of view. The topics in this lesson include the following:

- The standard UNIX shell (**sh**) features
- Shell commands and the interpreter
- Programs and processes

Some concepts and capabilities described in this lesson are difficult to grasp at first reading. Get as much as you can out of it, even if it's just terminology, and come back later to refresh your memory.

THE STANDARD UNIX SHELL

The standard UNIX shell, called the Bourne shell after its author, has been the standard shell since Seventh Edition UNIX. The program file for this shell is called **sh** and it resides in **/usr/bin** on System V, Release 4 and later UNIX systems. Earlier UNIX incarnations placed **sh** and most other high-use program files in **/bin**.

The **sh** program found on some UNIX systems, notably Berkeley-derived UNIX, is an older version, which does not have some of the features of the current version. On such systems, you should check for a shell program file called **sh5**. This is a UNIX System V shell.

Note: The shell is a program that, like any other program, can be replaced. As with mountains that must be climbed because they're there, some programmers feel that shells must be replaced because they're replaceable. The UNIX system has seen its share of shells, and there is nothing wrong with that. The urge to do the job better or to satisfy previously unrecognized needs is what has kept UNIX and its derivatives fresh for a long time.

In its current form **sh** is a big improvement over what it once was, having been modified to incorporate some of the features popularized by its primary competitors, **csh** and **ksh**, and some new ones of its own. Lessons 19 describes the alternatives to **sh** and shows you how to use some of their features.

FEATURES OF THE STANDARD SHELL

The shell is a *command interpreter* and a *command programming language*. It prompts for, reads, and executes user commands. The commands can come directly from a terminal or from a file.

The shell provides a collection of important features. These features are named and described briefly here. They are explained more fully later in this lesson and in other lessons:

- Customization by initialization files that are processed when the shell starts
- Mechanisms for background processing and conditional execution of user commands
- Redirection of program input and output
- Piping to connect programs in pipelines
- Packaging of repetitive tasks into script files
- Notification of new-mail arrival

If you invoke the shell as **jsh**, certain special commands are activated that implement job control. This topic is covered in Lesson 20. In addition, a version called **rsh** provides a restricted shell environment that is used for "guest" accounts, such as might be used for training, demonstrating products, and so on. The restricted shell limits the commands the user can execute and blocks attempts to move outside the restricted environment.

TYPES OF COMMANDS

The shell categorizes commands as *simple commands, command pipelines,* and *lists.* In the descriptions that follow, the term *blank* refers to a space or a tab character. A *name* is a sequence of letters (case sensitive—a–z and A–Z are distinct), digits (0–9), and underscores that starts with a letter or underscore. In addition, a *parameter* is a name, a digit, or one of the following characters:

```
    *    @    #    ?    -    $    !
```

Simple Commands. A command line consists of *words* and *blanks* that separate the words. The first word of a command line is taken to be the command file or program to execute. In the absence of symbols that cause redirection, piping, or command-list interpretation, (described later), the remaining words are passed as arguments to the command

You have seen commands of this form many times in the first two sections of this book. The command to display the contents of a file is a good example. Figure 15.1 identifies the components of a simple command. In addition to the filename arguments, a command line can also contain options that alter the default behavior of the program. The –v option tells **cat** to produce visible output of characters that have no graphical representations. This is handy for troubleshooting text files that contain unwanted nontext characters.

A command can terminate normally, or it can be terminated abnormally by various events (a user break or a signal from the operating system). Each simple command has a value called its *exit status.* If a command terminates normally, it usually returns a value of 0 to indicate success and a non-zero value to indicate a failure of some kind. If a command is terminated by the user (interrupt/break) or by the operating system, a signal code indicates the cause of termination. The exit status for abnormal termination is 128 (200 octal) plus the signal code.

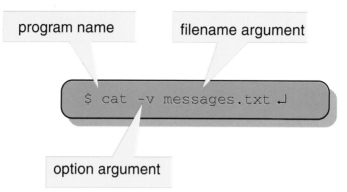

Figure 15.1 *A simple command consists of a program name, followed by an argument list. The arguments can be command options and filenames.*

These command exit status values are used by the shell for conditional command execution (see "Command Lists") and by driver programs that run other programs (the **make** utility and the C program driver, **cc**, are examples).

Commands Pipeline. The shell treats a sequence of commands separated by the pipe symbol (|) as a command pipeline. In this arrangement, the pipe takes the output of the command to its left and sends it as input to the command to its right. The last command in a pipeline writes to the terminal device or is redirected to a file or other device. (Even the case of a single command is referred to as a pipeline.)

An example of a pipeline was shown in Lesson 14 with the output of an **ls** command being paged by the **more** command. In Figure 15.2, a file is displayed by the **cat** program and the output is filtered by **grep**, which is a program that globally searches a file looking for lines that contain a specified pattern. Any lines that contain a match are printed. (The use of **grep** and other filter programs in pipeline commands is covered in detail in Section 7.)

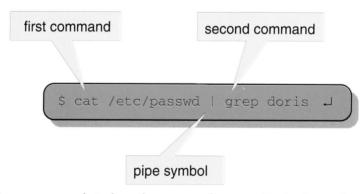

Figure 15.2 *Using a command pipeline, the contents of a system file, /etc/passwd, are examined to find lines that contain a specified pattern (a user name)*

The commands in a pipeline all run at the same time, and the exit status of the pipeline is that of the last command in the pipeline. The shell waits for the last command to terminate.

Command Lists. A *command list* is a sequence of commands separated by one of the following characters:

;   &   && ||

Figure 15.3 shows a command that sequentially executes two commands: **pwd** runs to conclusion and then **ls** runs.

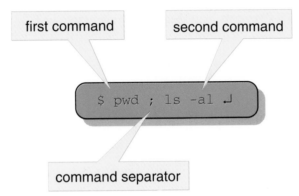

first command   second command

$ pwd ; ls -al ↵

command separator

*Figure 15.3 The semicolon used in this example causes sequential execution of the commands. The **pwd** command runs to completion and then the **ls** command executes.*

Use of the & separator (asynchronous execution) is covered in Lesson 20. The && and || separators (conditional execution) are covered in Lesson 38.

COMMAND EXECUTION

When executing your commands, the shell performs a series of actions on command lines. Some of the actions are fully described elsewhere in this lesson. The rest are covered in other lessons. The descriptions given here are deliberately brief and are intended only to give you an overview of the interpretation process:

- **Command substitution**   The shell interprets any command that is specified between grave accents and uses its standard output as words in the command line, as described in Lesson 38.

- **Parameter substitution**   The shell recognizes *positional parameters* (digits 0–9) and *keyword parameters*. Positional parameters are covered in detail in Lesson 38. Keyword parameters, also called *variables*, are covered in Lesson 16.

- **Blank interpretation**   After substitutions, a parameter called IFS (internal field separator—see Lesson 16) is used by the shell to determine how to break the resulting command line into arguments.

- **Input and output redirection**   Checks the command line to detect the use of redirection (see Lesson 17).

- **Filename generation**   The shell generates a list of filenames that match patterns specified ambiguously (using wildcards, described in Lesson 9).

QUOTING

As you have seen, certain characters have special meaning to the shell. In addition to the characters used to specify ambiguous filenames (*, ?, and [ ]), the special characters, or *metacharacters*, are the following:

```
;   &   (   )   |   ^   <   >   newline   space   tab
```

You will have problems if you need to use one or more of these metacharacters in a filename or in options to be passed to a program. To protect them from the shell, use one of the three available forms of *quoting*. Quoting a special character makes the character stand for itself.

Backslash. The basic quoting mechanism is to place a backslash in front of the special character. Thus * is seen by the shell as an ordinary character rather than as a filename wildcard. A \ followed by a real newline character removes the newline when processed by the shell. This allows you to break a logically long line into two or more shorter physical lines.

The quoting of metacharacters can be a confusing topic. It helps to be able to run simple demonstrations to see how things work. The following examples show how you can use the **echo** command to test quoted and unquoted command-line strings. Let's test the wildcard example. Run these three commands in your home directory. They demonstrate both filename generation and quoting. The filenames will differ, but the technique generally applies:

List all files:

```
$ echo * ↵
adv_awk awk_test bin contest courses group ham lib myls profile.bak
src test
$ ▢
```

Notice that none of the "dot" files are listed. This is because the expansion of * by the shell specifically excludes filenames that start with a dot. To see them, use this command:

```
$ echo .* ↵
.  ..  .exrc  .profile
$ ▢
```

In both of these examples, the * is seen by the shell as the metacharacter. To prevent expansion by the shell, quote the * with a \:

```
$ echo \* ↵
*
$ ▢
```

Single Quotes. A pair of single quote marks around a string causes all characters in the string to be quoted. The sequence '*?' when processed becomes *\?, preventing the shell from treating either as a special character. The backslash character doesn't have any special meaning inside a pair of single quotes.

If you need to protect a reference to a variable, such as $TERM, put it inside a pair of single quotes. Without single quotes, you get the value of the TERM variable:

```
$ echo $TERM ↵
vt100
$ ▢
```

Contrast this with the variable reference inside a pair of single quotes:

```
$ echo '$TERM' ↵
$TERM
$ ▢
```

The argument to **echo** ($TERM) is passed through without change. This quoting feature is used extensively in later lessons about programs, such as **sed**, that read processing command scripts from the command line.

Double Quotes. You can also quote a character or string by using double quotes. They behave the same way as single quotes except that the shell processes any $, `cmd`, and \ sequences in the quoted string. The impact of this processing is that parameter and command substitutions occur inside double-quoted strings. A typical use of double quotes is to permit single quotes in words (used as an apostrophe) within a string. First without double quotes:

```
$ echo You can't go home again. ↵
> ▢
```

Oops! What happened? The > symbol is called a *secondary prompt*. The shell has seen a construct that isn't complete (the single quote opens what is expected to be a quoted string), so it prompts for more with the secondary prompt. Get out of this mess by pressing the DELETE or BREAK key. Then use double quotes around the string:

```
$ echo "You can't go home again." ↵
You can't go home again.
$ ▢
```

That's more like it. One kind of quotes is protecting the other. It works the other way around, too.

PROGRAMS AND PROCESSES

A primary UNIX concept is the *process*. The UNIX system is process oriented. A process is an execution environment set up by the operating system kernel. An execution environment is a region of memory that has three major components: system data, user data, and program instructions.

Figure 15.4 depicts in a simplified way what happens when you execute a program. A *program* is composed of instructions and data. The files that we refer to as programs out on disk are just collections of bytes. To run, a program must reside in a computer system's primary memory.

The cloud-like image is used, perhaps because of its nebulosity, to represent processes. A single program file on disk can be used to create more than one process. In a multiuser environment, it is not at all uncommon for two or more users to be running the same program at the same time. Each process that is running the same program is called an *instance*.

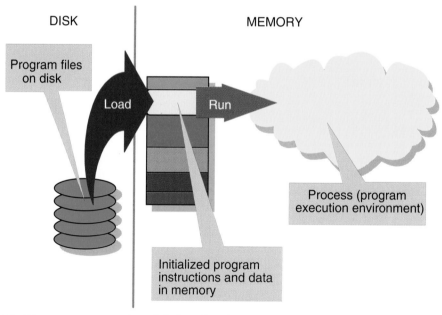

Figure 15.4 *Programs are stored on disk, but they do not run there. The UNIX kernel sets up an execution environment called a process. The process inherits system data and then program instructions and user data are read in from disk to initialize memory.*

Associated with each process is a unique ID (a number). To see what processes are running on you behalf, use the **ps** (process **s**tatus) command:

```
$ ps ↵
   PID TTY      TIME COMMAND
 16852  1a      0:02 ksh
 17819  1a      0:00 ps
$ ▢
```

The **ps** program has many options, most of benefit to system administrators.

WHAT YOU NEED TO KNOW

This lesson presents a lot of information about the shell and pointers to related coverage elsewhere in the book. Familiarity with shell-related terminology is important because it is a large part of the language of UNIX.

Many topics introduced in this lesson are developed and illustrated in other lessons. For example, the user environment is the topic of the next lesson. Check your understanding of these topics now and come back after you gain some experience with the shell to reenforce your knowledge:

- ☑ The UNIX shell is a command language interpreter that supports user customization, and input and output redirection

- ☑ The shell accepts simple commands, command pipelines, and command lists.

- ☑ Various forms of command processing, including conditional and background processing are supported.

- ☑ Three quoting mechanisms (\ and single and double quotes) can be used to protect special characters from shell processing.

- ☑ The UNIX shell creates additional processes to run most user commands. Each process has a unique ID. Multiple instances of the same program can run simultaneously, as separate processes.

Lesson 16

The User Environment

In the first two sections of this book references have been made to the user environment variables HOME, PATH, and TERM. These variables hold values that are important to you and to running programs, including the shell. This lesson describes the user environment in detail, showing you why it exists, how to set it up, and how to make the values available to programs that need them. The following topics are covered:

- The purpose of environment variables
- Setting and viewing variable values
- Setting variables on the command line
- Using read-only variables

THE PURPOSE OF ENVIRONMENT VARIABLES

An *environment* is simply a collection of variables and their values. A *variable* is identified by a unique name. Its value is represented by a sequence of characters (a *string*). Some variable names are commonly used by the UNIX system to establish a base environment and should be considered reserved words. Other variables spring into existence when you name them and assign values to them. Some variables are created and disposed of by running programs.

As you have seen in earlier lessons, environment variables provide the shell and other programs with needed information. For example, PATH tells the shell where to look for programs that you use in commands. If the PATH variable did not exist, or existed without being given a value, you would have to do more work to issue commands. The simple command **ls** to list your current directory would need to be specified fully, as in this example:

```
$ /usr/bin/ls ↵
...
$ □
```

The PATH variable supplies the shell with the leading path value, in this example **/usr/bin**, so that you need to type only the relative pathname of the program. It even relieves you of the need to know where this or any other UNIX utility program is located, as long as one of the colon-separated entries in PATH identifies the needed directory.

Other environment variables serve different purposes. TERM identifies your terminal type to visual programs, such as the **vi** editor, that need to know how to interact with it. Other variables, such as PS1 (primary prompt string), tell the shell about your preferences.

VIEWING AND SETTING ENVIRONMENT VARIABLES

If you want to see which variables are defined in your environment, run the **set** program. The program prints the variable names and their current values. This example is representative of a user's environment, but yours undoubtedly has different values for some of the variables and may include other variables:

```
$ set ↵
HOME=/home/rocky
IFS=

LOGNAME=rocky
LOGTTY=/dev/tp/12
MAIL=/var/mail/rocky
MAILCHECK=600
PATH=/usr/bin:/usr/dbin:/usr/ldbin
PS1=$
PS2=>
SHELL=/usr/bin/sh
TERM=ansi
TZ=:US/Mountain
...
$ ❑
```

If your environment defines more variables than fit on your screen, pipe the output to **pg** or **more** to page the output for viewing.

Being variables, their values are subject to change during your login session, although most don't vary, once set. If you need to change a variable, simply assign it a new value:

```
$ TERM=vt100-w ↵
$ ❑
```

The terminal type in this example, vt100–w, identifies a DEC VT100 terminal in wide mode (132 columns per screen row). It would be best for the user if his or her terminal is actually a VT100 in the wide mode, or at least a device that can emulate such a terminal.

To examine the value of a single variable, use the **echo** program, which simply displays or prints its arguments as text strings. Notice that you need to extract the value of a variable by appending a $ to the beginning of the name. If you echo the name without the $, you just see the name. This point is illustrated by this series of commands:

```
$ echo HOME ↵
$ HOME
$ echo $HOME ↵
/home/rocky
$ ❑
```

COMMONLY USED ENVIRONMENT VARIABLES

Let's take a closer look at some of the most commonly used environment variables with an eye toward understanding what they do. This list shows for each variable the name, a sample value (taken from the previous **set** example), and a brief description:

HOME (/home/rocky)   The fully-qualified pathname of the user's home directory. This is where your login session starts, and it is the default target of a **cd** command (you end up here if you don't give **cd** a directory argument).

IFS   Internal field separator. This string consists of characters that are used to separate fields and records. You can't see them because they have no graphical representations, but IFS has a default value of Space + Tab + Newline. The newline explains why this variable shows up with a clear line after it in the output of the **set** command. The shell uses IFS to determine how to break a command line into separate arguments.

LOGNAME (rocky)   This is the user's ID, or account name if you prefer.

LOGTTY (/dev/tp/12)   When you log in, a device file is associated with your session. This user is on a directly connected serial port. Workstation users typically see the name "console" as the value of this variable.

MAIL (/var/mail/rocky)   This identifies the user's mailbox, which is a file in the **/var/mail** directory. Electronic mail sent to you is saved here, and you are (eventually) informed of its arrival. A variable called MAILPATH provides the same capability with significant enhancements on newer UNIX systems. If both of these variables are defined, the MAIL value is ignored.

MAILCHECK (600)   The value is expressed as the number of seconds the system should wait between mail checks. This example shows the typical default value of ten minutes. When the specified waiting period expires, the system checks to see whether new mail has arrived for you. If so, you receive a message similar to "you have mail" the next time you receive the system prompt. Setting the value to 0 causes a mail check every time you are prompted by the shell.

PATH (/usr/bin:/usr/dbin:/usr/ldbin)   This value identifies the directories to be searched when you type commands. The system administrator maintains a default PATH that all users inherit, but you are free to modify it (see Lesson 18, Customizing Your Operating Environment).

PS1 ($)   This is the text of your primary prompt string. The standard UNIX default value is "$ ", but you can use whatever pleases you. Power users might like "Yes, master? " or something equally ego gratifying. DOS users might want the current path value (see Lesson 19, Alternative Shells).

PS2 (>)   If a command is not completed on one line, the shell prompts you for more with this string. This is used primarily for interactive shell programming purposes. If you mess up in forming a command, you might receive this prompt unexpectedly. To recover, simply press the DELETE (DEL or RUBOUT) key or the BREAK key.

SHELL (/usr/bin/sh)   This string identifies the shell to use when a subshell is requested. If the name of the shell begins with an r, a restricted shell is run (**rsh** for example). Otherwise the user's default login shell is run.

TERM (ansi)   The string value identifies your terminal to visually oriented programs that need to know how to position the cursor, clear the screen, set video attributes, and so on. Various software packages are used to provide video support on UNIX systems. As a user, you need only identify your terminal correctly in this variable. The rest is automatic.

TZ (:US/Mountain)   This variable identifies your system's time zone. Its form is either something like MST7MDT or that shown in the example. Both forms show that this user is the United States Mountain time zone. The first form shows that standard time is seven hours behind the GMT (or UTC) reference, and that daylight time is honored. Lookup tables, kept current by the UNIX vendors and system administrators, and programs use the TZ variable's value for internal time calculations. Be aware that if you call a system in another time zone, the time values are those of computer system's location, not yours.

In addition to the variables described in the foregoing list, various versions of UNIX use other variables. Check your local system documentation for details. Also, UNIX systems allow you to create your own for any purpose, as long as they don't collide with any of the variables used by the system.

INHERITANCE

In the previous lesson, you learned how UNIX uses separate processes to run commands. When the shell spawns a child process, a copy of all or a portion of the user's environment is passed on to the child as a kind of *inheritance*. It becomes part of the execution environment that is the child process. Figure 16.1 shows a generalized view of this inheritance mechanism. If the child process spawns another process, its environment is passed on in the same way. A child process can inherit from its parent process, but the environment of the parent is not affected by anything the child does to its copy.

The environment of a child process is assembled from up to three components:

- A copy of the UNIX environment, excluding variables that have been unset
- Any exported variables in the parents environment
- Variables set on the command line preceding the command

The first two components are automatically generated. The third component is optionally specified on the command line that invokes the command.

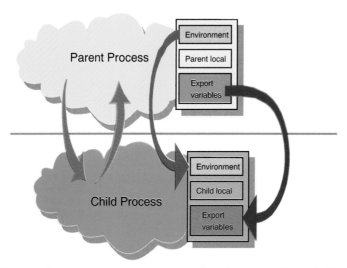

Figure 16.1 Each process has an environment associated with it. Your login shell is a process (identified here as the parent process). When you run a command, a new process (child) is created. It inherits a copy of portions of the parent's environment. Changes made to the environment of the child process at run time have no effect on the environment of the parent process.

THE SHELL ENVIRONMENT

A base environment is composed of variables passed on to your shell process from the system pro-grams that started it running. These variables are automatically passed from generation to generation. If you want to remove a variable and its value from your environment to prevent it from being propagated, use the **unset** command (not available in early UNIX shells other than Berkeley). Only the variables PATH, PS1, PS2, MAILCHECK, and IFS cannot be unset. If you have a variable PROJPATH that you want to remove from your environment, use this command:

```
$ unset PROJPATH ↵
$ ▯
```

EXPORTING LOCAL VARIABLES

If you define variables in your shell environment, they are known as *local variables*. They are vis-ible within that shell, but they are not inherited by child processes unless you export them. An example of this is the TERM variable. Recall that in Lesson 14, you had to set a value for TERM and export it (unless this had already been done for you) to use **pg** and **more** commands effec-tively. If you want to make a local variable visible in child processes, use the **export** command. In this example, it is used to immortalize the user's personal name:

```
$ PERSONAL=Rocky; export PERSONAL ↵
$ ▯
```

SETTING VARIABLES ON THE COMMAND LINE

UNIX provides a mechanism for a user or calling program to add variables or change the values of existing variables at the time a command is issued. The general form of the **env** command, which sets and exports variables on a command line is

```
env [-] varname=value ... command
```

You can provide one or more variable/value pairs in the command. The – option instructs **env** to ignore the inherited environment, passing to the command only the environment specified on the command line.

READ-ONLY VARIABLES

Variables can be marked *readonly*. A variable so marked is effectively a constant. Attempts to change its value by assignment will fail. The **readonly** command, without arguments, lists any variables currently marked as read-only:

```
$ readonly ↵
PPID=1
$ ❑
```

PPID is a variable that identifies the *parent process ID* of your shell. The system marks it as read-only. To protect a variable or a set of variables, run **readonly** with an argument list of variable names. You should set their values before marking them as read-only.

```
$ readonly PERSONAL PROJLIB ↵
$ ❑
```

WHAT YOU NEED TO KNOW

The environment is an important part of every UNIX process. Be sure that you understand the following points before moving on to the next lesson, which discusses standard input and output:

- ☑ The environment is a collection of variables and their values. UNIX maintains a set of variables that form the base environment inherited in total or in part by all processes.

- ☑ Use the **set** command to check the values of your environment variables or create new variables and set new values.

- ☑ Use the **export** command to identify variables that can be inherited by child processes.

- ☑ Mark variables read-only if you want them to be constant. Use **readonly** to mark variables or check their status.

Lesson 17

Standard Input and Output

An important aspect of the UNIX system design is the uniformity of program interactions with disk files, console and terminal devices, and many other input/output (I/O) devices. The uniformity is achieved by treating all such devices as files. This lesson examines how you can use special UNIX command operators to control your program's input or output. When you finish Lesson 17 you should have a good understanding of the following topics:

- Standard input and output files
- Input and output redirection
- Appending to files

STANDARD INPUT/OUTPUT FILES

Each UNIX process can have up to 20 open *file descriptors* as it executes. File descriptors are numbers in the range of 0 to 19. When you issue a command to run a program, the UNIX system automatically opens three of these and associates them with the device file that represents the users terminal. The open descriptors are known by these names:

> *standard input* (file descriptor 0)
>
> *standard output* (file descriptor 1)
>
> *standard error* (file descriptor 2)

The other 17 descriptors are available for use with other files the process might open itself. The process usually doesn't know how these file descriptors are connected on the outside. It expects to receive input on the standard input and deliver output to standard output and standard error. However, some programs, such as **more** and **vi**, will fail or behave strangely if they are not connected to a terminal device on the output streams. Figure 17.1 depicts standard input and output of a running program. This simplified view leaves out information about terminal drivers and other physical components. It focuses on the logical flow of data to and from the program and the user's terminal or console.

Standard input and standard output are *buffered* into lines. A *buffer* is equivalent to a reservoir that collects water when it is available and delivers it to a customer when asked. The line orientation of standard I/O means that the data collected in a buffer doesn't pass to its destination until the newline code is received.

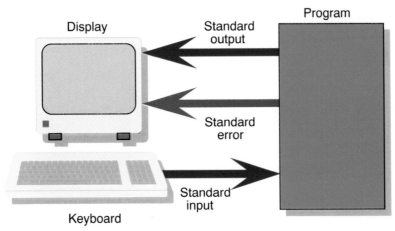

Figure 17.1 *When you run a program, the system automatically opens three file descriptors: standard input, standard output, and standard error. The default connections to these I/O channels in the case of a video terminal are keyboard to standard input, and both standard output and standard error to the display screen.*

The use of I/O buffers boosts system efficiency a bit and has other benefits. Buffered input gives the user a chance to correct input errors before the line is sent to the program. Output buffering tends to smooth the appearance of screen updates that might seem hesitant or jerky if sent a character at a time.

Standard error, on the other hand, is unbuffered. The reason for this is tied to its purpose. Error messages should be seen immediately (and heard if the terminal bell is rung). If an error message gets stuck in a buffer, the user might be deprived for a time of the information he or she needs.

Another reason, covered in detail later in this lesson, is that standard I/O can be *redirected* from your screen to another device or file. We don't want error messages being dumped into a pipeline or sent to a file, never to be seen or heard. (Although it is possible to redirect error output on UNIX, users typically redirect only standard input and output.)

INPUT REDIRECTION

Depending on your program's purpose, you might prefer to have a program receive its input from some source other than your keyboard. Figure 17.2 shows an example of such an arrangement. A user is sending Doris a mail message (electronic mail is covered in detail in Lesson 24), but rather than type the message cold, she prepares a "thank you" note in advance using an editor. Using a file to store her letter gives her the opportunity to get the note just right before sending it. The **mail** program normally operates interactively, collecting your message a line at a time and sending it immediately.

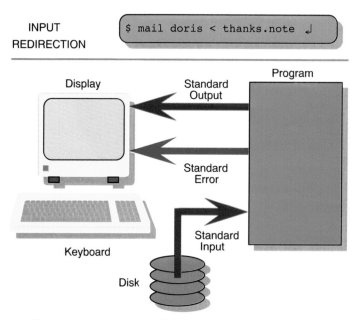

INPUT
REDIRECTION

`$ mail doris < thanks.note ↵`

Display

Standard
Output

Program

Standard
Error

Keyboard

Standard
Input

Disk

Figure 17.2 *Input redirection breaks the logical connection between the program's standard input and the keyboard. Input comes from the file.*

The command shown in the figure runs the **mail** program, identifies the user **doris** as the recipient, and takes the text of the mail message from the file **thanks.note**. While the **mail** program is running, the keyboard has only one purpose, which is to give the user a way of interrupting the running program by pressing the BREAK key. For input purposes, the keyboard is logically disconnected from the running program.

OUTPUT REDIRECTION

A program's output can also be redirected. Output intended for the screen can be captured in a file, sent to a pipeline, or rerouted to some other device. Use of output redirection was first described in this book in the discussion about collecting the text of several files into one using the **cat** program.

Figure 17.3 shows another use of **cat** with output redirection. This time **cat** is used to create a file and fill it with data collected from the keyboard. The session would look like this:

```
$ cat > noble.txt ↵
It is not rebellion itself which is noble
but the demands it makes upon us.
                    Albert Camus
CTRL-D
$ ▯
```
File text

Using CTRL-D to mark the end of the file

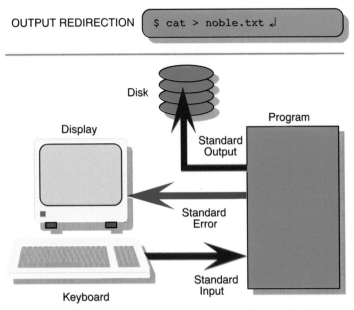

OUTPUT REDIRECTION `$ cat > noble.txt ↵`

Disk

Display

Program

Standard
Output

Standard
Error

Standard
Input

Keyboard

***Figure 17.3** Output redirection breaks the connection between the standard output stream and the user's screen, sending output to a different destination.*

As you type each line, use the BACKSPACE key and retyping to correct typing errors if you make any. Each line ends with a RETURN. To end the input session, press CTRL-D on a clear line. This nearly universal "end process" command terminates this session, causing the output file to be closed and the **cat** program to terminate. The text that you type at the keyboard fills the file **noble.txt**. To view the file you just created, use **cat** again, this time specifying the file to view but no redirection:

```
$ cat noble.txt ↵
It is not rebellion itself which is noble
but the demands it makes upon us.
                        Albert Camus
$ ▢
```

The difference in the appearance of the two commands is subtle, but the behaviors are significantly different.

Note: Be careful with output redirection. You can easily overwrite a file on most UNIX systems (Berkeley-derived systems provide a "noclobber" feature that helps you avoid this difficulty). When you redirect program output to a file, the first action performed is to create the destination file if it doesn't exist. If the file does exist, it is truncated to 0 bytes, effectively throwing away any previous contents.

If the command encounters problems, it delivers error message or diagnostic output to the user's terminal because standard error is still connected there. To capture error output of a program in a file, you can redirect it using the *command 2> errorfile* form of the command line. No space is allowed between the 2 and the > symbols that specify this redirection. The 2 refers to the file descriptor for standard error. In standard output redirection, the form 1> could be used but file descriptor 1 is assumed if you don't specify a descriptor.

APPENDING A COMMAND'S OUTPUT TO A FILE

You can append text onto the end of a file by using the >> syntax of redirection. A command of the form *command* >> *destfile* opens the destination file for writing at the end. Any output generated by the command is appended to the file. If the file doesn't exist, it is created. In the following example, a series of two commands is used to add an entry to a file of notes:

```
$ date >> notes.txt ↵
$ cat >> notes.txt ↵
...
$ □
```

The **date** command appends a date and time stamp to the **notes.txt** file. Then the **cat** command appends your note to the file. This is a simple way to keep a record of your progress on a project or anything else that you would like to track.

WHAT YOU NEED TO KNOW

This lesson provides an introduction to standard input and output. The general treatment of input and output as files gives you great flexibility in manipulating data, mixing and matching programs to build processing pipelines, and many other benefits. Before learning about how to customize your operating environment, review your knowledge of these topics:

☑ Processes can have up to 20 open file descriptors. Three file descriptors provide the standard input (0), standard output (1), and standard error (2) connections to the user's terminal file.

☑ Standard input can be redirected (<) to take input from a file or a device other than the keyboard. The input is buffered into lines.

☑ Standard output, which normally goes to the terminal display, can be redirected to other devices or files for overwriting (>) or appending (>>). It is also buffered.

☑ Standard error is an unbuffered output to the terminal display. It delivers error and diagnostic messages to the user immediately. Standard error can also be redirected (2>).

Lesson 18

Customizing Your Operating Environment

When a user account is created for you, certain assumptions are made about how you will use the system. The assumptions are primarily made by the system vendor and reflected by the default values built into the product. Additional configuration decisions are made by a system administrator during system setup.

Sooner or later you will want to have it your way. This lesson gets you started with the never-ending process of customization. The items covered in this lesson include the following:

- Altering your configuration file
- Finding out how to identify your terminal
- Changing erase and line-kill characters

ALTERING YOUR CONFIGURATION

Each time you log on, the UNIX system sets your initial operating environment. The environment has an inherited part and a part that you and your system administrator control. The base environment is inherited from the parent process of your login shell. You can't control the base environment any more than you can control what your parents bequeath to you at birth. However, you and your administrator can affect some aspects of your login environment.

Part of your initial configuration comes from the file **/etc/profile** (no dots in the name). This file contains settings that are common to all users. The file's contents can be modified by the system administrator. Another component of the configuration is more personal. Your **.profile** is used to modify your configuration by changing default values and by adding new environment variables. It also lets you automatically run commands for any purpose. You might want to take time now to print copies of these two files, so you can review the set commands they contain:

*Note: If you are using the C shell (**csh**), your configuration file is called **.login**. Other details of the configuration differ as well, so you need to translate some of the instructions in this lesson to an appropriate form.*

As you have read, **.profile** lets you specify commands that automatically run when you log into the system. Most of the commands you place in **.profile** will set environment entries that let you customize UNIX to meet your needs better. For example, in earlier lessons you learned how to alter the file-creation mask value using the **umask** command and how to set or change the TERM variable's value by assignment. But those changes were temporary—each time you log out of the system, the settings are lost, and you have to remake them manually each time you log in. If you want these and other actions to be made for you at every login, you need to modify your **.profile**.

Before doing anything else, make a backup of your **.profile**:

```
$ cp .profile profile.bak ↵
$ ▢
```

Now if you make a mistake or simply decide to restore the original configuration, you can recover easily by copying the backup file to the configuration.

Let's start simply by adding a command to the end of the configuration file. The command prints a message on your terminal each time you log in. To do this, you use output redirection with >>, as described in Lesson 17:

```
$ cat >> .profile ↵
echo Let the fun begin!
(end input with CTRL-D)
$ ▢
```

Having modified the file, you should log out and log in again to see the effect of the change.

If the text of your message contains any characters that are special to the shell, such as a single quote, you need to double quote the characters. For example, use **"You ain't seen nothin' yet!"** to protect the single quotes from the shell. Without the double quotes, the single quotes used as apostrophes are stripped out by the shell, and the message looks like bad typing instead of bad grammar.

SETTING YOUR *TERM* VARIABLE

Section 6 discusses the **vi** visual editor. A visual editor is so named because the editor immediately displays the result of your editing operations. The **vi** editor, being a visual program, needs to know your terminal type so that it can position the cursor, set video attributes, and perform many other actions. Unlike the PC environment, where the number of different video standards can be counted on one hand, the number of terminal types that can be connected to a UNIX system is numbered in the hundreds. Many of these terminal types adhere to the ANSI (American National Standards Institute) standards for terminals, but there are many earlier designs still in widespread use that don't. Writing a program that works on all terminals is a real challenge.

UNIX uses a *virtual terminal interface* to deal with this problem. Figure 18.1 depicts the virtual terminal interface that is implemented in various ways, depending on the vintage of your system and the support provided by your software vendor. The view presented here is generic. Programs written to the idealized virtual terminal can work with any video terminal that can be described in the terminal capabilities database. You set and export the TERM variable to identify your terminal to this software.

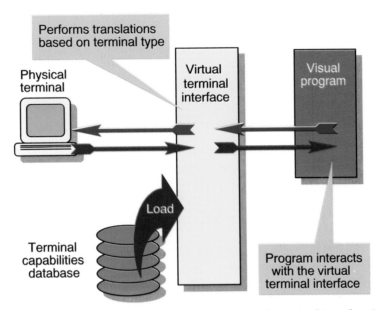

Figure 18.1 *A visually oriented program interacts with a virtual terminal interface (an idealized software terminal), which uses terminal capabilities data to translate input and output codes for the user's physical terminal.*

The setting of the TERM variable may already be automatic if your administrator or UNIX vendor has set up the configuration correctly. In fact, the value of TERM can usually be determined by a program that queries your terminal device to find out what make and model it is. Many terminals and communication programs respond with a recognizable code when asked to identify. For the purposes of this discussion, I'm going to assume that none of this is true.

Finding a suitable TERM value involves knowing the make and model of your terminal or terminal-emulator (software that makes a computer system costing thousands of dollars behave like a $200 terminal!). If you have a reasonably new terminal, you can probably get by with a TERM value of **ansi**, but you should use an entry that matches your terminal exactly if you can to obtain support for the terminal's features and the best performance possible.

Knowing the make and model, you can try to find a suitable identifier by examining systems files for a match. On older UNIX systems a file called **/etc/termcap** contains text descriptions of terminal capabilities. On newer UNIX systems, a facility called **terminfo** is used. A set of directories under **/usr/lib/terminfo** contain files for each supported terminal type. Let's poke around a bit (the tried and true way to learn about UNIX).

You can use a UNIX utility called **grep** to see if an entry exists for your terminal. The program does a global search (**g**) in a file for a specified string (called a *regular expression*, hence **re**), and prints (**p**) any lines that contain a match. If you have a Televideo 950 terminal, for example, you could check the file this way:

```
                                        —— Search string
                                        —— File to search
$ grep televideo /etc/termcap ↵
v5|tvi950|950|televideo950:\
v0|tvi910|910|old televideo 910:\
...
v3|925|925c|tvi925|newer televideo:\
$ ▢
```

Yup. There it is—first entry. Most names in this file are typed all lowercase, but if you get no "hits," try capitalizing the name of the manufacturer. The needed TERM value is the second one in the line (other fields contain alternate names). So tvi950 should do the job.

If you have a system that supports video terminals via **terminfo**, go to the database directory and check it out by do a few judicious listings. The first listing (using **ls -CF** to get columns and file-type indicators) shows the names of all the directories that are named for the first characters in the terminal designations.

```
$ cd /usr/lib/terminfo ↵
$ ls -CF ↵
1/        9/        d/        l/        t/
2/        A/        e/        m/        ti.src
...
7/        b/        j/        r/        y/
8/        c/        k/        s/        z/
$ ▢
```

A Televideo terminal might well have a designation that starts with a **t** (Humor me—forget what you know from the **grep** example, but only briefly!). Change to that directory and list again. I have used an argument of **tvi*** to limit the list, but you don't have to do that. You might find it helpful to pipe the output of **ls** to **pg** or **more** because there are a lot of terminal types that start with **t**.

```
$ cd t ↵
$ ls -C tvi* ↵
tvi           tvi912-2p     tvi9202p      tvi950-4p     tvi9502p
tvi-2p        tvi9122p      tvi920b       tvi950-ap     tvi9504p
...
tvi910        tvi912cc      tvi925        tvi950-rv     tvi950rv
tvi910+       tvi920        tvi950        tvi950-rv-2p  tvi950rv2p
tvi912        tvi920-2p     tvi950-2p     tvi950-rv-4p  tvi950rv4p
$ ▢
```

Wow! Fifteen tvi950 types. Don't panic. You can use the base tvi950 designation to get started and home in on the best match for your terminal later. The variations on the theme handle different settings of the terminal (such as page width) and different production versions of the terminal. First check the value of TERM that is stored in your environment:

```
$ echo $TERM ↵
dumb
$ ▢
```

Excuse me? Is that any way to talk about a terminal? The designation **dumb** is used for a terminal of unknown type. The assumption is that it can't do anything useful. Next use **grep** to see what TERM is set to in the configuration file:

```
$ grep TERM .profile ↵
eval `tset -m ansi:ansi -m $TERM:\?${TERM:-ansi} -r -s -Q`
$ ▢
```

If you see something like this, don't mess with it. If the **tset** program can identify your terminal, it's automatic. If not, you'll be prompted at each login to identify your terminal manually. Just be sure to identify your terminal correctly next time you log in. Here's a sample login sequence:

```
(Preliminary log-on stuff)
TERM = (unknown) vt100 ↵
Terminal type is vt100
$ ▢
```

This method accounts for the fact that you might not always use the same terminal. Hard-coding a value in **.profile** is not a good idea if you move around a lot. If you see a hard-coded value, you can edit **.profile** to change it either to match your terminal type or to put in the **tset** command shown above, if the program is available on your system. To determine whether **tset** is available on your system, run the following command. If you see the response **/bin/tset**, as shown here, the command is available:

```
$ ls /bin/tset ↵
/bin/tset
$ ▢
```

To make such changes to your **.profile**, you should learn to use one of the many editor programs available to you. Section 4 teaches you to use the **ed** line-oriented editor and Section 6 covers the visual editor, **vi**.

SETTING THE ERASE AND LINE-KILL CHARACTERS

When you attempt to log into a UNIX system, you are asked to provide a login ID and one or more passwords. If you make a typing mistake, you need either to try again, rerunning the entire question-and-answer sequence, or know how to correct typing errors during input.

The traditional erase (destructive backspace) on UNIX systems is the # key (usually a shifted 3), but many UNIX systems use CTRL-H, which is the code the BACKSPACE key sends, if your terminal has one. The line-kill character, which erases the current line contents, is either the @ key (usually SHIFT-2) or CTRL-U.

If the values have been changed and you want to restore the default values for the erase and kill characters, use **stty ek**. On the other hand, if you're not happy with the default values on your system, you can use **stty** to change them. For example, to set erase to backspace and kill to CTRL-U, issue this command:

```
$ stty erase "^H" kill "^U" ↵
$ □
```

When you type this command, use the caret character, ^ (usually SHIFT-6), followed by the associated control letter. The double quotes are needed to protect the ^ from processing by the shell, and the resulting two-character sequences are interpreted by **stty** as their single-character control-code equivalents.

WHAT YOU NEED TO KNOW

The UNIX system gives you the power to control the way the system works for you. Various configuration files and commands let you have it your way. Before learning about alternative shells in the next lesson, check your knowledge of these points:

☑ Use your **.profile** (or **.login** for **csh**) to personalize your operating environment.

☑ A virtual terminal interface provides a mechanism for programs to work with any terminal that can be described in the terminal database. You can find the needed TERM variable value by searching system files and directories.

☑ Use the **stty** program to control terminal interface options, such as the choice of erase and line-kill characters.

Lesson 19

Alternative Shells

There has been a big shell game going on for many years in the UNIX world. Typical of games of chance, there have been a few big winners and a lot of losers. This Lesson describes two shells that have come up winners. Calling these shells alternatives tends to diminish their importance, but **sh** is still the standard shell. The material in this lesson is on these two worthy alternatives:

- The C shell (**csh**) from Berkeley UNIX
- The KornShell (**ksh**) command language

MAINSTREAM UNIX SHELLS

There has been a lot of personality and ego involved in the development of UNIX. Whether driven by a quest for immortality or just lacking enough imagination to come up with meaningful names, many UNIX programmers have named programs after themselves or "family" members. The **awk** program, for example, is named by the last initials of its authors (Aho, Weinberger, and Kernighan). The **biff** program, which alerts you to newly arrived mail on some systems is reputedly named after Ken Thompson's dog Biff, who announced the postman's arrival.

AT&T UNIX shells are often referred to by the author's names. The standard UNIX shell, **sh**, described in Lesson 15 and used as the basis of examples up to this point in the book was written by Steve Bourne at Bell Laboratories. His shell replaced an earlier one written by John Mashey. A more recent AT&T offering is the KornShell (**ksh**) by David Korn.

Due to the early and continuing educational uses of UNIX, which has been available in source code form, many programmers have attempted to improve on the original design. Some individuals and organizations have succeeded and have inspired significant changes to the de facto UNIX standard over the years.

The University of California at Berkeley has had a lasting impact on the UNIX universe, contributing to changes to the kernel, the file system, numerous utility programs, and the shell. Figure 19.1 shows a simplified diagram of relationships among the three primary interactive shells. The Berkeley branch produced the C shell, which introduced many improvements and innovations. Later, many features of the C shell were incorporated into the AT&T Korn shell, which was based on **sh** for programming compatibility.

The Bourne shell is found on all UNIX systems. The C shell dominates on Berkeley-derived systems, as you might expect, and is available for DOS, OS/2, and other environments. KornShell, which has become very popular since introduced in 1982, is now used by nearly 80% of the UNIX user population within AT&T and is also available on a wide range of other systems. The versions of C shell and KornShell that run on other systems are limited by the capabilities of those systems.

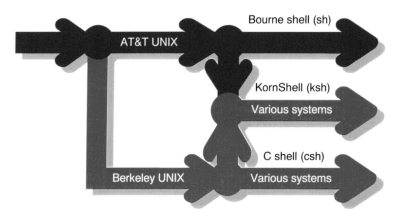

Figure 19.1 *The three major UNIX shells and numerous others are all derived from the early Bourne shell from 7th Edition UNIX. Wide availability of UNIX source code for educational purposes has made it relatively easy to modify the system, including the user interface.*

C SHELL FEATURES

The C shell quickly gained a reputation as a preferred shell for interactive use. It offers many conveniences and safety features that are welcomed by new users and programmers alike. Here are some of the more popular **csh** innovations:

INITIALIZATION AND TERMINATION FILES
The C shell uses two configuration files for initialization and another for termination. The **.cshrc** and **.login** files are read at startup of **csh**. When you end your session, the **.logout** file is read.

COMMAND HISTORY
The shell maintains a history list of previous commands. You can reexecute previously run commands in total or by using substitutions with basic editing commands. The history list size and the substitution command (!) name can be modified by changing the values of control variables.

JOB CONTROL
This feature allows you to manage a set of foreground and background processing jobs in a variety of ways. See Lesson 20 for more information about this topic.

DIRECTORY MANAGEMENT
The C shell maintains a stack of directory names. By using a set of directory commands (**cd**, **dirs**, **pushd**, and **popd**), you can quickly and easily return to directories you have visited before. (Some **csh** versions don't provide this feature.)

PROGRAMMING ENHANCEMENTS

For shell programmers, **csh** offers a more C-like syntax than **sh**. It also provides enhanced variable substitutions and a wider range of intrinsic (built-in) commands.

FILENAME COMPLETION

When enabled by the **filec** variable, **csh** can complete partially typed unambiguous names for you. Various commands let you complete filenames and user names with minimal typing.

COMMAND ALIASES

You can package frequently used or complicated commands and give them aliases. A list of aliases is kept for you by the shell and you can modify it by using the **alias** and **unalias** commands.

KORNSHELL FEATURES

Based on the Bourne shell, the KornShell command language uses a compatible programming language syntax with additions. The latest update was released in 1988. It is an official UNIX component as of System V, Release 4. The shell is available in both binary (executable, machine-specific) and source forms. It merges the best of C shell features with a sprinkling of its own enhancements.

FEATURES ADOPTED FROM C SHELL

The original purpose of **ksh** was to make the most used and admired features of **csh** available on AT&T brand UNIX. The features lifted from **csh** include

- Command history list
- Command aliases
- Job control
- Tilde expansion
- General numeric expression processing

NEW ENHANCEMENTS

Here are highlights of the new features and improvements in the KornShell command language.

COMMAND-LINE EDITING

KornShell has two built-in visual editor modes for command-line editing. You can choose to use either **vi**- or **emacs**-style commands to edit your commands. This works with the history file, so you call recall previous commands, edit them, and execute the modified versions.

IMPROVED CD CAPABILITIES

This feature makes it easier to get to another directory using abbreviated or partial names. It also simplifies the process of returning to the previous directory and, by extension, toggling between two directories. You can also define a function to replace **cd** with your own version.

PROGRAMMING LANGUAGE ENHANCEMENTS

For shell programmers, **ksh** includes many additions and improvements, including arrays, a generalized user-defined function facility, internationalization support, improved security, integer arithmetic, substring operators, and menu-programming tools.

PUTTING THE CURRENT PATH IN YOUR PROMPT

Frequent DOS users who have grown accustomed to having the current directory displayed in their prompt string will like this feature. Most alternative shells automatically set the environment variable PWD, or something comparable, to the value of the current path when it is changed by a **cd** command. To obtain a pathname prompt under KornShell, for example, use the following assignment in **.profile** or other configuration file:

```
PS1='$PWD: '
```

The single quotes are required and you probably want a separator, such as the : used in the sample or perhaps a > symbol. Also, leave a space at the end of the prompt string to get some visible separation between the prompt and your commands.

WHAT YOU NEED TO KNOW

The C shell and KornShell alternative shells offer many features for both general users and programmers that, once you start using them, become indispensable. This lesson is intended to peak your interest in **csh** and **ksh**, but the book does not depend on their use. What you learn about **sh** is generally applicable to any of the shells. Differences among the shells are noted in this book where necessary.

Check your knowledge of these points before you go to Lesson 20, which describes background processing and a related topic, job control.

- ☑ The Bourne shell, **sh**, is the standard UNIX shell on virtually all systems.
- ☑ The Berkeley UNIX shell is **csh**. It introduced numerous improvements and additions to the shell. It is primarily used interactively, but it has a C-like programming capability that is favored by some users.
- ☑ The KornShell (**ksh**) command language is a merging of **sh** and **csh** features and a sprinkling of new features. It is quickly becoming the shell of choice for UNIX and other systems.

Lesson 20

Background Processing and Job Control

All UNIX systems have the ability to run multiple commands simultaneously, on behalf of one user or a whole community of users. The command process that has the read and write access to the controlling terminal is said to run in the *foreground*. Other processes for the same user are said to be running in the *background*.

This lesson examines the capability and its consequences. In addition, it describes an extension of background processing called *job control*, which allows users to manipulate foreground and background processes, stop or terminate jobs, and so on. This lesson examines the steps you must perform to run commands in the background and how to use job control commands. By the time you finish this lesson you will understand the following topics:

- Running jobs one after another (synchronous execution)
- Continuing foreground processing while running other jobs in the background (asynchronous execution)
- Using job control for managing multiple jobs

FOREGROUND VERSUS BACKGROUND PROCESSING

What you see on your terminal display is whatever program is running in the foreground. That's usually the shell, interspersed with the output of the commands you run. Your terminal standard I/O (input, output, and error) is active with the foreground process. Background processes run essentially out of sight and out of mind. Your shell continues to run, and you can run additional programs at the same time.

EXECUTION OF COMMANDS

The shell executes commands either directly in the current shell process or in a fresh subshell process. Direct execution is done with *intrinsic commands* (those commands built into the shell program itself), such as **pwd**, and with *user-defined functions*. The advantage of direct execution is that it is considerably faster than execution in a subshell. If changes are made to variables, the changes affect the shell and remain in effect as long as the shell is running.

Most commands, however, are executed in a subshell process. In this dominant form of command execution, the shell starts a subshell (a new copy of itself) and runs the command(s) directly in the subshell process or in a command process that replaces it. Figure 20.1 shows how the shell runs a typical foreground process of this type. While the command is running, the shell waits, and you can't type any more commands (although you can use type-ahead to queue up some keystrokes in advance).

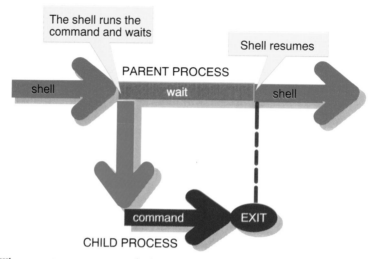

Figure 20.1 When you issue a command, the shell finds the associated program file(s) and runs the program. The program usually runs as a separate process. While the program is executing, the shell is waiting for it to terminate. Upon completion of the command, the shell resumes execution.

USING . TO EXECUTE COMMAND FILES

Changes made to environment variables in a subprocess are temporary and have no effect on the variables of the parent shell. Such changes endure only as long as the subshell process or command process is running. Normally this is not a problem. Indeed, it's the way you want to work most of the time because it protects your environment and local variables from harm.

However, if you want to package some variables and values in a file and execute them to modify your environment, the one-way copying of variables is a problem. Assume, for example, that you are trying to set up an environment for some project you're working on. You want an easy way to set several variables.

You could just type each one interactively at the shell prompt, but that is tedious and potentially error ridden. How about making a file with the commands in it, and run it as a program? Let's try it. First create the command script file by redirecting the output of **cat**:

```
$ cat > setvars ↵
book="Rescued by UNIX" ↵
author="Augie Hansen" ↵
```

```
publisher="Jamsa Press" ↵
(CTRL-D pressed here)
$ ▯
```

Next, change the file mode to executable by using **chmod** with the **+x** option:

```
$ chmod +x setvars ↵
$ ▯
```

OK. Let's run it and then check the list of variables by using **set**. We'll pipe the output through **tail** to look at just the last few lines:

```
$ setvars ↵
$ set | tail - 5 ↵
SHELL=/bin/ksh
TERM=vt100
TMOUT=0
TZ=MST7MDT
_=setvars
$ ▯
```

The variables are nowhere to be found. That's because they were created and destroyed in the sub-process and have no effect on the parent shell.

Let's try something else. If you run a command of the form . *file*, the shell reads and executes the commands in the file in the current process (the dot must be followed by a space or tab). If the commands set or changes variables, the new values stick, as you can see from this sample run:

```
$ /usr/augie/test: . setvars ↵
$ /usr/augie/test: set | tail -5 ↵
TZ=MST7MDT
_=./setvars
author=Augie Hansen
book=Rescued by UNIX
publisher=Jamsa Press
$ ▯
```

Great—there they are, in the parent shell's local environment. If you use this technique to set up projects or for any kind of special initialization, be careful not to clobber variables that shouldn't be altered. If you mess up in a really big way, log off and on again to revert to your default configuration.

BACKGROUND PROCESSING

The background processing model looks similar to the foreground model at first glance, but the differences are substantial (see Figure 20.2).

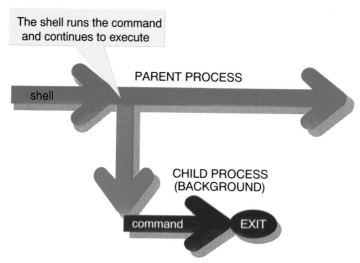

The shell runs the command and continues to execute

PARENT PROCESS

shell

CHILD PROCESS (BACKGROUND)

command   EXIT

Figure 20.2 *Asynchronous processing occurs when two or more processes run simultaneously and independently of each other. Here, a command executes in the background as the shell continues executing. The shell returns a prompt to the user immediately, rather than waiting for the child process to complete.*

When you type a command that ends with a **&**, a subshell process is created, and the command is run independently of the parent shell. That has several effects of interest to you. The primary effect is that the shell process doesn't wait for the command to complete.

Typically background processes don't have a visible screen appearance in nonwindowed environments. For example, assume that you have several accounting programs, one that generates payroll, one that updates your accounts payable, one for accounts receivable, and one for general ledger updates. When you run these programs, they normally do not display screen output. Instead, the programs update your accounting files and possibly print reports or paychecks. Because these programs don't require keyboard input and don't display screen output, you can run the programs in the background, while you issue other commands in the foreground. Figure 20.3 illustrates the execution of foreground and background tasks.

When you run a program in the background, the process ID of the background process is displayed when it is started, and error messages are still directed to your screen (where they might get mixed in with output from a foreground process). But you normally send the standard output of a background process to a pipeline or redirect it to a file. Input to a background process is typically taken from files or redirection.

Processes running in the background die if the parent process is terminated. You can keep them alive if you plan ahead. Run exactly the same command, but put the command **nohup** (no hangup) ahead of the command you are putting in the background. If the parent terminates, the protected background processes continue to run (unless the death of the parent is caused by a system failure or shutdown, of course).

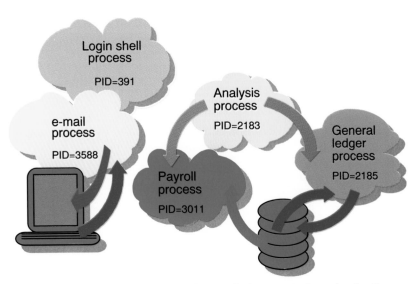

Figure 20.3 *When you run processes in the background, they run independently of your terminal, interacting with the file system and, by various interprocess communication mechanisms, with each other. The foreground process is in control of your terminal.*

In the following example, a large data file is sorted and any duplicate records eliminated, all in the background. Input to **sort** comes from a named file and output is piped to **uniq** to eliminate the duplications:

```
$ sort names.lst | uniq > names.out &         Run command in background
19883                                          Process id of background process
$ (user continues with other commands)
...
$ ☐
```

The **&** puts a command in the background, and a command pipeline is a command. Therefore, you don't need to use parentheses or braces around the pipeline.

If the command is likely to take a long time to run, you might want to check the status of the command. Use **ps** (described in Lesson 15) with a **-p** option to limit output to the process of interest. You may also want to use the **-f** option to get a full listing. If you don't see any output (other than the column headings) from this command, the process has terminated.

Adjusting Process Priorities

If you don't need fast processing of your background command, you can lower its priority. Use the **nice** command, so named because you are being nice to other system users when you use it. It lowers the priority of any command by the amount given as its argument. It takes an optional increment in the range of 1 to 19 (a default increment of 10 is used if one is not specified). You still need to put the command in the background by using &. The following example runs a background command at an increment of 15 below normal priority:

```
$ nice -15 reportgen & ↵
$ ☐
```

A privileged user can raise a a background command's priority by using a negative increment (--*value*), as in the command

```
$ nice --19 i_am_special ↵
$ ☐
```

TERMINATING PROCESSES

Just as there are times when you end a foreground process by typing CTRL-D, there will also be times when you need to end a background process. To terminate a process, use the **kill** command.

The command takes the process ID as an argument and zaps the specified process. If you forget the process ID, use the **ps** (process status) command to find out what it is. To terminate the background process we started earlier, if it's still running, we would type this command:

```
$ kill -9 19883 ↵
$ ☐
```

JOB CONTROL

First introduced in Berkeley UNIX with C Shell support, *job control* is a facility that lets you control multiple *jobs* from a single terminal. A group of related processes, usually a simple or compound command, or a pipeline, is called a job.

One job, the foreground job, has read and write access to your terminal. Any other jobs may be either running in the background or stopped. Associated with each job is a unique ID. You can use the IDs with various job-control commands to specify actions, such bringing a background job to the foreground, terminating a job, and others.

Job control is enabled by default for an interactive **csh** or **ksh** session. To use job control with the standard shell, start the session as **jsh** instead of **sh**.

The following set of sample screens walk you through the sequence of getting a background job going, checking the jobs that are running, peeking at the output, and terminating the job. First, let's create a command that keeps on running, and running ...

```
$ cat > who_log ↵
while true
do
        date >> who_log.out
        who >> who_log.out
        sleep 60
done
$ chmod +x who_log ↵
$ ▢
```

Don't worry about how this works; we'll cover that and more in Section 7. The program is designed to save the current date/time stamp and a list of logged in users, and then marks time for a minute (**sleep 60** [seconds]).

To put the job in the background, start it with the trailing **&**. In this example, the **./** ahead of the program name is needed because PATH doesn't include the current directory, so it has to be specified explicitly: The second command, **jobs**, lists the current jobs. The current shell is not listed as a job:

```
$ ./who_log & ↵
[1]      20200
$ jobs ↵
[1] +  Running                 ./who_log &
$ ▢
```

The number in square brackets is the job ID, which we'll use shortly to deep-six this job. The background job does its thing, which is building the data file called **who_log.out**. Here are the last ten lines (the default for **tail**) showing a change as the superuser logs in:

```
$ tail who_log.out ↵
Tue Jan 11 23:06:43 MST 1994
...
Tue Jan 11 23:07:43 MST 1994
arh             tty01           Dec 25 19:43
augie           tty1a           Jan 11 14:42
Tue Jan 11 23:08:43 MST 1994
arh             tty01           Dec 25 19:43
root            tty02           Jan 11 23:08
augie           tty1a           Jan 11 14:42
$ ▢
```

A more elegant program would only add entries for new logins and not waste all this space on repeats. To terminate this job, use the job-control kill command with the job ID (preceded by a % sign) as an argument:

```
$ kill %1 ↵
$ ▢
```

WHAT YOU NEED TO KNOW

To make the most efficient use of your computer system, you might find it useful to run multiple programs. This lesson has shown you some valuable tools for running and managing foreground and background processes. The next section teaches you how to use the line-oriented editor, which you may find useful in interactive sessions and in batch-orient command files. Before switching gears, verify your knowledge of these points:

☑ Commands usually execute in a subprocess. The parent shell waits for the command (child process) to terminate.

☑ You can run jobs in the background while you continue interactive foreground processing.

☑ Use the . command to run commands directly in the current shell process.

☑ Job control lets you control multiple jobs from a terminal.

BASIC TEXT EDITING

The UNIX system is strongly oriented toward the use of text files, which contain letters, numbers, and standard punctuation symbols, much like the paragraphs that make up this page. To be sure, there are many compiled program files, and some applications use special binary formats to store their data, but, in large measure, the data files used by the system and the user community are ordinary text files.

As you work with UNIX, you will being using text files for creating and storing mail messages, writing shell command (script) files, and a wide variety of other purposes. It is in your best interest to become familiar with text editing tools (that let you create and change text files) as quickly as possible. This section introduces you to basic text editing using the line-oriented editor **ed**. What you learn here will be valuable to you when you tackle the visual editor **vi** because it is based directly on **ed**.

UNIX has no standard word-processing program. Instead, it uses separate text-processing programs, such as **nroff** and **troff** to convert text files containing ordinary text and formatting commands into formatted documents. Although this approach offers some interesting benefits, it is difficult to learn and use, forcing you to be a programmer of text and images. I choose not to cover the text-processing programs in this introductory book and recommend instead that you (or your system owner) obtain an established integrated word-processing program. If you prepare documents of any complexity beyond simple memos, this may be the best UNIX-related advice you ever get.

Lesson 21

Line-Oriented Editing

This lesson and the next two lessons teach you to use the **ed** line-oriented editor. You can use it interactively or in command files (shell scripts). You can do essentially the same and more with **ex** (an extended version of **ed** available with Berkeley-derived UNIX and System V). The following topics are covered in this lesson

- Starting and quitting the editor
- Getting help
- Entering text
- Printing and listing text
- Addressing lines

THE *ed* EDITOR

The UNIX editor **ed** is line oriented. You issue commands to perform all actions, such as displaying lines, appending or inserting text, making substitutions, deleting lines, reading and writing files, and others. As you edit a file, the editor maintains a buffer in the form of a temporary file on disk. When you edit a file, **ed** performs the requested actions on the buffer (the temporary file). When you exit **ed**, you can choose to save your changes to the a permanent file or discard them.

Editors of this type don't use a cursor to point to a particular character in a line. At any time, the editor maintains a *current line* indicator. Most editing operations take place relative to the current line. Text in the editing buffer is not displayed unless you ask to see it or request a command that prints text as a side effect. The editor is, by design, terse in its interactions with the user.

Given the availability of visual editors, such as **vi** (see Section 6) and **emacs** (not officially supported but widely available), why bother at all with line editing? In short, the answer is efficiency and compatibility.

The **ed** editor is small and fast. Its efficiency in terms of system resource use is outstanding, and if you know how to use it, you can complete an **ed** session to make a change in a file in the time it takes just to load **vi** or another visual editor into memory.

Compatibility with thousands of shell scripts that use **ed** is, perhaps, a more compelling reason to know something about the editor. In addition, because it can be used in batch mode and driven by editing script files, **ed** plays a pivotal behind-the-scenes role in several major programming and documenting systems.

Yet another reason to learn about **ed** (or **ex**) is that the search and replace features of the line-oriented editors are used within the visual editor, **vi**, for those tasks that affect more than the current character or line in the editing buffer. Nearly everything you learn here will be of use to you when you learn about visual editing.

STARTING THE EDITOR

As with all UNIX programs, **ed** is summoned by typing its name. You can start **ed** with or without a filename argument. In this example, the filename **quote.txt**, is used:

```
$ ed quote.txt ↵
?quote.txt
❏
```

The **?** is an error message from **ed**. This message is a little more helpful than most issued by **ed** in its default mode. To get a more detailed message for this error, type **h** (help) and press RETURN (all commands must be followed by a RETURN) to see the full text of the help message:

```
h↵
cannot open input file
❏
```

That's a little more helpful, but it doesn't say why the file couldn't be opened. On a UNIX system, a file-open failure occurs if the file does not exist or the user does not have needed access.

If you want to have error messages printed in full without having to ask each time, use the **H** command. The first time you use **H** it turns the feature on. The next time turns it off. This is called a *toggle*.

Other editor variables that control its interactions with you are toggles also. The editor normally provides no prompt. The cursor just sits there at the left end of a line waiting for you to type a command or text. To turn on a prompt, type **P** (toggle prompt) and press RETURN. The prompt is a *. You might find it helpful to use the prompt at first because it helps you know when the editor is waiting for a command (the * is showing) and when it is waiting for text input (no prompt). The examples that follow show the editor appearance with prompting turned on.

ENTERING AND SAVING TEXT

The **a** (append) command appends text to the editing buffer. Let's use it to create some text. When you type **a** and press RETURN, the editor adds text *after* the current line in the editing buffer. In this case, because this buffer is empty (you are creating the file), text is added at the beginning.

When you use the **a** (append) command to add text to a file, **ed** enters *input mode*. Within input mode, everything you type is considered to be text to be added to the file. You end each line of input with a RETURN. To end the input mode, use the **.** (dot) command at the start of a clear line:

```
*a⏎ ────────────────────────── Begin input mode
Work consists of whatever a ⏎
body is obliged to do... ⏎
Play consists of whatever a ⏎
body is not obliged to do. ⏎
            Mark Twain ⏎
.⏎ ─────────────────────────── End input mode
*▯
```

The new text is in the editing buffer, but it is not yet saved in the disk file. To save the text on disk, use the **w** (write) command. We started **ed** with a filename argument, and it remembers the name. It saves the contents of the editing buffer to the remembered filename:

```
*w⏎ ───────────────────────── Write file to disk
121 ─────────────────────────── Number of bytes in file
*▯
```

The number printed by **ed** when you save a file is its size in bytes (characters). By default, the **w** command saves the entire buffer to the remembered filename.

USING THE ED EDITOR

Using the **ed** editor line editor, you can create or change text files. **ed** is a line editor, which means that you issue commands that work with one line of text at a time. The editor displays no prompt unless you request one (an asterisk) with the **P** command. You request editing actions by issuing single-letter commands. Start **ed** with a command of the following form:

```
$ ed filename ⏎
```

Note: *The editing commands you issue within* **ed** *are case sensitive, meaning you need to enter the commands in either upper or lowercase exactly as they appear in the examples shown.*

QUITTING THE EDITOR

When you are ready to end your editing session, enter the **q** (quit) command and press RETURN. If you have saved your additions or changes, the editor exits without complaint:

```
*q⏎
$ ▯
```

If you have not saved your work, the editor responds with its usual expression of puzzlement (?)—the ancient equivalent of "say what?". At this point, you can either save and quit to preserve your work or simply issue the quit command a second time to force the editor to terminate your session without saving.

ADDRESSING LINES

Many **ed** commands accept a preceding line number or a range of lines (a pair of numbers separated by a comma). You can use several different methods to specify a line number:

- Shorthand symbols (. [dot] for current line, $ for last line)
- Absolute line numbers (such as 2 or 100)
- Relative line numbers (such as . + 3 or $ - 1)
- Search (using /*string*—see Lesson 22))

If you don't provide a line number or range to commands that accept them, reasonable default values are used. For example, the **w** command assumes 1,$ (the entire buffer) unless you restrict the range. The **a** command takes a single line number, which specifies the line after which text is to be appended. The command assumes the current line (.) unless you specify another.

For example, Figure 21.1 depicts an editing buffer that contains descriptive text. If you decide to save a piece of it, not the whole buffer, you can use a command of the form *startline,endline* **w** *filename*, where the line numbers identify the inclusive range of lines to write to the named file.

Note: If the named file exists and you have write access, its contents will be overwritten by this command. See Lesson 23 for a way to run UNIX commands from within the editor. Doing this allows you to check the file first (possibly to see if it exists) before writing to it.

If you start the editing session with a filename argument, **ed** remembers that name. Using a different name in the write command shown does not change the name associated with the editing buffer.

PRINTING AND LISTING TEXT

As you edit, **ed** gives you several ways of displaying text in the editing buffer. The **p** command prints (or displays if you prefer) the current line. If you give the command an address range, **ed** attempts to display all lines in the specified range. Specifying a range that goes beyond the end of the buffer elicits an error indication.

*Note: If the file contains any nonprinting characters that you would like to see, use the **l** (list) command. This command prints all characters, even those with no visible presentation, in an unambiguous way. The tab character prints as >, and other control codes are printed as octal numbers.*

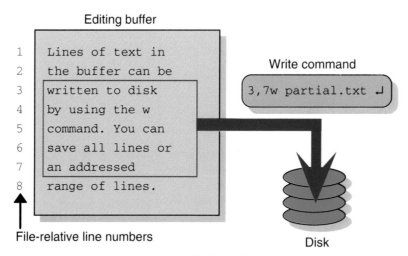

Editing buffer

1	Lines of text in
2	the buffer can be
3	written to disk
4	by using the w
5	command. You can
6	save all lines or
7	an addressed
8	range of lines.

Write command

3,7w partial.txt ↵

File-relative line numbers

Disk

Figure 21.1 *Each line of text in the editing buffer has a file-relative line number. You can use these numbers to form address ranges for* **ed** *commands. This example shows lines 3 through 7, inclusive, being written to a file called* **partial.txt**.

To see line numbers with the text, use the **n** command. A line number indicates the relative position of the line to the beginning of the file. The first line is numbered 1. The editor maintains an invisible line 0, which can be addressed by some commands, such as append.

To display a specific line only, use one of the print commands with a preceding line number. To display the entire buffer, use a range of **1,$** (shorthand is ,). If you provide no number or range, these commands print the current line.

INSERTING VERSUS APPENDING

In the **quote.txt** file example, you appended text to an empty buffer to create the text of a new file. You can also use the append command to add text to an existing file. Figure 21.2 shows an image of a portion of an editing buffer into which a file containing a list of creatures has been read.

Initially, the current line is the last line read into the buffer from the file. This is a specific case of the general rule that the current line is set to the last line affected by a command. You can use several methods to find a particular line in the file:

- Search for text in the line (see Lesson 22 for details)

- Go to the beginning of the buffer and step through the lines one at a time (press **1↵** to get to the beginning, then display each line by pressing ↵)

- Address the line directly if you know its number (as in **2↵**).

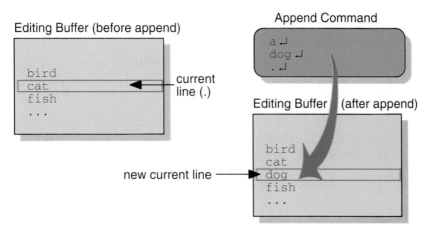

Figure 21.2 Appending text to a file adds the new text after the addressed line, which is the current line if no address is provided. The buffer opens up to accept one or more lines of input. To append text at the beginning of the buffer, address line 0.

When you append text, the text is added *after* the addressed line (current line if no address given). Therefore, the append command in the figure adds the text "dog" on a new line after "cat."

You can also use the **i** (insert) command to add text to the buffer. It operates the same way as append, except that the new material is inserted *before* the addressed (or current) line. Line 0 is not a suitable address for insert. To insert text at the beginning of the buffer use **1i** instead. Remember, to exit input mode, type a dot (.) at the start of a clear line.

WHAT YOU NEED TO KNOW

This lesson has taught you the basic operation of **ed** and has shown you how to enter text. The next lesson shows you how to go on "search-and-destroy" missions in which you locate and delete or change text. Before moving on to the more dangerous aspects of **ed**, check your knowledge of these topics:

☑ The **ed** editor operates on a buffer of lines. The last line affected by a command usually becomes the current line, which indicates your position in the buffer.

☑ Enter text by using the **a** (append) or **i** (insert) commands. End input with . (dot). Changes made to the buffer have no effect on the your disk file until you use the **w** (write) command.

☑ Most **ed** commands take an address or a range to specify the portion of the buffer they affect.

☑ Use **h** for help on an error. Use **H** to turn help on/off. Use **P** to turn prompting on/off.

Lesson 22

Searching and Replacing

In Lesson 21 you learned the basics of using the **ed** editor to create text and how to save the text to a file. This lesson describes the commands and methods used to find and modify text in the editing buffer. The topics you will learn include the following:

- Deleting text from the buffer and changing lines of text
- Undoing commands that affect the editing buffer
- Searching for text strings
- Using a regular expression to match a set of strings
- Substituting text for matched strings
- Performing global search-and-replace operations

DELETING AND CHANGING TEXT

To delete lines from the editing buffer use the **d** (delete) command. The delete command accepts a line number (assumed to be the current line if not specified) or an inclusive range of lines. The current line is set to the line *after* the last line deleted. If the deletion occurs at the end of the buffer, the current line is set to last line of the resulting buffer.

Figure 22.1 shows the effect of deleting a range of lines from the editing buffer. Notice that deleted lines are saved in a buffer, permitting recovery. The lines are effectively forgotten, but not gone.

The = command prints the number of a line that is referred to symbolically. For example, to find out what the line number of the current line is after a deletion or any time you need to know, use the command .=, which prints the file-relative line number of the current line. If you want to know how many lines are in the buffer, use $= (the = command without the $ works, too, because that is the default). The current line is not affected by these commands.

The **c** (change) command combines a deletion of lines with text insertion. You specify a line or lines to be changed and type the new text as you would with an insert or append command. Exit the input mode with . as usual. The current line is set to the last of the new lines entered. If no text is input, the current line is set according to the rules for delete.

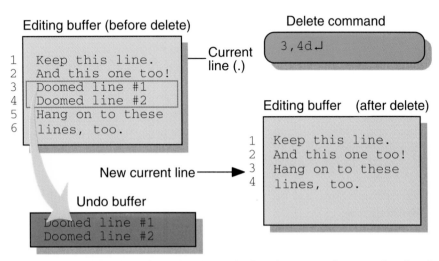

Figure 22.1 *When you delete lines from the editing buffer, the current line is updated to the line after the last line deleted (or the end of the buffer if the deletion was at the end). The deleted lines are kept in an undo buffer for possible recovery.*

UNDOING CHANGES TO THE EDITING BUFFER

If you change your mind about a deletion or any other command that affects the contents of the buffer, you can reverse the most recent command by using the **u** (undo) command. Undo the effects of an errant command immediately. Anything else that modifies the buffer prevents you from using undo on an earlier command.

Undoing the effects of a command changes the buffer, so you can also undo the effects of an undo. In fact, you can key in an alternate version of some text and toggle between the two versions (by pressing **u⏎**) until you determine which is the better version.

SEARCHING FOR TEXT

Thus far you have seen how to get to a line by typing its number (if you know it) or starting at the beginning or somewhere else in the buffer and indexing through the buffer a line at a time. When your text files become long, however, traversing the file a line at a time can become very time consuming. There must be an easier way, you say, and indeed there is. The editor has a search facility that can look forward or backward in the buffer for a text string.

Use commands of the form */text/* to look for matching *text* toward the end of the buffer from the current location. If the search reaches the end of the buffer, it wraps around to the beginning and continues up to the starting point, if necessary. The text specified for the search is called a *regular expression* (the next topic in this lesson). For now just use literal text (each character stands for itself exactly).

To search backward in the buffer (toward the beginning) use a command of the form *?text?*. Wrapping at buffer boundaries occurs as with the forward-search form. After finding a match, you can continue the search with */ /* or *??*. It is not necessary to retype the search string because **ed** remembers it. You don't need to use the closing */* or *?* if the following character is a RETURN.

In the following example, you adjust the current line by searching for the word "obliged." First load the **quote.txt** file.:

```
$ ed quote.txt ↵
121
❑
```

Check the current line, which should be the last one in the buffer:

```
.=↵
5
❑
```

It is. Now search for the word "obliged" by using a forward search, which will have to wrap around to the beginning of the buffer, and check the current line number again:

```
/obliged↵ ────────────────────────── Search command
body is obliged to do... ──────────── Line containing desired text
.=↵
2 ──────────────────────────────────── Line number
❑
```

Looks good so far. Let's go for a double. Search again, but this time just type the search command without the search string, and once again check the current line number:

```
/↵ ───────────────────────────────── Continue the search
body is not obliged to do. ────────── Another line containing the text
.=↵
4
```

Good. It's working. Now let's embellish the topic of searching for text by adding the ability to search for text that is specified in ambiguous ways. This gives you ways of expressing searches more generally and more compactly.

REGULAR EXPRESSIONS

A *regular expression* (RE) specifies a set of strings (a *string* is a sequence of characters such as a word). This means that you can use one expression involving ordinary characters (literal) and special characters (metacharacters) to match different strings in a text file. Hidden behind this disarmingly simple definition is a mass of detail. The topic is covered further in Sections 6 and 7. The formal details of REs can be found in the user documents, such as the command reference manual pages for the **ed** and **ex/vi** editors, **lex**, and **grep**. This brief introduction lets you get started using some of the more common regular expressions forms.

The **ed** editor provides support for a limited form of regular expression notation. You can use REs to search for text strings, form line addresses for **ed** commands, and match text to be replaced in a line (see the next topic). To get started you need to know about these regular expression constructs:

c Any ordinary character c is a one-character RE that matches itself. The letter a matches the letter a in a string.

$\backslash c$ An escaped special character is a one-character RE that matches itself. The special characters include ., *, [, \, ^, $, and /. While . has a special meaning (see the next item), \. does not. It matches a single dot used as a decimal point or a period, and so on.

.   The dot is a one-character RE that matches any single character.

*   The asterisk matches 0 or more occurrences of the preceding one-character RE. It is often used with . (.*) to mean any string of 0 or more characters of any kind (abcdef, for example). See the description of *closure* in Lesson 35.

^   At the beginning of an RE, the ^ anchors the match to the initial segment of a line. (**^electron** matches the word "electron" only at the beginning of a line, but not in its interior.)

$ At the end of an RE, the $ causes an RE to match only the final line segment. (the RE **shirt$** matches the string "shirt" only if it falls at the end of a line.)

[s]   A string, s, of characters (one or more) within square brackets is a one-character RE called a *character class*. It matches any one character in the set. You can use – to represent a range of consecutive characters, so [A–E] is equivalent to [ABCDE]. The – is not special at the beginning or end of the set. Use ^ as the first character to invert the sense of the match (match any character that is not in the set). The ^ is not special if it is not first in the set.

To search in a file about sports for all references to games that include the string "ball" in their names, use the search **/.*ball**, which would match "baseball", "basketball", "football", and "volleyball", to name a few. This RE would also match the word "ball" by itself. To constrain the search to sports that start with B or b and end with "ball", tighten the RE a bit: **/[Bb].*ball**. This RE doesn't match the word "ball".

Other examples of RE notation and use follow in this lesson and in other lessons throughout the remainder of the book.

SUBSTITUTING TEXT

The way you change text within a line is a bit arcane. You use a regular expression to specify text to match and a replacement string. The **s** (substitute) command has the form **s/**RE**/**repl**/p** where *repl* is the text to be substituted for the matched text. The trailing **p** on the command instructs the **s** command to print the modified line. For example, to change the word "obliged" to "required" (sorry, Mr. Twain), use the following command:

```
s/obliged/required/p↵ ——————————— Substitute "obliged" with "required"
body is required to do... ——————— Line with substitution
u↵ ————————————————————————————— Undo the change
❑
```

The use of literal text is reasonably safe, but it requires more typing than a carefully constructed regular expression. Undo the change, **u↵**, and try to use a regular expression that matches obliged instead of the literal text: The **o.*d** expression looks promising at first glance, but see what happens:

```
s/o.*d/required/p↵ ——————————— Substitute command
brequiredo... ———————————————— Result of substitution
❑
```

The expression matched the longest sequence of characters from the o in body to the d in do—not quite what we need. Let's undo the change and try again. This time, we limit the match by specifying a start of "ob" and an end of "ed":

```
u↵ ——————————————————————————— Undo the previous substitution
s/ob.*ed/required/p↵ ————————— Substitute command
body is required to do... ———— Result of substitution
❑
```

Not elegant, but it works. We used almost as many characters in the regular expression as in the literal text, but on average an RE will save you some typing. Again, undo the change and try yet another variation of the **s** command.

The **s** command accepts line and range specifications, so you can make substitutions that affect all or a portion of the editing buffer. In this example, the command searches the entire buffer for a word. Any matched words are converted to uppercase letters:

```
1,$s/ob.*ed/OBLIGED/p↵ ───────────── Substitute throughtout the entire file
body is not OBLIGED to do.
,p↵ ──────────────────────── Display the file's new contents
Work consists of whatever a
body is OBLIGED to do...
Play consists of whatever a
body is not OBLIGED to do.
                Mark Twain
❏
```

The substitute command prints only the last line changed. To see the full effect, use **p** command to print the buffer The example uses the **,** shorthand range in place of **1,$**.

GLOBAL SEARCH AND REPLACE

The commands you have learned to this point operate on a line or a block of adjacent lines. The following commands let you operate globally on the editing buffer. These can be combined with any **ed** command or list of commands except the global commands themselves. An undo can be applied to a global command just as with any other editing command.

Use the **g** (global) command to search the entire buffer (or a block of lines if you specify a range). The global command first marks each line in the buffer or range that contains a match, then it visits each marked line and runs the command list. In the following example, you need to replace all occurrences of the company name IBM in a document with its full version:

```
g/IBM/s//International Business Machines Corporation/g↵
❏
```

Look at this command carefully. The global is used as a prefix and as a suffix. The first **g** is the global command that makes the editing command (**s**) operate globally on the editing buffer. The second **g** is a parameter to the **s** command that tells it to operate globally within the matched line(s). Without it, only the first occurrence of "IBM" in a line would be replaced.

In the substitute command, note that the place where the RE would normally go is empty (*s//repl/*). The value of the RE is known from the global search, so **ed** uses the same value. You don't have to type it again unless you want to use one RE to locate a line and another to indicate what part of it is to be replaced.

To invert the sense of global command, use the **v** command instead of **g**. This form of the global command runs a list of commands on any lines that do not match the specified search pattern.

WHAT YOU NEED TO KNOW

This lesson shows you how to search for strings and modify text in the editing buffer, rounding out the coverage of **ed** by describing additional commands for manipulating text (copy and move blocks, add text from a file to the buffer) and altering the buffer's connection to a disk file.

Check your understanding of the following topics before proceeding:

☑ The **d** command deletes lines from the buffer. The **c** (change) command does the same and then takes your input as replacement text.

☑ Use the **u** (undo) command to reverse the effects of the previous buffer-affecting command.

☑ The forward and reverse search commands (/ and ?) take regular expressions (RE text patterns) to specify the search target. Use the command without an RE to repeat the previous search.

☑ The **s** (substitute) command replaces text that matches a pattern specified by an RE with text you provide. Use a **g** parameter suffix on substitutions to act globally within lines.

☑ Use the **g** (global) command to mark lines containing a specified pattern and run a list of commands on the matched lines.

Lesson 23

Additional Editing Commands

The first two lessons in this section introduced you to the major features of the **ed** editor. This lesson adds to your editing prowess by teaching you how to use additional editor commands. These commands provide you with the following features:

- Verify or change the currently remembered filename
- Join adjacent lines and groups of lines
- Mark positions in the buffer for addressing and quick access
- Move text around (cut and paste) and copy blocks of text
- Edit a new file and read text into the buffer from a file
- Execute external shell commands from within the editor

DISPLAYING OR CHANGING CURRENT FILENAME

If you need to check the name associated with the file you are editing, use the **f** (file) command. Without a filename argument the command simply displays the currently remembered filename.

If you provide an argument, *file*, the command changes the editor's filename association to *file*. This is a useful feature for two primary reasons. If you start **ed** without providing a name, you need to assign one either with the write command (**w** *file*) or set it before issuing a write command. Also, if you read a file by name into the editor at startup, or while editing by using the **e** (edit) or **r** (read) commands, you can use the **f** command to change the name of the file you will write to. This lets you create new files based on the contents of existing files without modifying the originals.

In this example, you read in a file called **old.txt** from disk and then change the name to **new.txt** before saving the buffer to disk. If you make any changes to the text between reading in the old and writing out the new, the changes have no effect on the old file:

```
$ ed old.txt ↵
68
f new.txt↵
( possible editing commands )
w↵
85
q↵
$ ▯
```

JOINING LINES

At times you may find that two or more short lines of text would be better if collected into a single line. Use the **j** (join) command to join adjacent lines into one. The join command expects a pair of line addresses that indicate the inclusive range of lines to join. If it doesn't get a range, it does nothing. The following command joins lines 2 through 4:

```
2,4j↵
❑
```

MARKING AND RETURNING

As the size of your text files become long, finding your last edit location within the file can become time consuming. To help you locate specific file locations quickly, you can place a mark on a line by using the **k** command. The mark is any lowercase letter, so you can create up to 26 "bookmarks" in the editing buffer. Setting a mark has no effect on the value of the current line. To mark the 23rd line in the buffer, if there is one, with an x use this command:

```
23kx↵
❑
```

After moving around in the buffer you can quickly return to the marked line by typing 'x. You can also use marks in forming addresses for commands, such as 'y,.d, which deletes from the line marked **y** up to and including the current line.

MOVING AND COPYING TEXT IN THE BUFFER

The **m** (move) command takes a range of lines and relocates them after a specified line in the buffer. The line specified as a destination must not be within the range being moved. When the move is finished the current line is set to the last moved line.

Figure 23.1 shows a pair of lines being relocated to the beginning of the buffer. The command illustrates the use hidden line 0 as a destination.

You can also copy lines by using the **t** (copy to) command. The copy command makes a copy of the specified range of lines and puts it after the targeted line. It sets the current line indicator to the last line copied. For example, the following command copies lines 1 through 3 of the file to the end of the file:

```
1,3t$↵
❑
```

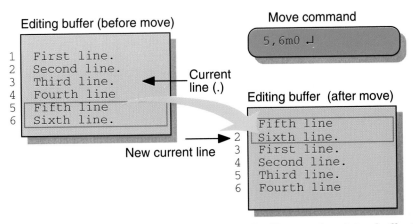

Figure 23.1 The move command relocates a line or a block of lines in the editing buffer. The hidden line 0 is a suitable target for a move because the command places moved lines after the targeted line.

READING TEXT FROM A FILE

You have two ways to bring text into the editing buffer. The first is to use the **e** (edit) command to begin editing a new file. The command clears the editing buffer and reads in the contents of the specified file. The remembered filename is used if none is specified:

```
e words.txt↵
21
□
```

Another method lets you insert text into the editing buffer by reading from a file. The **r** (read) command takes a filename argument and appends the lines at the end of the buffer. If you need to put the lines elsewhere in the file, use the move command to relocate them.

An interesting twist on both of these commands is that the filename can be replaced by the construct !*command*. This form runs the specified command in a shell and takes the output as editor input. The following read command brings the current date and time into the buffer:

```
$ r !date ↵ ———————————————— Read the output of the date command
29 —————————————————————— Number of bytes added to the file
,p↵ ———————————————————— Display the file's contents
(previous buffer contents...)
Fri Jan 12 21:42:02 MST 1994
□
```

EXECUTING SHELL COMMANDS

If you need to run a program at the shell level quickly, you can do so without leaving the editor. Type ! followed by the shell command. The command is executed by the shell and when it completes control is automatically returned to the editor. To check the files in your current directory, use this simple shell command:

```
!ls ⏎ ─────────────────────────── Run the ls command
noble.txt
numbers.txt
quote.txt
who_log ─────────────────────── Command result
who_log.out
words.txt
!
❑
```

Use !! to repeat the previous shell command at any time. Also, the remembered filename is available as %, so you can do neat things like this:

```
!pr % | lp & ⏎
!
❑
```

The command formats the contents of the disk file (not the buffer, so save changes first) and sends them to the print spooler in the background. Control returns to the editor immediately.

WHAT YOU NEED TO KNOW

The editing commands described in this and the previous two lessons cover the essential editing features of **ed**. Other commands and variations on those introduced here are available and may be of interest to you after you gain some experience. Refer to your user documentation for more detail. Check you knowledge of the following topics before embarking on a tour of user-to-user communication tools in the next section:

☑ Use the **f** (file) command to check or change the currently remembered filename associated with the editing buffer.

☑ Join a range of adjacent lines into one line by using the **j** (join) command.

☑ Mark positions, bookmarks, in the buffer by using the **k** command.

☑ Move text blocks around with the **m** (move) command and copy blocks of text by using the **t** (copy to) command.

☑ Use the **e** (edit) command to begin editing a new file and read text from a file by using the **r** (read) command.

☑ Use the **!** command to execute shell commands from within the editor.

Section Five

UNIX COMMUNICATION TOOLS

With the explosive growth of networked computers and with the advent of the information superhighway quickly approaching, the ability of a computer system to communicate with other computer systems has become an increasingly important criterion in evaluating a system's worth. From its early days, UNIX has provided excellent user-to-user communication capabilities. In addition, it has strong support for computer-to-computer communication.

This section describes some of the many communication tools that are available to UNIX users. The three lessons in this section focus on the programs that are available to virtually all UNIX users. Other tools may be available to you in certain operating environments.

Lesson 24

Communicating with Other Users

One of the joys for most new UNIX users is communicating with other users. One reason is that it's very easy to do. Another reason is probably that it builds a sense of community. The reasons aren't important. The fact is that communicating with other users, especially via electronic mail, has been popular on UNIX since the earliest days and continues to grow in popularity.

This lesson introduces you to the primary user-to-user communication tools available on virtually all UNIX systems (**write** and **mail**) and one (**talk**) that may be available to you.By the time you finish this lesson you will understand how to

- Use the **write** and **talk** programs to communicate directly with other users on your system

- Send and receive electronic mail

DIRECT COMMUNICATION

An interactive form of user-to-user communication is implemented by the **write** program. It is a line-oriented program in the pattern of all early UNIX programs. A more recent program, **talk**, uses video terminals, with a split screen display that eliminates potential ambiguities.

BLOCKING ACCESS

Before you check out the communication programs, let's deal with the issue of access. All users have privacy rights. The commands described next allow you to write directly to another user. When you do, the other user sees your message on his or her screen in the midst of their work.

The UNIX system gives each user a way to control such interruptions. You can set your terminal device to accept or reject writes to the terminal. To find out how yours is set, use the **mesg** command without an argument:

```
$ mesg ↵
is n
❏
```

This means that attempts to write to you are blocked. If you want to let other users interrupt you, give an argument of **-y** to the command:

```
$ mesg -y ↵
❑
```

On Berkeley-derived systems, the argument is **n** for no and **y** for yes, without a leading dash. The merged UNIX system accepts either form. Regardless of your terminal setting, the superuser can always write to your terminal (for shutdown messages, for example).

USING THE WRITE PROGRAM

The **write** program results in your messages and those of your correspondent being mixed together. This interleaved operation requires that you adopt a convention for taking turns. The usual method is to type **o** on a line by itself to mean "over". At the end of a conversation you can type **oo**, meaning "over-and-out".

Here is a sample conversation between two users. The contact is initiated by the root account user (text shown in plain typeface). System prompts and my responses are shown in bold typeface. System-generated messages are shown in italic typeface:

```
$
            Message from root on hansen (tty02) [ Wed Jan 19 23:13:05 ]
Hi Augie.
o
write root ↵
Go ahead...
o
I need to do a backup soon. Can you log off for about 30
minutes or so?
o
Sure. Give me 5 minutes to finish this program. OK?
o
Fine. See you tomorrow AM about the test run. Bye. Doris
(end of message)
(Press CTRL-D)
$ ❑
```

The first system message is produced when the root user initiates the contact by issuing a **write augie** command. The second system message is generated when the root user terminates her end of the conversation by pressing CTRL-D. On earlier versions of **write**, the string "end of message" may show up as <EOT>, meaning end-of-transmission, which is the ASCII name for CTRL-D.

USING THE TALK PROGRAM

The **talk** program does essentially the same thing as **write**, but it uses a split-screen display on video terminals. Figure 24.1 shows a sample **talk** session between two users.

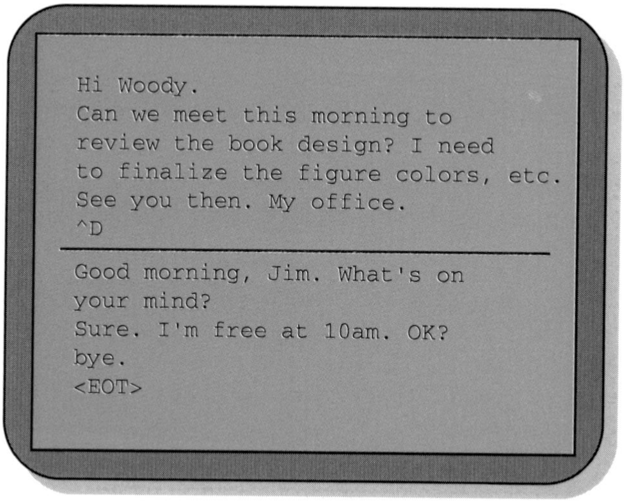

Figure 24.1 The **talk** *program provides direct communication between two users. A split-screen display provides separate views for sender and receiver.*

The **talk** program is designed to work in a networked environment and supports account names with network node names (such as **mars!rover**, **rover@mars**, or other forms that are acceptable) if needed to specify the correct account. See Lesson 26 for information about networks and network addresses.

All characters are displayed as they are typed. There is no line buffering. Use your erase and line-kill characters to correct keying errors. End your conversation by pressing CTRL-D or the BREAK key. When you end the session, the screen clears, and the cursor goes to the lower-left corner of the screen.

ELECTRONIC MAIL

The major problem with direct writing is that it is *synchronous:* the users must both be on line and willing to participate at the *same time.* If the recipient is in the middle of some task—editing a file, for example—he or she might not be too happy about being interrupted. Perhaps the user has "put the shields up" (**mesg -n**) to deflect such intrusions. Or maybe the user is not logged in.

An *asynchronous* means of communicating, electronic mail, is far more respectful of others user's time and avoids the inevitable "tag" game played by users trying to contact each other in real time.

To implement electronic mail, the system maintains a set of directories and files for mail messages. Each user has a file in the system's mail directory. As new mail arrives it is added to the file for the recipient and the user is informed of its arrival (see Lesson 16 for information about mail-related variables).

The mail system is implemented by the **mail** program, the old standby on UNIX systems since the Seventh Edition, or by one of its many descendants. This coverage is based on the widely used **mailx** program, which blends features from several popular electronic-mail programs. (On the SCO Open Desktop system used for the examples in this lesson, **mail** is linked to **mailx**.)

Figure 24.2 illustrates the major features of an electronic mail system. A logged-in user, rocky, sends a message to another user, doris, who is currently not logged in. The message is appended to the appropriate mail file in the mail directory. Next time Doris logs in, her system displays a "you have mail" message. Doris, in turn, can display the message using the **mail** command, or Doris can wait to read the message at a more convenient time. Many users add the **mail** command to their startup file so that they can dispense with mail as soon as they log in.

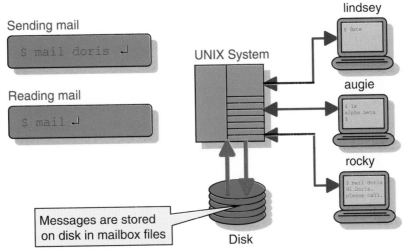

Figure 24.2 *Use the* **mail** *command (possibly* **mailx** *or some other name) to send and read mail. Messages sent to a user are stored in his or her mailbox file for later retrieval. When you read your mail, you can discard or save received messages. Type the command ? while running* **mail** *in command mode to see a help screen that describes your options.*

SENDING MAIL

To send a mail message, run the mail program with the login name of the intended recipient or recipients. If you have the older mail program, the cursor just goes the next line and waits for you to type your message. Current mail programs prompt for a subject. Respond appropriately and type the text of your message.

As you input text, check each line for errors before pressing the RETURN key. With the old mail program, you can't go back to previously entered lines, so when you quit, the message goes out, warts and all. With the newer programs, you can invoke an editor to correct errors before sending the message. The **ed** program is the default, but you can set the EDITOR variable in your environment to specify your preference.

In this sample session, **mailx** is invoked directly. Pressing CTRL-D on a line by itself ends input and sends the message on its way:

```
$ mailx doris ↵ ——————————— Send mail to the user Doris
Subject: Project X Meeting ————— Subject of mail message

Hi Doris:
We have a meeting scheduled for 3pm today
to go over the field trial results. We could
use your help with the review. Can you make it? ——— Message text

Bye. Rocky.
EOT ———————————————————— CTRL-D pressed to end message
$ ▯
```

READING MAIL

You use the same command to read your mail as to send mail to other users. Typing the command with no arguments starts the process. Here, I am informed on one new message:

```
$ mailx ↵
SCO System V Mail (version 3.2)   Type ? for help.
"/usr/spool/mail/augie": 1 message 1 new
>N 1 arh        Thu Jan 20 10:47   13/417    Emergency station setup
& ▯
```

Pressing RETURN at the & prompt causes the message to be displayed:

```
& ↵
Message  1:
From sparks Thu Jan 20 10:47:09 1994
From: sparks@hansen.UUCP (J. S. Donnelley)
X-Mailer: SCO System V Mail (version 3.2)
To: augie
Subject: Emergency station setup ——— Message header
Date: Thu, 20 Jan 94 10:47:08 MST
Message-ID:   <9401201047.aa29015@hansen.UUCP>
Status: R

Hi Gus:
We'll be going to the ham station to set up and
handle traffic for the earthquake emergency. Leaving in ——— Message
one hour. Are you riding with us or separately?       text
73, Sparks.
& ▯
```

Now what? If you need to find out what to do next, you can press **?** to summon a condensed page that highlights the primary mail commands. You issue mail commands using single letters. To save the current message, press **s**↵ to append to your mailbox file, or **s** *filename*↵ to append to a named file. Use the **w** command instead of **s** to save the message without the header information.

Other options available to you at this point are too numerous to mention and a good reason to tell you to read the manual if you want to know more. For now let's just delete the message (**d**↵) and quit the mail program (**q**↵):

```
& d
& q
Held 0 messages in /usr/spool/mail/augie.
$ ▢
```

After messages have been marked from deletion (marked automatically by **save** and **write** commands), they are usually removed from the mailbox file when the mail program exits. You can override this feature with configuration variables or by exiting with **x** instead of **q**.

Some mail programs offer other features, such as forwarding of mail to other systems (handy if you have accounts on different systems), and delivery notification (handy if your associates have convenient memory lapses). Again, check your manual and also find out about local customs.

WHAT YOU NEED TO KNOW

The programs described in this lesson let you reach out an touch someone on your system. These programs provide a basic level of user-to-user communication. Other communication tools, described in the next two lessons, extend your reach to users on other systems. Before setting sail on this new adventure, check your understanding of the following topics:

☑ Use the **write** program to interact directly with another user's terminal on the same system. Attempts to write can be blocked if the other user has disallowed writes.

☑ The **talk** program allows you to communicate directly with other users on your system and on those of a local area network.

☑ Use **mesg -n** to block attempts to connect to your terminal or **mesg -y** to allow such access.

☑ The **mail** and **mailx** programs, among others, are used for sending and receiving electronic mail. This asynchronous form of user-to-user communication continues to grow in popularity.

Lesson 25

Communicating with Other Systems

If you have accounts on more than one system, you might find it necessary to connect to one while using another. Copying files between the accounts is a good reason to do so, as is reading electronic mail that was sent to a different account than the one you are using at the time.

This lesson introduces you to the **cu** program. It gives you a basic way to establish an interactive communication between two UNIX systems or between a UNIX system and a non-UNIX system. This lesson covers the following topics:

- Calling other UNIX systems using the **cu** program
- Transferring text files (upload and download)
- Connecting with non-UNIX systems, such as bulletin boards

CALLING OTHER SYSTEMS

A connection between two computer systems, no matter how close or far apart they are, is described in rather parochial terms. The system your terminal is connected to, by whatever means, is the *local* system. You could even be connected by a radio link from the Moon to the host that serves your terminal. It's still your local machine. The computer system that your local system calls is the *remote* system. Of course, a user on the other system sees it the same way from his or her point of view, so yours is the remote system as far as the other user is concerned.

If you have an account on another system, you can use the **cu** program to call it and log in as you would from any terminal or PC running a terminal-emulation program. Figure 25.1 shows a typical arrangement, in which two systems communicate via a *full duplex* (allows two-way communication) connection. The remote system could be another UNIX system or it can be any other system that is capable of answering the phone and connecting to a terminal device. A bulletin board system (BBS) is a primary example.

To start an interactive communication session with another UNIX system, start **cu** with a command of the form cu [*opts*] [*dest*], where *opts* is a collection of connection- and line-configuration options, and *dest* is either a telephone number or a system name. A system name must be one of the names known to **uucp** (see Lesson 26). For example to call a system called helios9 with 9600 bits-per-second transmission rate and even parity, type this command:

```
$ cu -e -s9600 helios9 ↵
```

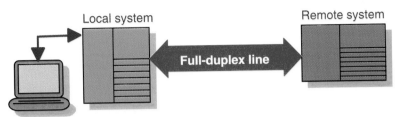

*Figure 25.1 The system your terminal or console is connected to is the **local** system. The system called by your system is the **remote** system, which can be running UNIX or some other operating system. You must have an account on the remote system.*

Check your manual and local customs for command options and communications settings to use. The system names that are available to you can be found by using the **uuname** command. Here is an example taken from one of my UNIX systems:

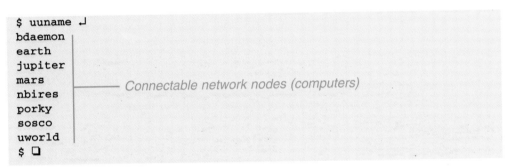

```
$ uuname ↵
bdaemon
earth
jupiter
mars            ——— Connectable network nodes (computers)
nbires
porky
sosco
uworld
$ ▢
```

When a connection is established, you should see the response CONNECTED from the remote. Press BREAK a time or two to receive a login prompt. Proceed as you normally would if you had called the remote system directly from your terminal.

INTERACTING WITH OTHER UNIX SYSTEMS

After you have logged in, you can run commands on the remote system and on the local system. The **cu** program lets you run commands on one system while delivering output to the other. You can also transfer text files using awkward-looking, but simple commands.

RUNNING COMMANDS

The **cu** program runs as two separate processes: a *transmit* process and a *receive* process. The transmit process reads from standard input (usually your keyboard) and sends what it reads to the remote system. Lines with the ~ prefix (used as an *escape* character) are treated as local commands. As shown in the table, commands prefixed by ~$ run locally and send output to the remote system. Other variations are available.

The receive process takes output from the remote system and sends it to the standard output on your local system. Some remote system output may be directed to files on the local system.

To get system-specific information from the remote system, for example, use the **uname** (UNIX system name and information) command:

```
$ uname -a ↵
omniware hansen 3.2 2 i386
$ ▢
```

The remote system is a microcomputer running a desktop UNIX system. To get the same information on the local system, type the same command with the escape prefix:

```
$ ~!uname -a ↵
UNIX_SV mars 4.2 1 i386 386/AT
$ ▢
```

This system is also a PC-class system running a different desktop UNIX version. (The command reports the system incorrectly—it's really a 486 chip, but PC UNIX systems are currently based on the 386 "porting" base.)

Table 25.1 presents an abbreviated list of commands that **cu** runs locally. Numerous other commands are supported, with some variations among the versions of the program.

Command	Description
~.	Terminate the interactive session
~!	Run an interactive shell on the local system (stopped by a CTRL-D or **exit** command)
~!*command*	Run command in a subshell (exits upon *command* completion)
~$*command*	Run *command* on the local system and send its output to the remote system
~%cd [*newdir*]	Change directory on the local system (~!cd [*newdir*] runs **cd** in a subshell so its effect is transient)
~%put *from* [*to*]	Copy the file *from* on the local system to the file *to* on the remote system (uses same name if *to* is not specified)
~%take *from* [*to*]	Copy the file *from* on the remote system to the file *to* on the local system (uses same name if *to* is not specified)

Table 25.1 This abbreviated list shows some of the commands that are run locally (because of the ~ prefix). Commands without the prefix run on the remote system.

TRANSFERRING FILES

From your perspective, when you copy a file from your local system to a remote system, you are *uploading* the file. Copying a file from the remote system to your local system is called *downloading*. (No other field of endeavor is richer with opportunity to invent new words and phrases except, perhaps, government!)

UPLOADING A FILE

As Table 25.1 shows, the command to upload a file has the form ~%**put** *from* [*to*]. The file transfer can occur only if the remote system supports the standard UNIX command **stty** and **cat**, which set the required terminal mode and generate the output data stream. Also, both systems must use the same control characters for erase and line-kill.

Figure 25.2 shows the command that copies a file called **cqww.log** to the remote system. Only the *from* name is specified, so the copy ends up with the same name in the directory that is current on the remote system. Provide a *to* name if you want to rename the file during the transfer. The red arrows show the effect of the command.

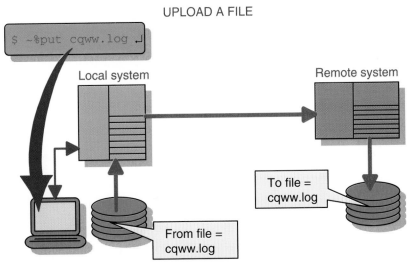

UPLOAD A FILE

```
$ ~%put cqww.log ⏎
```

Local system

Remote system

To file = cqww.log

From file = cqww.log

Figure 25.2 *Use the ~%put command to upload a file. The same name is used on the remote system as on the local system unless you provide a different destination pathname. The upload process works for standard text files (not binary) and no error checking or recovery is done.*

DOWNLOADING A FILE

Use a command of the form ~%**take** *from* [*to*] to transfer a file from the remote system to the local system. This command requires the UNIX programs **echo** and **cat** be available on the remote system. Set tabs mode on the remote system (see your documentation on **stty**) to guarantee that tabs won't be expanded to spaces during the transfer.

Terminating a Session

Use the ~. command to end your **cu** session. Before ending the session, log off the remote system by the normal means (CTRL-D or **exit**).

Using cu with Non-UNIX Systems

When you use **cu** to call a non-UNIX system, you accept some severe limitations. The remote system probably doesn't know how to handle a video terminal, so you're stuck with a "dumb" terminal interactions even if your terminal has a high IQ. The other serious limitation is that file transfers are not supported. This is a side effect caused by the likely lack of certain UNIX-style commands and capabilities needed to do the transfers.

In spite of these limitations, you can still log on to a remote system and carry on an interactive session (read and write mail messages, "shop 'til you drop," or whatever. And you can still run local commands on your UNIX system without leaving the **cu** program.

What You Need to Know

The **cu** program is a basic interactive communication program. This lesson shows you how to invoke it and use its primary features. The next lesson introduces you to a set of programs that provide flexible, error-corrected, unattended file transfers and remote command execution. Before taking the plunge into UUCP and networks, be sure you understand the topics presented in the lesson:

- ☑ You can call other UNIX systems and even non-UNIX systems by using the **cu** program.

- ☑ Ordinary text files can be copied between UNIX systems. Copying to a remote system from your local system is uploading (~**%put**) and copying from the remote to the local system is downloading (~**%take**).

- ☑ The **cu** program provides no error detection or correction on file transfers. Use an error-correcting protocol if data integrity is important (see Lesson 26).

- ☑ Connecting with non-UNIX systems, such as bulletin boards, is supported by **cu**, but without file transfer. Remote commands are those acceptable to the remote system.

Lesson 26

UNIX and Networks

In the previous two lessons you were introduced to some simple methods of communicating with other users on your own system and on other systems. This lesson extends your knowledge of these topics by giving you an overview of the major networking features of UNIX systems. The following topics are covered:

- The UUCP family of programs
- Creating and using a UUCP-based network
- TCP/IP and internetworking
- Internet access and programs

The coverage of these topics is at a high level, intended primarily to give you a feel for what can be done and a reason to explore the details in your system documentation. The Internet topic described in detail in the Jamsa Press book, *Success with Internet*.

UNIX AND UUCP-BASED NETWORKS

Some of the programs described earlier in this section depend on UNIX system networking features. The UNIX mail programs, for example, use the system's UUCP (**UNIX-to-UNIX Copy**) programs to transfer files among systems. The name **uucp** is used in this book to specify the user-level program itself, and UUCP refers to the complete set of **uucp**-related programs.

THE UUCP PROGRAMS

Collections of UNIX systems use UUCP over dedicated and dial-up lines to create networks. Other computer systems running compliant software can participate also. The UUCP package is the basis of UNIX electronic mail and other communications features. Table 26.1 lists the UUCP user-level programs.

You can run these programs directly, although they are usually run on your behalf by other programs. For example, you run a program such as **mail**, which calls on UUCP programs to do the work of copying files to other users and between systems. Remote execution of commands, including printing, are other examples of UUCP use.

147

Program	Description
uucp	Request a file copy operation between cooperating systems
uux	Execute commands on a remote UNIX system (restricted set for security)
uuname	List names of connected systems
uulog and **uustat**	Get status of **uucp** and **uux** requests

Table 26.1 The user-level programs of the UUCP package request and track file transfers and remote command execution of programs. Other UUCP programs work in the background to effect the requested transfer and command actions.

You can send a file or a group of files to a user on another system by using the **uucp** program. To send the file **outline.txt** to a user named **inky** on a remote system called **macho**, use a command like this one:

```
$ uucp outline.txt macho!inky ↵
$ ▢
```

The form of this command should be familiar. It's just like **cp** *from to* that you use on your local system except the destination is now on a different system. The **!** separates the components of the path, with the machine name on the left and the path to the user on the right.

The pathname of the public directory is represented by PUBDIR, which is a symbolic name for a directory called **/var/spool/uucppublic**. The path **/usr/spool/uucppublic** is used on earlier UNIX releases. This directory may contain files and other directories that are used for temporary storage of files in transit. Two new programs that were introduced with System V are effectively friendly front ends for **uucp**. The **uuto** program sends a file to a remote system's PUBDIR, and **uupick** allows the user on the remote system to retrieve the file.

The **uuname** program, introduced in Lesson 25, is one that you might need to use from time to time. It lists the system names that your host system is connected to or can call. The telephone numbers, transmission rates, and other parameters for each named system are stored, so you can specify a call by system name alone.

A Sample UUCP Network

Figure 26.1 is a partial view of a network that shows how a file can be transferred from one user to another user on a different system. This network uses modems and the switched telephone system as a transport medium.

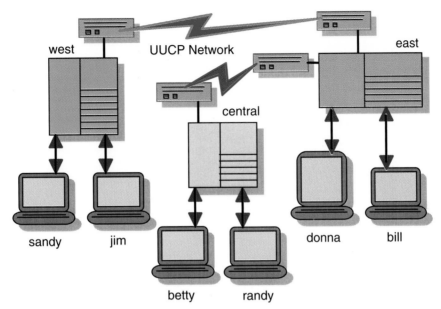

Figure 26.1 A dial-up arrangement of three widely scattered systems illustrates how an informal UUCP network can be easily assembled.

Direct connections between nearby systems, high-speed leased lines between offices in different cities, and even microwave and satellite links are used in practice. UNIX systems connected in this way and running UUCP software are called UUCP networks.

A mail message or other file is relayed from system to system until it arrives at its destination. A UUCP-style address is a pathname formed by specifying the system name and the user name combined with a separator (!). If other systems are involved in relaying the file, the concatenation of system names prefixes the user name. From the user **sandy** on the **west** system, the UUCP path to **donna** is **east!donna**. From **sandy** to **randy** on the central system, two hops are required: **east!central!randy**.

C shell users need to protect the ! from processing by the shell. The addresses shown in this example become **east\\!donna** and **east\\!central\\!randy**. In fact, addresses formed this way work with all shells, so if you use different shells on a regular basis, you might as well adopt this form to avoid confusion.

Several major networks have been constructed to the UUCP model. USENET, started as an academic bulletin-board system, is such an arrangement. What began as a network of a few systems at the University of North Carolina and Duke University turned into a large news-distribution network. As the burden on USENET grew, various network service providers have come on line to relieve and supplement the overburdened systems in the USENET community.

INTERNETWORKING

In addition to keeping the world safe from tyrants and madmen, the U.S. Defense Department has played a significant role in the computer business—one that benefits us all. In the early 1970s, the DOD sponsored work in the form of ARPAnet, which supported military research efforts. The network was, in fact a network of networks. It was built on a set of protocols that have evolved and become the basis of a world-wide network called the *Internet*.

TCP/IP

TCP is the Transmission Control Protocol and IP is the Internet protocol. Software written to these standards provides the "mirrors and magic" of *internetworking* (networks of networks). UNIX systems can take full advantage of the world-spanning networks of computer systems. Traditionally, most of the systems have been UNIX-based, but an increasing number are not.

Each of the cloud-like objects in Figure 26.2 represents a network of some kind that supports TCP/IP connections. Each of the networks can be linked to other networks, as represented by the red lines. Such linkages are usually high-speed, dedicated circuits. The networks in the figure form a *backbone* of systems that provide the primary path for data flowing through the internet arrangement.

Note: The word internet—all lowercase—refers to any interconnected set of networks, whereas Internet refers to the specific network arrangement that has ARPAnet roots.)

Satellite networks, shown in the figure as grouping of small squares, and even isolated systems, can participate in the network by gaining access through any other connected system. The network called MyNet in the figure might be connected via a dial-up, on-demand arrangement, or even via a radio link, while the one labeled YourNet probably has a dedicated-line connection to one of the primary sites. The network is constantly changing as new systems are added, renamed, moved, or disconnected.

NETWORK APPLICATIONS

If you have access to a computer system or network at work, you might already have Internet access. If not, you can usually obtain access by connecting to a commercial service provider, a public network, an educational system, or one of the many organizations that already have access. Just as almost everyone, in the U.S. at least, has a TV set and a telephone, it won't be long before nearly everyone will have his or her own Internet ID. In fact, your Internet connection just might come through your TV via cable or other means.

So, once you're connected, what can you do? You know about electronic mail already. But there is a lot more in store for you. Two primary application programs provide access to network features: **telnet** lets you log in on remote systems and **ftp** lets you transfer file to and from remote systems. The systems don't have to be UNIX-based.

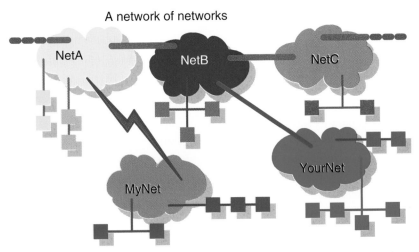

A network of networks

Figure 26.2 This illustration shows how a collection of diverse networks and their subnetworks can be hooked together by using TCP/IP software to form a large network of networks.

The telnet application is a user interface program for remote system access. You can call any remote system that is accessible on the network, but you need an account on the remote system. To start a **telnet** session, simply type the command name. Use the **?** command to see the manual page:

```
$ telnet ↵
telnet> ? ↵
Commands may be abbreviated.  Commands are:

close           close current connection
display         display operating parameters
...
open            connect to a site
quit            exit telnet
send            transmit special characters ('send ?' for more)
set             set operating parameters ('set ?' for more)
unset           unset operating parameters ('unset ?' for more)
...
z               suspend telnet
!               invoke a subshell
?               print help information
telnet> ❏
```

The **ftp** application is an interface program for the ARPAnet standard file-transfer protocol (FTP). You can transfer text and binary files to and from remote systems of any supported type. *Anonymous FTP* is a popular use of this application. It lets you access public databases without the need for an account on the system where the data resides. Many systems allow the posting of data, source code for programs, and other information that you can copy for the cost of a call.

The **ftp** program is complex and varies from one implementation to another. Check your system reference documentation for details about your version and how to use it. As with **telnet**, you can start just typing the command name and get a manual page by typing **?** at the **ftp>** prompt.

UNIX-STYLE PROGRAMS FOR NETWORKS

The **telnet** and **ftp** programs work on any system within the network. The commands described in Table 26.2 are UNIX specific. They offer some advantages in terms of ease of use. These programs were designed to mimic standard UNIX commands and are named accordingly. Thus, **cp** for copy becomes **rcp** for the remote version.

Program	Description
rlogin	Remote login program
rsh	Remote shell (called **remsh** on some systems to avoid a conflict with the restricted shell, **rsh**)
rcp	Remote file-copy program

Table 26.2 These commands are designed to work with remote UNIX systems on a network. The names and behaviors mimic standard UNIX commands, with the initial r in each name meaning "remote" version.

NETWORK ADDRESSES

In the early days of the Internet, addressing was a relatively simple matter if you knew the login name and system of a user. As the size of the Internet has increased, more clever means of specifying addresses of individual systems and users have been developed and employed. The essence of addressing is that a user is accessible on a machine somewhere in the overall network in much the same way that individuals have a street address or post office box in the world outside the computer.

For users on the same local-area network, the address of another user is typically just the user name. This works always if the recipient is on the same machine as the sender. It usually works on a LAN, too, because a directory service or mail database keeps track of which users have accounts on which systems. Things get a bit murky if a user has multiple accounts on more than one system or if no user directory is maintained. In situations like these, use a qualified path that follows the Internet-style address format: *user@system*, as shown in Figure 26.3.

Complicating things quite a bit is the fact that the Internet serves millions of users scattered about the world in a complex web of interconnections. To bring order to as potentially chaotic situation, the systems on the network have been identified by *domains*. The original high-level domains were formed along organizational lines, as shown in Table 26.3. Other domain naming is done based on geographical alignments.

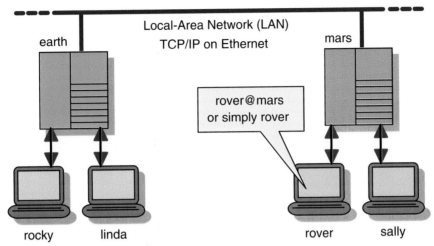

Figure 26.3 *The address you use to reach another user on a local-area network is determined by the presence of absence of a mail database or other address-resolution server. If unique login names are used across a network and a user directory is maintained, all you need is the login name. Otherwise, use the form **user@system**, where **system** is the name of the destination computer system.*

Domain	Description
com	Commercial/business-oriented user community
edu	Educational users at universities, in high schools, and so on
gov	Nonmilitary government users
mil	Military organizations and related research laboratories
org	Other organizations that don't fit neatly into the other categories (there always has to be a "none of the above" choice)
net	Any resources related to the network itself

Table 26.3. *The six original high-level domains are based on an organizational scheme. Other high-level domains are geographical.*

Within each of the organizational domains are numerous systems and networks of systems. Therefore, each of these domains is divided into lower level domains. For example, under **edu** are numerous universities, such as the University of Denver (domain name **du**). Within the university are departments, so a further subdivision produces even lower-level domains, such as **cs** for the Computer Science Department. Within that departmental domain are machine and network names.

When sending e-mail or transferring files to another Internet user, you need to specify the user's account name and a recognizable system address. It may be necessary to specify a domain and its subdomains, as depicted in a general form in Figure 26.4.

The Internet address format places the system name on the right side of the @ symbol. The system name is composed of domain names separated by . (there's that dot again!). The domain name at the right end of the sequence is the highest level (**com** in this example). Working toward the left brings you to increasingly lower levels in the domain hierarchy until you get to a specific system or network name.

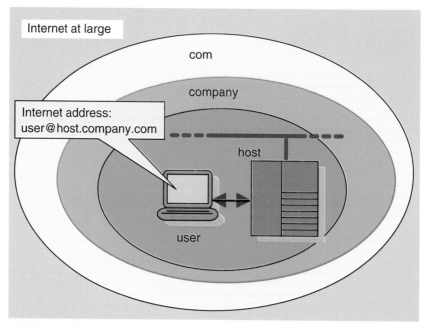

Figure 26.4 *The use of domains permits a flexible addressing scheme that adapts to a rapidly growing worldwide network.*

The address shown in the figure identifies **user** at the domain **company.com**. The actual host machine is not named in the example because a local directory on the company's network figures out which system to send the item to. For some users, you may need to specify the domain completely to the machine level (for example, **user@host.company.com**).

TRANSFERRING BINARY DATA

Some segments of distributed networks can handle files composed of only ordinary text characters. Such files are called *text* files. Files that contain any control codes other than the usual format effectors (tab, newline, and carriage return) or non-ASCII characters are called *binary* files. In addition to possible network limitations, the **cu** program described in the previous lesson can not reliably transfer binary files. The mail-forwarding programs are similarly limited.

If you need to send a file that contains binary data, typical of compiled program files, you may need to alter the file to make it pass through the communication program or network software without damage. The process involves converting the file to an acceptable form before transmission and then converting it back to its original form after reception. A pair of programs called **uuencode** and **uudecode** do the job. The programs are available on some UNIX systems and from network archives in source-code form for systems that don't have them.

The **uuencode** program converts sequences of three characters that possibly contain binary data to sequences of four printable ASCII characters. In addition, some control information is added. The overall effect is to inflate the file by some 35%.

A command of the form **uuencode [*file*] *file-label*** encodes the **file** and labels it in its control information header, which is used during decoding to give the file a name. The program writes to standard output and is used with redirection or as part of a command pipeline using the techniques described in Section 3. The following command converts a binary file to an acceptable form for transmission:

```
$ uuencode listdir listdir > listdir.uu ↵
$ ▢
```

I used the **.uu** extension on the redirected output file to give a clue about its contents. This is not required, but it's good practice.

On the receiving end, the **uudecode** reverses the effects of **uuencode**, stripping out the header to identify the filename and permissions, and converting the contents back to binary form. This command is all you need:

```
$ uudecode listdir.uu ↵
$ ▢
```

WHAT YOU NEED TO KNOW

There is a lot more to know about the networking features of UNIX than can be told even in an entire book. This lesson is intended only to spark your interest in pursuing the matter more fully if it interests you.

The next section introduces you to the visual editor, **vi**, and shows you how to create and edit files interactively. You can set up your mail program to use any editor you like. The default editor is **ed**, but you can add **EDITOR**=*path*/**vi** to your configuration file (.**profile**, .**login**, etc.) to use **vi** automatically instead. Before starting the next section, review these points:

☑ The UUCP family of programs extends basic UNIX commands so that they can work across system boundaries.

☑ Using UUCP programs and dial-up circuits, leased lines, or other media, it is easy to create local- and wide-area networks.

☑ Using software built to TCP/IP standards, a worldwide network of networks, the Internet, has been established.

☑ Internet access is available to nearly anyone who has a computer and a telephone line. Most UNIX users already have access through their employer's or school's networks.

☑ Whether based on UUCP, TCP/IP, or other protocols, the networks provide convenient and efficient electronic mail and file-transfer services.

Visual Editing

In Section 4 you learned how to use **ed**, a UNIX line editor that lets you create and change text files using commands that work with one or lines of a file. When you work with **ed**, you normally issue one command that changes your file and then a second command to display the file's new contents.

This section instructs you in the use of the UNIX *visual* editor **vi**. A visual editor is so named because as you work, the results of your commands (the file's contents) are always immediately in view. In other words, you don't have to issue an editing command and then a second command to display the file's contents.

The **vi** editor is the standard UNIX visual editor as of the introduction of UNIX System V. Prior to that release, UNIX had no official visual editor, although **vi** and several other worthy contenders were widely available as unsupported software. Being the official standard, **vi** is an editor that you should know how to use. It is the most widely available on UNIX systems of any vintage. When you complete the seven lessons in this section, you will have a good working knowledge of the **vi** editor. The lessons cover the following topics:

Lesson 27

Getting Started with the Visual Editor

This section builds on your knowledge of basic editing with **ed** and **ex** (see Section 4) by describing and illustrating the main features of the visual editor **vi** and the methods you use to create and edit text files in an interactive, visual mode.

This lesson gets you up and running quickly with **vi**. The material presented covers the following topics:

- Starting **vi** from the UNIX command line
- Entering text interactively and reading text from a file
- Viewing text
- Using special input characters
- Quitting the editor

STARTING THE VISUAL EDITOR

The **vi** editor is an interactive editor that lets you create and modify text on a character-by-character basis with constant visual feedback. In other words, the changes you make to your file immediately appear in front of you on the screen. Most users find this method more comforting than the "flying blind" approach that some users attribute to the use of line-oriented editors like **ed**.

Starting **vi** is easy. To create a new file, just type the **vi** program name and press RETURN (**vi** ↵). The editor starts up with an empty editing window and a message about this being a new file. We'll create a file from scratch later in this lesson. To get started we'll use an existing file to get some text into the editing buffer.

Providing a filename argument causes **vi** to start with the file's text fully or partially displayed (depending on the file's size), as shown in Figure 27.1. The command line that starts this session looks like this:

```
$ vi quote.txt ↵
(starts vi session on named file)
```

Figure 27.1 also illustrates the initial screen appearance of a **vi** session. The upper portion is the editing window, and the bottom line is the command-line and message window. If your terminal is capable of special video attributes (inverse video, underline, and so on), the editor may use one of them to highlight the last line:

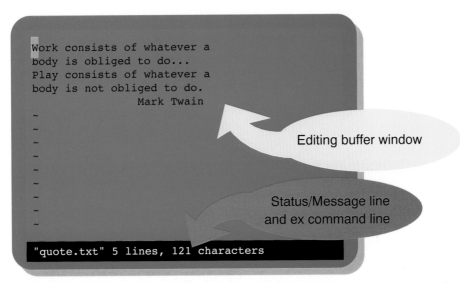

```
Work consists of whatever a
body is obliged to do...
Play consists of whatever a
body is not obliged to do.
                    Mark Twain
~
~
~
~
~
~
~
~
"quote.txt" 5 lines, 121 characters
```

Editing buffer window

Status/Message line
and ex command line

Figure 27.1 When you start editing a file, vi displays the file's contents in an editing window, which on a typical terminal is the whole screen except for the last line. The last line is reserved for messages and line-oriented commands.

Once the editor is running, **vi** acts upon your commands immediately (no RETURN necessary), except when you use the **ex** command mode (see the next lesson for more details about editor modes such as **ex**). The editor accepts single-character commands in its initial mode.

Some of the single-character **vi** commands instruct the editor to position the cursor. Others put the editor into the input mode so you can insert or append text. The cursor, usually a blinking block or underline on a terminal screen, shows you where you are in the editing buffer. The cursor location is the focal point of most editing and text insertion actions.

The tildes (~) down the left edge of the editing window indicate that these lines contain no text from the file. This situation occurs when there is not enough text left in the file to fill the editing window. The file either has fewer lines than the window can display or has been scrolled or paged down to the end of the file.

QUITTING THE VISUAL EDITOR

The **vi** editor is actually just the visual mode of the **ex** editor. The quit command and all of the file commands that follow in this lesson are issued on the bottom line of the visual editor screen, which is, in effect, a one-line **ex** editor window.

To quit the editor, you press the : (colon key), which puts the cursor on the bottom screen line. On this line you can type most **ex** and **ed** commands and you can also issue operating system commands. The **q** command takes you out of the editor unless there are unsaved changes to the editing buffer. You must follow all **ex** commands with a RETURN.

If you have made changes to the editing buffer and you want to save them, you can issue separate **w** and **q** commands, but it is easier and quicker to do them together:

```
:wq ↵ ──────────────────────── Write the file's contents to disk and quit
$ ▢
```

Note: Current versions of *vi* also give you a pure visual mode command, ZZ, that does the same job. This one doesn't need a RETURN—its immediate.

If you have made changes and decide not to save them, you can quit by using the following command:

```
:q! ↵ ──────────────────────── Quit without editor prompts
$ ▢                                for saving your changes
```

The appended ! tells the editor to turn off the safety checks (such as a reminder that you have not saved your changes) and to do what you told it to do: quit. When you use the ! in this way, **vi** assumes that you've grown up and are now responsible for your actions. By the way, **vi** won't laugh if you mistakenly discard changes you really wanted to save, but it won't help you recover them either.

REEDITING THE CURRENT FILE

Another alternative is to start editing the same file again, throwing away any changes you have made to it in the current session. This is the "fresh start" command:

```
:e! ↵
```

INSERTING TEXT

When you issue certain visual mode commands, the editor switches to the text input mode. It adds the text you type to the editing buffer (also called the *work file*). You end text input with the Esc key, which completes the input operation. Exceptions are the **r** and **~** commands, which are self-completing (and don't require you to press Esc). Here are the primary commands that initiate text input:

    i   (insert)   Input text with the new text being inserted to the *left* of the current character. As you input text, the line opens up and shifts to the right as you type. You can type as much text as you want during the input session. A variation on the command is started by using the **I** command, which inserts text at the beginning of the current line.

a (append)   The append operation is the same as insert, except the new text goes into the editing buffer *after* the current character. The variation **A** causes the appending of text to occur at the end of the current line.

s (substitute)   The substitute command is usually given a multiplier that specifies how many characters to delete before the new text (any amount) is put in its place. For example, **5s***text***Esc** replaces the current character and the next four with the replacement characters identified as *text*.

o (open)   Opens a line below the current line and switches to input mode. The **O** variation opens a line above the current line.

R (replace)   Replaces characters with new text (works as an overtype mode).

r (replace one character)   Replaces the character at the cursor with the next character typed.

~ (convert letter case)   Replaces the character at the cursor, if it is a letter, with the opposite letter case.

Other commands that cause a switch to input mode are described in Lesson 31. In addition, you can read text from a file using the **ex** (and **ed**) **r** (read) command. Use a command of the form **:r** *file* ⏎, where *file* is either a real filename or the output of a command execution (**!ls -l**, for example).

SCROLLING AND PAGING

If the editing buffer contains more than one screen or window of text, you can scroll and page the editing buffer by using simple commands. To test the commands described, let's use the **r** (read) command to get a lot of text into the buffer. The command **:r !ls -1 /usr/bin** adds a large number of lines to the buffer. The actual text will vary from one system to another, but it will serve nicely for demonstration purposes.

The editor leaves you on the last line of the new input. You can jump quickly to a line by using the **G** command. A numeric count specifies the line to go to. Use **1G** to get to the first line. **$G** (or simply **G** because **$** is assumed if you don't type a number) takes you to the last line.

Note: When you type these visual mode commands, you do not see what you type. The editor accumulates the characters you type and acts on them as soon as it sees a complete command.

If the file you are editing contains more lines than one screenful, you can scroll through the text by using CTRL-D (down) and CTRL-U (up). The number of lines scrolled is set initially by the editor to allow some overlap. You can control the number of lines scrolled by providing a preceding count (for example, **18**CTRL-D). The count is remembered and used in future scrolls until the session ends or you change it again.

The scroll commands roll the screen a line-at-a-time. You can jump by "pages" using CTRL-F (forward a page) and CTRL-B (backward a page). These commands clear the screen and redraw a screen-page away from the current line, where a page is the number of lines in the editing window minus one for overlap. A preceding count causes these commands to jump by that number of pages.

SPECIAL INPUT CHARACTERS

Use the TAB key to insert a standard hardware tab (repeats every eight columns). Tab is a control character that is input as CTRL-I on keyboards that lack a TAB key.

The editor also offers a *shift*, which defaults to eight columns, but you can set other values. A popular value used by many programmers is a shift width of four columns. Use CTRL-T to insert a shift during input mode.

Most of the time you use control characters for their effects, but at times you may want to insert their codes into the file. Use the \ to quote the erase (Backspace) and line-kill characters. You can generally quote any non-printing character by preceding it with CTRL-V. The resulting code in the buffer is actually a single character, but it displays as a ^ followed by the control-code letter or other symbol. For example, the ESC key ends text input, but typing CTRL-V before the escape leaves the sequence ^[in the buffer and input continues.

WHAT YOU NEED TO KNOW

This first lesson in a series of seven has introduced you to a core set of commands for getting into the editor, performing a few simple text-creation commands, and getting out of the editor. The next lesson describes the major modes of the **ex/vi** editor and the tasks you perform in each mode. Verify your understanding of these topics before you advance to the next lesson:

☑ You starting the **vi** editor from the UNIX command line either with or without a filename argument.

☑ Enter the text input mode by using various commands, such as append (**a**), change (**c**), and substitute (**s**).

☑ Text can be read from a file or from program output by using the **:r** command.

☑ Use the **G** command to go to a specified line. **1G** moves to the first line and **G** ($ assumed) moves to the last.

☑ You can scroll the text with CTRL-D (down) and CTRL-U (up) and page text with CTRL-F (forward) and CTRL-B (backward) in the file.

☑ Quit the editor by using **:q**. If you want to save changes, use with a preceding write command. The shortcut **ZZ** is equivalent to **:wq↵**.

Lesson 28

Editor Modes

When you edit files using **vi**, as briefly discussed in Lesson 27, you can advantage of special **ex** commands. This lesson introduces you to the **ex/vi** editor modes and gives you a model that helps you to know what happens when you press a particular key. The topics covered include the following:

- The **ex/vi** editor modes and commands that cause transitions among them
- The visual command mode and some simple commands
- The **ex** command (last-line) mode and shell escapes
- Text input modes

EDITOR MODES AND TRANSITIONS

The ideal editor, if there is such a thing, works in harmony with the way you work. *Modeless editors*, which have a single action associated with each key and key combination, are the most natural type of editor because they act predictably in virtually all situations. These editors are likened to a typewriter because they were designed to put what you type into the editing buffer unless you use special keys to issue commands.

The **ex/vi** editor is a *moded* editor: Because of this, most keys have more than one meaning. The default mode is *visual command mode*, which is used for cursor positioning, searching for text, reading and writing files, and so on. You have to issue commands to get to the text input mode and a special command to get out of it. Although this design offers some interesting features, it is generally hard to learn and often troublesome to use, especially if you regularly use a modeless editor on some other system.

The **vi** editor is really just the visual mode of the **ex** editor mentioned in Section 4. In fact, the **ex** program is known by several names, each eliciting a different kind of editing behavior:

- **ex**—the extended line-oriented editor
- **edit**—a simplified line-oriented editor (**ex** for beginners)
- **vi**—the visual mode of **ex**
- **view**—**vi** run as a read-only file viewer
- **vedit**—a simplified setup of **vi** for beginning users

In this lesson, we concern ourselves with the four modes shown below the line in Figure 28.1, although there are other editor modes of interest to hard copy terminal users. Don't let your eyes glaze over at this point. The figure simply shows the editor modes of interest and the actions that cause transitions from one mode to another. Keep this model in mind as you work with **vi**.

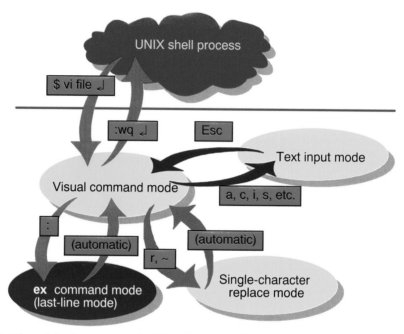

Figure 28.1 *The **ex/vi** editor uses modes. Visual command mode is the initial and primary mode.*

VISUAL COMMAND MODE

When you run **vi** from the UNIX command line, the system starts your editing session. If you specified a file on the command line, **vi** retrieves and displays the named file. Then you are placed in the *visual command mode*.

Characters that you type in this mode are acted upon immediately as visual-mode commands. The bulk of the commands are for cursor positioning, window size control, scrolling and paging, searching for text, and getting file information.

EDITING COMMANDS

The basic editing commands, described here, have immediate effects on the contents of the editing buffer. Many other visual-mode commands have an *action/object* orientation that lets you perform a variety of editing actions (copy, change, delete, move) on a wide range of textual objects (characters, words, lines, sentences, and so on). Lessons 30 through 32 describe and illustrate the use of these visual-mode commands

DELETE CHARACTERS

Two visual-mode commands perform simple deletion operations. Use **x** to delete the character at the cursor location. Use **X** to delete the character to the left of the cursor. A number typed before the commands multiplies their effects. For example **5x** deletes five characters starting with the one at the cursor.

PUT TEXT

The **p** command puts back the text of the most recent deletion or copy command. The restored text is put to the right of the current location. Use **P** to put text back to the left of the cursor. An interesting combination of visual commands lets you easily transpose characters. Move to the first of the two out-of-sequence characters and press **xp**. The **x** deletes the current character and the **p** puts it back to the right of the new current character, effecting the transposition.

JOIN LINES

The **J** command joins adjacent lines into one line. (Note that **vi** uses **J** for this purpose, whereas **ed** and **ex** use **j**. The conflict with a cursor-motion command is the reason.) A number prefix of 3 or greater joins more than the default of two lines.

CORRECTIONS

Use **u** to undo the effects of the most recent change to the editing buffer. If you need to reverse a change, do it right away because any intervening change to the buffer prevents you from undoing the earlier change. Any number of changes to the current line can be undone by the U command as long as you have not moved off the line before issuing the command.

THE ex COMMAND MODE

From visual command mode, you can activate a temporary **ex** command mode session (one command) by pressing the **:** key. The visual editor displays the **:** prompt on the last line of the screen or window. You respond by typing a command and pressing RETURN. Other visual-mode commands that use the last screen or window line are **/** and **?** for text searches and **!** for filtering all or a portion of the editing buffer through external commands.

ISSUING ex EDITOR COMMANDS

Virtually all of the line-oriented editing commands are available here, but global search-and-replace (**g**), and file-interactions, such as read (**r**), write (**w**), rename (**f**), and quit (**q**) are the most often used commands. Upon completion of the command (except quit, of course), an automatic transition back to visual mode takes place.

This example writes a range of lines from the current file to a different file:

```
:.,.+30w extract.txt ↵
```
Range of lines to write
Target file

You can also make a permanent transition to the full-time **ex** editor mode by typing **Q**. If the visual editor gets hopelessly confused, it puts you in this mode. The way back to visual mode is to type the command **vi↵** at the **ex** prompt.

RUNNING SHELL COMMANDS

You can use this mode to issue various operating system commands from within the editor. Two forms are permitted. The first, **:!**_cmd_**↵**, runs one command and returns to visual-editing mode. This form of command execution is demonstrated by the following command, which runs the **mailx** program on the current file (assumed to be a message of some kind).

```
:!mailx doris < % ↵
[Hit return to continue]
```

Note: *Be sure to save the file before issuing this command because the mailer gets the text from the disk file, not the editing buffer. If you don't save, you might send a rancid (outdated) version of the message.*

The % symbol used in the command is a shorthand notation that represents the name of the current file—the one remembered by **vi** if you used a file name on the command line or provided one in an **f** (file) command within the editor. The example command mails the message taken by input redirection from the file you are editing and sends it to the specified user.

The second form, **:sh↵**, invokes a permanent subshell. You can run in the subshell for as long as you wish. When you are ready to return to the editor, type **exit** or issue a CTRL-D command to kill the subshell. You are returned to the editor on the line that was your previous editing context. Here's a sample session:

```
:sh ↵
$ (run your commands)
$ exit ↵
```

Any shell commands are allowed in either form of shell access, but firing up another **ex** or **vi** process is frowned upon.

TEXT-INPUT MODES

Many visual-mode commands cause a transition to a text-input mode, possibly after deleting or rearranging text.

Input Mode

Characters that you type in the input mode are stored in the editing buffer. When you enter text initiated by an **a**, **i**, or **s** command, it is saved starting at the current location (cursor or line). Lines are spread or opened up as needed to take all of the input you provide. You end text input by pressing the **Esc** key, which causes a transition back to visual command mode.

Single-Character Replace Mode

This mode is similar to the standard text input mode except that it inserts only one character, replacing the one at the cursor location, and returns to command mode without waiting for an Escape code. Use this mode to make quick spelling corrections or change punctuation (**r**), and change letter case (**~**).

For example, to fix the spelling of "randot" to "random," get the cursor on the t somehow (see Lessons 30 and 31) and type **rm**, which replaces the character at the cursor with the one following the **r** (replace) command. To capitalize the word "father," move the cursor by any suitable means to the letter f and press **~** to obtain "Father." (Only alphabetic characters are affected by this command.) You can repeat the case-change effect to get "FATHER" by repeatedly pressing **~** key. This works because each press of **~** advances the cursor one position.

What You Need to Know

The **vi** editor-mode model presented in this lesson shows you the way **vi** switches modes and the effect of the current mode on the interpretation of your keystrokes. Before you venture on to Lesson 29, which describes methods of customizing the editor, be certain of these points:

- ☑ The initial and primary **vi** mode is visual command mode, which is used for cursor positioning, controlling your view of the editing buffer, searching for text, and checking file status.

- ☑ Several basic editing commands let you easily delete characters (**x**), put back previously deleted text (**p**), join lines (**J**), and undo changes to the editing buffer (**u** and **U**).

- ☑ The **ex** command mode (last-line mode) lets you issue UNIX system commands and line-editing commands.

- ☑ The text input mode is used to add text to the editing buffer. This mode is entered when you execute insert, append, substitute, replace, and change commands. You end input by pressing the **Esc** key.

- ☑ The single-character input mode is a self-completing replacement of the current character.

Lesson 29

Customizing the Editor

In order to meet a wide range of potential uses and attendant user demands, the **ex/vi** editor is highly configurable. This lesson tells you how the editor configuration is controlled and how you can put your own spin on it. The topics covered include the following:

- Understanding editor variables
- Using the **set** command to view and set variables
- Configuring the editor by external means

EDITOR VARIABLES

The **ex/vi** editor configuration is controlled by a large number of variables. These variables fall into three categories: numeric, string, and Boolean. The following paragraphs describe each type and tell you how they are used.

NUMERIC
The numeric variables specify many aspects of the editor's operation, such as how many lines to display in the editing window, how many lines to scroll, how wide a displayed line is, and so on.

STRING
Several editor variables are stored as strings. These identify your shell (full pathname) for use in executing external programs, your terminal type, and the special codes used by the editor to determine the extent of paragraphs and sections in document files.

BOOLEAN
Most of the editor variables are Boolean. Such variables are either on or off (true or false). The variable name by itself means it is on or true. With a "no" prefix, it is off or false. For example, the variable **showmode** is on when written that way and off when written as **noshowmode**.

THE SET COMMAND

To view the settings of what is called the *short list* of editor variables, use the :**set** command, as shown in Figure 29.1. The command results in a response being displayed on the message line (in place of the command itself).

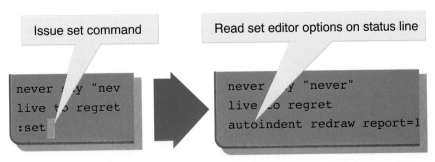

Figure 29.1 The short list of editor variables is summoned by the **ex** *mode's* **set** *command. You can see that autoindent and redraw features are on in this example.*

If viewing all editor variables is your intent, use the command :**set all** ⏎, which results in a display like this (output edited to save space):

```
:set all
noautoindent        nomodelines          noshowmode
autoprint           nonumber             noslowopen
noautowrite         nonovice             tabstop=8
                    ...
nolist              shell=/usr/bin/ksh   wrapmargin=0
magic               shiftwidth=8         nowriteany
mesg                noshowmatch
[Hit return to continue]
```

The last line tells you to hit RETURN, but a gentle press will probably suffice.

You also use the **set** command to change the value of a variable or a group of variables. Setting a specific variable requires that you know its type and provide a suitable value on the right side of an equal sign, which is used to make an assignment of a value. To set the wrap-margin to ten columns, for example, use this command:

```
:set wrapmargin=10 ⏎
```

You can use abbreviations for many of the variables (see the manual page for **vi** in your command reference documentation). For example, **wrapmargin** can be reduced to **wm**. A **wrapmargin** value of 0 turns off automatic line wrap. This setting is preferred by programmers. Any other value sets the column position in from the right side of the editing window where lines are wrapped. Users who are entering text for documents, mail messages, and other page-oriented files would find a **wrapmargin** helpful.

If the text of a word falls within the specified margin, the line is wrapped at the delimiter (normally a space or tab) before the word, as shown in Figure 29.2.

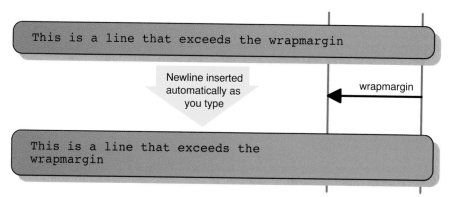

*Figure 29.2 Use a **wrapmargin** setting other than 0 (10 is a good value for most situations) to enable wrapping at the right end of input lines. The feature inserts Return codes (converted to newline codes by UNIX) for you automatically so you can concentrate on typing your text.*

This is one example of the many editor features that are controllable to some degree by each user, independently of all other users. I recommend that you set **showmode** and **number** initially. (The show-mode feature, which tells you which mode the editor is in during input operations, is not available with earlier **vi** versions.) If you are a programmer, you should also set **showmatch** and **autoindent**. Read your command reference to familiarize yourself with other variables and their uses.

EXTERNAL CONFIGURATION

Two files, **.profile** (or **.login**) and **.exrc**, participate in configuring the editor for your use. The first of these configuration files identifies your terminal type, as discussed in Lesson 18. The second file is called **.exrc** in the tradition of other UNIX system configuration files. The name means "**ex run commands**." This file should be created in your home directory.

Each time the editor is started in any mode, the commands in this file are run to set up the editor the way you want it. You normally put any variable assignments that you need in this file. In addition, you can define input abbreviations (shortcuts for input strings using the **abbr** command) and keyboard map commands (visual-mode command shortcuts created by **map** commands).

Prepare an **.exrc** file using **ed** or any other method you know. Here we use the venerable **ed** editor to give it some time in the spotlight:

```
$ ed .exrc ↵
?.exrc
a
set autoindent
set showmode
```

```
set report=1
set number
.
w
52
q
$ □
```

You need to have read permission for this file (see Lesson 12), but that's all, so your default permissions should be fine. The file in your home directory is used unless you have one in the current directory. This lets you set up different configurations for different purposes. I set up a plain text-oriented **.exrc** in my home directory, but put special versions for programming (**wrapmargin** off, **autoindent** and **showmatch** on, and so on) in my source code directories.

*Note: Some versions of the editor can also use the environment variable EXINIT for configuration. The variable takes a string value with **set**, **map**, and other commands in a blank-separated list, enclosed in parentheses. The advantage over using .exrc files is speed of loading, but this advantage has been nullified by the compiled **terminfo** entries used by current versions of the editor.*

WHAT YOU NEED TO KNOW

This lesson has shown you how the **ex/vi** editor is configured. Use this knowledge to tweak the editor to suit your preferences. Before moving on to Lesson 30, which shows you how to get around the editing buffer with ease and teaches you about some of the primary editing objects, confirm your understanding of these topics:

- ☑ The **ex/vi** editor uses numeric, string, and Boolean variables to control its configuration and command behaviors.

- ☑ Use the **set** command to view the values of editor variables and to set variables to suit your operating habits and circumstances.

- ☑ Use external files and environment variables to configure the editor automatically.

Lesson 30

Moving Around in the Editing Buffer

One of the primary command-mode actions while editing with **vi** is positioning the cursor. This lesson shows you how to perform the following actions by issuing visual mode commands:

- Move the cursor in editing buffer using basic positioning commands
- Move forward and backward by words
- Jump to editing window positions

MOVING BY CHARACTERS AND LINES

The line that contains the cursor is called the *current line,* and the character on which the cursor lies is the *current character.* Except for global operations, such as search-and-replace, commands that modify text in the editing buffer take place beginning at the cursor location. Some editing actions affect lines and others affect strings (sequences of characters).

If your keyboard has arrow keys that are recognized by the **vi** editor, you can use them to move left and right by characters and down and up by lines. If your keyboard has no arrow keys or if they fail to work, use the **h**, **j**, **k**, and **l** keys. The actions performed by these keys are shown in Figure 30.1. (The "**hjkl**" keys are used for cursor positioning because the Lear-Seigler ADM3a terminal used in the initial development of **vi** had no cursor keypad, but it had direction arrows marked on the front edges of these keycaps.) Touch typists often prefer to use these "home row" keys, even when arrow keys are available.

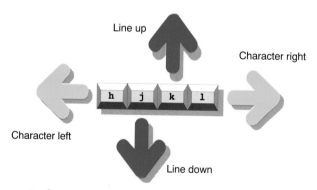

Figure 30.1 If your terminal is not equipped with direction arrows keys, use these letter-key commands to move the cursor by characters and lines. Some models of terminals that have no separate direction keys mark these keys with arrows.

You can multiply the effect of these commands by typing a number before typing the command letter or special key. The command **3h**, or **3←**, for example, attempts to move the cursor to the left by three character positions. For this command, if three or fewer characters are on the line to the left of the cursor, the cursor lands at the beginning of the line. A beep sounds (or the screen flashes) if the cursor is already at the beginning of the line and you attempt to move left. Equivalent behaviors greet attempts to move past the right end of the line with the **l** command, or past the buffer bottom or top with **j** or **k** commands respectively.

Here is a summary of the basic cursor commands and some synonyms that you might prefer to use. The control key versions are needed only for some very early versions of **vi**.

Command	Cursor Movement
H, CTRL-H, BACKSPACE	Left a character
L, CTRL-L, SPACEBAR	Right a character
J, CTRL-N	Down a line
K, CTRL-P	Up a line

Table 30.1 This summary of basic cursor positioning commands also shows some synonyms that you might find useful.

The line up and down commands attempt to hold the same column position in the destination line as the cursor has in the current line. If the destination line is too short for this, the cursor lands on the last occupied position of the line.

Three additional commands move the cursor by a line or lines, but deposit the cursor at the beginning of the destination line. Both the + key and the RETURN key (⏎) move to the beginning of the next line. The – key moves back to the beginning of the previous line. All of these take a numeric multiplier. To move to the beginning of the fourth line down from the current line in the editing buffer, type **4+** or **4⏎**, for example.

MOVING BY WORDS

Moving the cursor through text a character at a time is a slow process. You will usually want to move more quickly to locate text. One way to accelerate your cursor-positioning movements is to jump forward and backward by words.

FORWARD AND BACKWARD BY WORDS

Table 30.2 summarizes the commands that jump to the next and previous "beginning-of-word" locations.

Command	Motion
w, W	Next beginning-of-word location
b, B	Previous beginning-of-word location

Table 30.2 *To move the cursor quickly through text, use these commands to jump by words. Each takes you to the beginning of the next or previous word, where a word is a sequence of characters delimited by separators.*

The lowercase commands (**w, b**) use punctuation marks and other nonalphabetic characters as delimiters. To include such characters as part of a word, use the uppercase version (**W, B**). Program source code often contains constructs like **scrn->col** and NAME_SIZE, which look like multiple words to **w** and **b** commands but are treated as single words by **W** and **B**.

Figure 30.2 illustrates these behaviors for the next-word commands. You can use multipliers on the basic commands to jump by more than a single word at a time. The command **5w** moves the cursor to the fifth beginning-of-word after the current location.

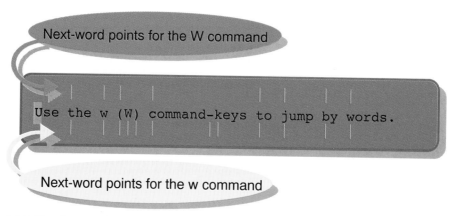

Figure 30.2 *Use the **w** and **W** commands to move forward (right and down) through text in word-sized chunks. The **w** command stops at punctuation and other special characters. The **W** command doesn't. Use **b** and **B** to jump backward (left and up).*

The next-word and previous-word commands *wrap* at line boundaries. This means the cursor moves onto the next or previous line, if one exists, if a command tries to take the cursor past the end or beginning of the current line. The cursor can be anywhere in the current word when you enter these commands. However, the behavior of the previous-word commands varies with the starting cursor position. If you jump backward using **b** or **B**, the current word is counted as one of the beginning-of-word points if the cursor is not on the first character.

MOVING TO THE NEXT END OF WORD

The **e** and **E** commands move forward (right and down) in the editing buffer to the next end-of-word location. A preceding numeric argument multiplies the effect. As with the other word-motion commands, **e** stops at special characters and **E** does not. These commands are handy for seeking the end of a word to append an s to make the word plural or to add "ing" or other suffix.

MOVING TO WINDOW LOCATIONS

Locations within the editing window provide good targets for quick cursor movements. The **H** command (SHIFT-H) moves the cursor to the home position, which is the upper-left corner of the editing window. **vi** always paints the screen starting from this location.

The **L** command (SHIFT-L) moves the cursor to the lower-left corner of the editing window. If there is not enough text to fill the window, **L** moves the cursor to the last displayed line regardless of its physical location. In addition, the **M** command puts the cursor at the beginning of a line near the middle of the displayed lines.

The use of these commands is illustrated in Figure 30.3, which shows the **H** and **L** command effects. Both of these commands take numeric arguments that specify offsets from the window boundaries. For example, **5H** places the cursor on the fifth line and **5L** places it on the fifth line from the bottom of the window or last displayed text line.

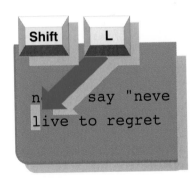

*Figure 30.3 The upper-left corner of the editing window is called the home position. Use the **H** command to move the cursor directly home (this is called "homing the cursor"). Similarly, use the **L** command to jump to the lower-left corner of the editing window.*

Requests that are out of range are handled gracefully by **vi**, which satisfies as much of the request as possible. Unreasonable requests, such as using a numeric argument with **M** are simply ignored.

WHAT YOU NEED TO KNOW

The commands described in this lesson give you precise control over the positioning of the cursor. Each of these commands is a cursor-motion command. The commands position the cursor when used alone. They can also be combined with *actions* to produce other useful effects.

In the next lesson you will learn about a general approach to objects and actions that give you additional positioning options and introduce you to basic **vi** editing features. Try to understand these topics before starting Lesson 31:

☑ Arrow keys or the **h, j, k,** and **l** keys move the cursor horizontally by characters and vertically by lines.

☑ Use the **w, W, b,** and **B** commands to move the cursor to the beginning of the next or previous word. Use **e** and **E** to move to the next end-of-word location.

☑ The commands **H, M,** and **L** move the cursor quickly to editing window positions.

☑ Most **vi** commands allow a preceding number to multiply their effects.

Lesson 31

Objects and Actions

Your knowledge of the visual editor is about to take a quantum leap. When you edit, you can think of your file as containing several different types of objects (things, such as characters, words, lines and so on). As you edit, you perform operations (*actions*) on *objects*. For example, you might transpose two characters or you might delete a word. If you understand the concept and application of objects and actions, you can easily perform many of the tasks the editor can handle. This lesson introduces you to a few more of the words that compose the language of the visual editor and then teaches you to how to speak the language fluently. Topics covered in this lesson include

- The text and window objects known by the editor
- The actions you can perform on those objects
- Applying the action-object model for visual editing

OBJECTS

In Lesson 30 you met a few of the motion commands that **vi** knows about: positioning by characters, words, lines, and windows. Table 31.1 lists the basic cursor-motion commands that you use to specify editing objects. The motion command positions the cursor. The characters, words, and other items delimited by the current cursor location and the new location comprise the editing objects that you can use in editing commands.

Motion Command	Description
^ (caret)	First displayed (nonblank) position in the current line
0 (zero)	First position in the current line even if the character there is not visible (space/tab)
*n*G	A positive nonzero number (default = $) with the goto command
$	The end of the current line (very last position even if blank)
n| (bar/pipe)	An occupied column in the current line (with no *n* means column 0)

Table 31.1 This summary of cursor-motion commands shows you the many ways that the visual editor lets you specify cursor locations. The text between the current cursor location and the new one is, effectively, an editing object. (continued on next page)

Motion Command	Description
'x (single quote)	Beginning of the line (first nonblank) at a mark ('x) or previous current line ('')
`x (back quote)	Cursor location in the line at a mark (`x) or previous current line (``)
%	The balancing parenthesis, brace, or bracket for the one currently at the cursor
) and (	The beginning of the sentence in the forward (right/down) and reverse directions
} and {	The beginning of the paragraph in the forward and reverse directions
]] and [[	The beginning of the section in the forward and reverse directions
H, M, and L	The home (upper-left), approximate middle, and lower-left corners of the editing window
b and B	Next beginning of word backward (left/up) from the current cursor location
e and E	Next end of word forward (left/up) from the current cursor location
w and W	Next beginning of word forward (left/up) from the current cursor location
fc and Fc	Find a character looking right (f) and left (F) in the current line
tc and Tc	Move to a character looking right (t) and left (T) in the current line
/str and ?str	Search for a string looking forward (/) and backward (?) in the editing buffer
h, j, k, and l	Cursor movements by characters and lines (includes various synonyms such as Space, Return, +, –, arrow keys, and so on)

Table 31.1 This summary of cursor-motion commands shows you the many ways that the visual editor lets you specify cursor locations. The text between the current cursor location and the new one is, effectively, an editing object. (continued from previous page)

Each of the cursor-motion commands listed in the table affects the cursor position if an object of the specified type is accessible. For example, 37G moves the cursor to the beginning of line 37 if there are at least that many lines in the editing buffer.

Figure 31.1 shows an example of positioning the cursor by finding a character. The **f** cursor-motion command takes an argument that is the character to find—the letter s in the following example—looking to the right of the cursor location in the current line only. The **F** version looks left to the beginning of the line for a character—e in the example. You can repeat a find in the same direction you started by using the ; (semicolon) command. To look in the opposite direction, use the , (comma).

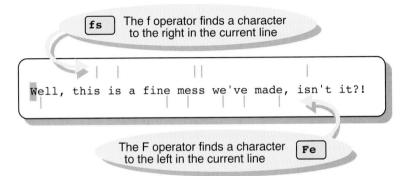

Figure 31.1 *The find operators, f (forward) and F (backward) attempt to find a specified character in the current line. After a matching character is found, you can repeat the search in the same direction by using the ; operator or reverse direction with the , operator.*

Other motion commands behavior similarly. The) command looks right to the next beginning-of-sentence location. Envisioning the command as the surface of an eyeball looking to the right may help you to remember this. The]] command uses a doubled character to remind you that this command moves by sections of a document file, often all the way to the end.

ACTIONS

The action words of the visual editor are called *operators*. Table 31.2 lists the operators, which are used to delete, change, copy, shift, and filter text. The operators do nothing by themselves. You combine them with editor objects to affect the contents of the editing buffer.

Operator	Description of Action
d	Delete
c	Change
y	Yank a copy
> and <	Shift right and left
!	Filter through an external command

Table 31.2 *The operators are combined with objects (specified by cursor-motion commands) to form visual-mode commands. The commands affect all text that is traversed from the current cursor location to the new location. A doubling of the operator, for example cc, causes the action to affect whole lines. Commands can take optional multipliers to magnify their effects*

If you double the operator name (for example, **dd**, **cc**, and **yy**) the resulting command means operate on whole lines. Therefore, the command **3dd** means delete three lines. Similarly, **>>** means shift the line containing the cursor one shift width to the right, providing a convenient way to indent lines. Of course a multiplier can magnify the effect: **5>>** shifts five lines to the right by one shift width.

USING ACTIONS AND OBJECTS TO EDIT TEXT

You have seen that cursor-motion commands by themselves move the cursor to a location in the editing buffer. A side effect of the cursor motion is that the movement from the current cursor location to the new one identifies a text object. And you just saw how simple combinations of operators and objects make editing commands—those that affect the contents of the editing buffer.

GENERAL FORM OF VISUAL-MODE COMMANDS

As you will see in the next two lessons, some *named buffers* and *numbered buffers* are at your disposal. These go at the front of the basic command to identify temporary storage locations, leading to this general visual-mode command form:

   [*buffer*][*operator*][*number*]*object*

The interpretation of the *number* part varies. A few cursor-motion commands (z, G, |) treat a number as a line or column number. The scroll commands use a number as a scroll amount in lines, and nearly all others use a number as a multiplier.

SOME SAMPLE COMMANDS

Here is a sampling of editing commands that demonstrate some of the basic combinations of operators and objects. Use commands like those shown in Table 31.3 and variations on the themes to modify text.

Command	Editing operation performed
dw	Delete a word.
d4w	Delete four words (can also be written **4dw**).
cw*new*Esc	Change a word to *new*.
3cc*new*Esc	Change three lines to *new*.
y$	Yank a copy of the end of the current line
5dd	Delete five lines (current and four more)

Table 31.3 This sampling of visual-mode commands shows some of the many ways you can combine actions and objects to edit text. (continued on next page)

Command	Editing operation performed
dG	Delete from the cursor to the end of the buffer
cfx*new*Esc	Change text from the cursor to the first x found looking to the right with *new*.
d/*keep*	Delete all text from the cursor up to but not including the *keep* text.
R*new*Esc	Replace (overtype) existing text with *new*.

Table 31.3 This sampling of visual-mode commands shows some of the many ways you can combine actions and objects to edit text. (continued from previous page)

REPEATING A BUFFER-MODIFYING COMMAND

Use . to repeat the most recent command that modified the contents of the editing buffer. For example, you delete a word with **dw** and repeat the command by pressing . one or more times.

If you perform a succession of command repeats with . , only the last one can be reversed with **u** (undo). If all of the deletions occur on the same line and you have not moved off the line, you can use **U** (restore line) to reverse the changes. However, it is usually safer and faster to count the words to be deleted and issue a command of the form **d***n***w** (or *n***dw**) because the effect of the command can be reversed in its entirety without regard to how many lines are affected.

REPEATING SEARCH COMMANDS

Figure 31.2 shows the effect of repeated text searches. Use the last-line command /*text* to initiate the search. If a match is found, you can repeat the search in the same direction by typing **n** to continue in the same direction or **N** to reverse the search direction.

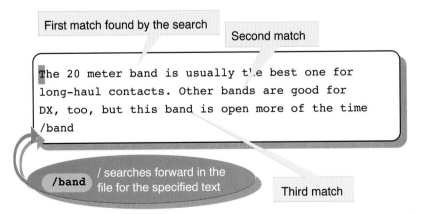

*Figure 31.2 Use the / to search forward for a string (? searches backward). If a match is found, the cursor stops on its first character. Repeat a search with **n** (same direction) or **N** (reverse direction).*

You can fabricate an interactive search-and-replace-command by using a text search and then a change-text command to start. Then repeat the **n** command to find the next match and conditionally execute a . command to do the replacement. This approach lets you decide which matching text to replace and which to keep.

WHAT YOU NEED TO KNOW

The visual editor was designed to manipulate text in a very general way. The ability to apply an action to virtually any text objects lets you tailor your editing actions to the problem at hand. The next lesson exposes you to the cut-and-paste capabilities of the editor within a file and between files. Check your mastery of these topics before picking up the electronic scissors and tape:

☑ The objects (text and window locations) known by the editor specify cursor motions. Used by themselves, they reposition the cursor.

☑ Editor actions are specified by operators. You can perform various actions on each of the editor objects. The generalized form of a visual-mode command is [*buffer*][*operator*][*number*]*object*.

☑ If you learn how to apply the action-object paradigm, you will greatly enhance your visual editing technique and speed.

Lesson 32

Cutting and Pasting

This lesson teaches you how to perform a variety of cut-and-paste operations that let you move or copy text within a file and between files. The **ex/vi** editor manages numerous buffers and temporary files in the course of an editing session. The topics covered in this lesson include the following:

- Understanding current and alternate files
- Using named buffers
- Copying and moving text between files

EDITING BUFFERS

The **vi** editor displays only one file at a time, but it can keep track of two editing buffers (temporary files) and a raft of associated named and numbered buffers. The editing buffer that you see while editing is called the *current file*. Any actions you perform are done on the current file. Behind the scenes is a second editing buffer called the *alternate file*. It is dormant until you switch buffers, bringing the alternate file to the foreground and sending the current file to the background. This process changes the identifications of the two files.

While operating in visual command mode and editing **file1** you can start editing another file, **file2**, by issuing the command **:e file2↵**. If you have made changes to **file1** that have not been saved, use the write command to save changes before switching files. The editor warns you about unsaved changes, but it lets you force a switch without saving, if that's what you want to do, with the exclamation point (**:w!** *filename↵*). Use **:e!** to reedit the current file.

Switching between files is easily achieved using commands you have already used. The only additional detail you need to know is that the name of the alternate file is symbolized by **#**. You can use this shorthand name in commands issued on the **ex** command line. Switch back and forth between the two files by using the command **:e #↵**. The command tells the **vi** editor to swap the files.

NAMED BUFFERS

A set of *named buffers*, **a–z**, provide storage locations for uses such as moving and copying text. You access the named buffers by using a " followed by the letter name. Thus, **"x** refers to the named buffer **x** for both write (save) and read (retrieve) operations.

When you save text to a named buffer, you overwrite any previous contents of the buffer. To append to a named buffer, use the uppercase version of the buffer name (**A–Z**). Use this method to accumulate chunks of text to be inserted as a block somewhere in the current file or the alternate file.

COPYING TEXT BETWEEN FILES

Let's put this knowledge of files and buffers to work. Use a named buffer, **a**, to copy text from **file1** (initially the current file) to **file2** (the alternate file). The process of copying text from one file to another involves several steps. First you position the cursor to the line that begins the block (or string) to be copied. Then you copy the text to the buffer. Figure 32.1 shows these two steps.

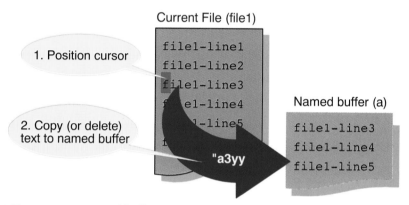

Figure 32.1 *You can use a named buffer to capture text to be copied between files. First position the cursor to the start of the block, then yank lines to the named buffer.*

For demonstration purposes, the text in the files is self-identifying, each line indicating its initial file and line number. Use any form of cursor positioning that makes sense in your circumstances. The example shows three lines being copied, but you can copy any number of lines and even line fragments. Use commands such as **"xyw** (copy one word into buffer **x**), **"yy$** (copy to the end of the line into buffer **y**), and so on.

Figure 32.2 shows the effects of editing a second file. When the second file is brought to the foreground (made current), the first file is pushed into the background (made alternate). When the second file is current, you position the cursor to the insertion point.

To get the text from the named buffer into the file involves the put command. Whole lines go after the current line (**p**) or before the current line (**P**). Similar rules apply to putting line fragments (**p** puts right, **P** puts left). Figure 32.3 shows the effect of putting the lines after the insertion point. The cursor can be anywhere in the current for whole-line insertions, but must be on the exact character location for fragment insertions.

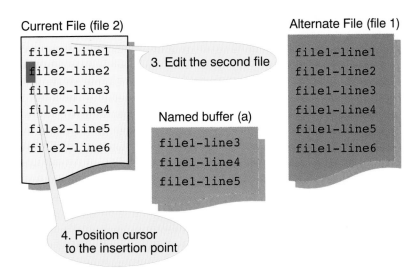

Figure 32.2 The third step in copying text between files is swapping the files by using the :e # command. The current file becomes the alternate and vice versa. Then you position the cursor to the insertion point of the new current file.

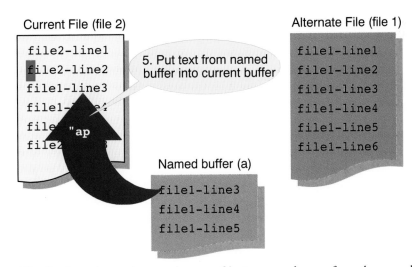

*Figure 32.3 The final step in copying text between files is to put the text from the named buffer into the current file. Use **p** to put new lines below and **P** to put them above the current line.*

Note: The contents of named buffers and the editing buffers are lost when you exit the editor.

Moving Text Between Files

Moving text between files is identical to copying, except that you delete lines from the source file instead of taking a copy. Because of this action, you should save the source file before switching to the destination file.

What You Need to Know

This lesson introduces you the cut-and-paste facilities and methods supported by the **ex/vi** editor. The next lesson uses similar editor features to help you with recovery operations. Check your knowledge of these topics before moving on:

- ☑ The editor keeps a current file, which is the editing buffer for the active file.

- ☑ An alternate file is also maintained when more than one file has been loaded. The alternate file is dormant until made current.

- ☑ You can copy text between files (and within files) by using named buffers.

- ☑ Moving text between files is the same as moving except the moved text is deleted from the source file.

Lesson 33

Recovering from Errors

Errors happen. Sooner or later, you'll get bitten by a system or software error, a power loss, or some other problem. This lesson gives you some error-recovery tools that can save you a lot of grief. The following topics are covered:

- Correct errors during input

- Recover previously deleted text from buffers

- Recover files saved from previously-interrupted sessions

CORRECTING INPUT ERRORS

The **vi** editor provides means of correcting errors as they occur if you discover them before leaving the current line. Figure 33.1 shows how the insert-mode error-correction keys work.

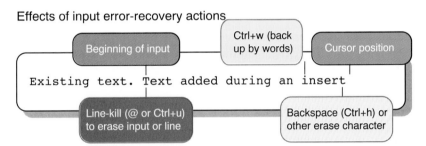

Figure 33.1 Use the erase, line-kill, and CTRL-W *keys to correct errors in the current input line without leaving input mode. No error recovery command can go back past the end of the current input or the current line.*

To erase the previous character or series of characters, use the BACKSPACE key or the CTRL-H equivalent or the character you have elected to use for erase. You can back up only to the beginning of the current input or the beginning of the current line, whichever comes first.

You can also erase the most recently typed word by using CTRL-W. Used more than once, the command erases additional words back toward the beginning of the current line or input. To erase back to the beginning of the current input or line in one shot, use the line-kill character (usually @ or CTRL-U).

RESTORING PREVIOUS TEXT DELETIONS

The editor manages a set of numbered buffers (1 through 9) that receive copies of deleted lines (fragments of text less than a line in length are not saved after the initial delete to an unnamed buffer). You can use the numbered buffers to recover text that was removed by the last nine commands that deleted blocks of lines. As you delete more text, the earlier deletions are pushed to higher numbered buffers and are eventually lost forever. When you quit **vi**, all deleted text in these buffers is lost, but they are carried between editing buffers just like named buffers are when you switch files.

Use a command of the form "*n*p, where *n* specifies the numbered buffer that you think contains the text you want to recover. If the text is not what you wanted, use the **u** command to undo the process and try again with a different buffer. This error-recovery technique is depicted in Figure 33.2, which shows three lines of previously deleted text being put into the editing buffer from recovery buffer number 2.

If you don't know which buffer contains the text you need to recover (the usual situation), start with buffer 1 and use this special form of the recovery command to work your way through the buffers one at a time:

```
"1pu.u.u.u.u.u.
```

The command initially recovers text from buffer 1. If that's not what you want, the **u** command undoes the recovery. The **.** , as you have learned, repeats the previous command. But in this one situation it automatically increments the buffer number before putting text again. Use the **.** and **u** commands alternately until you either find the text you want or run out of buffers to examine.

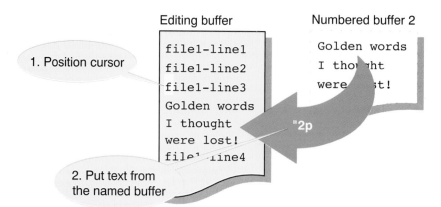

Figure 33.2 Use the numbered buffers to recover lines of text from previous deletions in the current editing session. This figure shows three lines from buffer 2 being inserted (put) after the current line.

RECOVERING FILES

If your editing session is terminated by a hang-up on the phone line, a system "crash" (an unexpected and unwanted hardware failure or power loss), or an editor crash, the work file associated with your session remains on disk and can be used for recovery at a later time. (You can simulate an editor crash by using the **:preserve** command.)

The next time you log in, or finish a command in the current session if the system is still running, you receive mail informing you of the saved file's existence. The following message (edited to fit the page format of this book) was received after I simulated a crash:

```
A copy of an editor buffer of yours was saved when the editor was
killed. No name was associated with this buffer so it has been
named "LOST". This buffer can be retrieved using the "recover"
command of the editor. An easy way to do this is to give the
command "vi -r ". This works for "edit" and "ex" also.
```

This message is from the SCO Open Desktop system. Your UNIX system might use different wording and might specify the recovery procedure differently.

Current versions of **vi** use a command option of -L to get a list of saved files. You start the recovery procedure by using this command:

```
vi -L
```

This version conforms to modern standards for commands options and command line construction. Older **vi** versions use the -r option without a filename argument to get the list of saved files.

For new and old versions alike, to recover a particular file identified in the list, use the **-r** option with a filename argument. To recover the LOST file identified above, for example, use this command:

```
vi -r LOST ↵
```

This starts an editor session. You can then decide whether to save the contents of the file under this or some other name, or simply abandon it (**:q!↵**).

REDRAWING THE SCREEN

If you find that line noise or messages from **write** trash your editing window, don't worry. The contents of the editing buffer are not affected unless you are in input mode and line noise generates "monkey type" for you.

To recover the appearance of your editing window, press Escape to be sure you're not entering text, and press CTRL-L (lowercase or uppercase L). This command redraws the entire screen, restoring the displayed text from the contents of the editing buffer.

WHAT YOU NEED TO KNOW

The techniques described in this lesson help you to recover from errors. This concludes the formal coverage of the **vi** editor, but other editing techniques are described and demonstrated throughout the rest of the book.

The next section extends your knowledge of command pipelines, filters, and shell command files. The visual editor will be your constant ally in this work, so be sure you understand these topics before proceeding:

☑ Use erase, line-kill, CTRL-W commands to correct errors during text input sessions.

☑ You can recover previously deleted text from a set of numbered buffers. The last nine deletions of blocks of lines are recoverable.

☑ You can recover files that were saved from previously-interrupted editing sessions. You can simulate an editor crash by using the **:preserve** command.

☑ If your editing window is trashed by messages, use CTRL-L to redraw the screen.

Section Seven

USING THE UNIX SHELL AND UTILITIES

By now you should have a fairly good handle on how to use the major user-level UNIX facilities. These aspects of the UNIX system were designed to give users the ability to create and manage files, print documents, and interact with other users and systems without having to deal with too many options and special cases.

Inevitably you reach a point where you are not completely satisfied with someone else's canned solutions, or your tasks become involved enough or nonstandard enough to warrant custom solutions. If this description fits you, you've run smack into the "p word"—programming.

The material presented in this section fills in some of the details glossed over or only alluded to in earlier lessons and introduces you to a whole new level of interaction with the UNIX system. The coverage of the programming features of the UNIX shell and its major utility programs includes the following topics:

Lesson 34

Filters and Command Pipelines

The design of the UNIX system adheres to several principles, one of which is that each program should do one clearly defined task as well as possible. The details of how the program does its job are hidden, but the program's inputs and outputs are well defined. Also, UNIX programs are usually terse, favoring no output at all over a silly message that says essentially "I have no output." This design permits UNIX programs to be pasted together into *command pipelines* that provide ad-hoc solutions to a wide range of processing problems.

You have seen various examples of simple command pipelines in earlier lessons. The examples showed output from commands being piped to **more** or **pg** for screen viewing or to **tail** to see the last few lines of a file. This lesson builds on that experience by introducing the general topic of *filter* programs and shows you how to use them at the UNIX system command level. Topics covered in this lesson include the following:

- Using programs that filter data streams

- Understanding and applying standard UNIX filter programs

- Splitting data streams with the **tee** program

FILTER PROGRAMS

A *filter* is a program that reads standard input, performs some data manipulation on the data, and writes standard output. As is true for most UNIX programs, input and output can be redirected. (Review Lesson 17 if necessary to be sure you understand the purpose and application of standard input, standard output, and standard error, and redirection.)

It is convenient to think of standard input, standard output, and standard error as *streams*. Picture yourself standing beside a stream of water with a net in your hand. As the stream flows by, you use the net to remove chunks of debris found in the stream. You are, in effect, the filter with the output stream being cleaned to some extent by the actions you perform on the input stream.

Using the stream analogy, data flowing into the standard input of a filter program can be modified in some way to produce an output stream that differs in some way from the input stream. Figure 34.1 playfully shows how we might brighten the world a bit by filtering out all the grumps. The filtering agent is called **happy**, which takes a stream of faces, mixed in appearance (nobody is neutral in this example), and provides a stream composed solely of smiley faces.

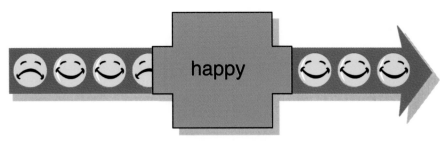

*Figure 34.1 The filter **happy** produces a stream of smiley faces from a mixed input stream. How it works is one of the great mysteries of the universe.*

The details of how the filter works are unknown, but several possibilities spring to mind. The filter might simply turn back any frowning faces, in which case there will be fewer faces in the output than in the input. Where the frowns go is not stated. Maybe the filter tells the incoming frown faces a great joke, in which case the number of faces in the output is the same as in the input. I prefer this solution because we don't have to deal with the potentially thorny issue of frown-face disposal.

UNIX FILTERS AND COMMAND PIPELINES

The UNIX filter **grep**, first used in this book in Lesson 18 to identify a terminal type, is a filter of the kind that reduces the output by passing only lines that either match or don't match a pattern. The **sort** filter, on the other hand, is of the second type. It produces as much output as there is input, but performs a translation on the input to put it into some specified sequence.

Let's experiment with a few of the standard UNIX filter programs to see what they can do and how we can combine them to process data in various ways. A data file called **phone.lst** used in the next example contains a list of names and telephone numbers. Using **cat** to examine the file's contents, you can see that the names are not in any particular order:

```
$ cat phone.lst ↵
wanda    306
betty    511
john     459
bill     111
jane     466
doris    307
will     399
kent     555
bob      333
linda    388
gus      473
$ ❑
```

THE sort PROGRAM

Let's use **sort** to order the file by name. If you provide a filename on the command line, **sort** reads from the named file. However, **sort** is most often used as a filter in the interior of a command pipeline. In the following example, we use the output of the **cat** command as a source of data for a command pipeline. The output of **sort** is redirected to a file, which you then display by using **cat** again:

```
$ cat phone.lst | sort > sorted.lst ↵
$ cat sorted.lst ↵
betty    511
bill     111
bob      333
doris    307
gus      473
jane     466
john     459
kent     555
linda    388
wanda    306
will     399$
$ ▢
```

This example sorts by using each line in its entirety as a sort key. You can provide options to the **sort** program that cause it to use a different field as a key (*+pos*, *-pos*), to sort in reverse order (**-r**), to sort numerically rather than by string comparison (**-n**), and many other variations. The following modification of the previous command line sorts the list by phone number in reverse order:

```
$ cat phone.lst | sort -rn +1 ↵
kent     555                      ———— Sort second column
betty    511
gus      473                      ———— Use reverse order, sorting numerically
jane     466
john     459
will     399
linda    388
bob      333
doris    307
wanda    306
bill     111
$ ▢
```

Without the -n option, **sort** would order the list of numbers 1, 2, 12 as 1, 12, 2 because of the way character strings are treated. The +1 option specifies one field after the initial (leftmost) field up to the end of the line. In our example list, that's the second field by itself. The default field separator is a blank (space or tab). You can change the separator to any other character if the data file uses a different character (a colon is commonly used in UNIX system data files).

The *tr* Program

The filter program **tr** translates characters in the data stream according to your specification. The program doesn't accept filename arguments; just two strings and a few options: **tr** [-**cds**] [*string1* [*string2*]] Any characters found in *string1* are translated into the corresponding characters in *string2*. Characters not found in *string1* pass to the output without change. The -**c** option complements the set of characters represented by *string1* and -**d** deletes all input characters specified by *string1*. The -**s** option causes each string of repeated characters in the output to be squeezed into one character (aaaa -> a).

Create a file **wisdom.txt** using your favorite method. I use **ed** for this demonstration. This file is used in several examples that follow.

```
$ ed wisdom.txt ↵
?wisdom.txt
a↵
Fear is the main source of superstition,↵
and one of the main sources of cruelty.↵
To conquer fear is the beginning of wisdom.↵
↵
                    Bertrand Russell↵
w↵
146
q↵
$ ▢
```

This file contains words with mixed letter case. To turn Bertrand Russell into an e e cummings, pass the file through the **tr** command:

```
$ cat wisdom.txt | tr [A-Z] [a-z] ↵
fear is the main source of superstition,
and one of the main sources of cruelty.
to conquer fear is the beginning of wisdom.

                    bertrand russell
$ ▢
```

Lord Russell's prose still makes a lot of sense, even when diminished this way. The translation is straightforward. Any character in the set of uppercase letters is converted to its lowercase equivalent. The notation [*min-max*] is the **tr** way to express a range of contiguous characters. The brackets [and] are required characters. In the example, A is mapped to a , B to b, and so on by the natural one-to-one correspondence set up by the two string ranges specified in the command.

The *uniq* Program

The sorting process may bring identical lines to adjacent positions in the output. Use the **uniq** program to filter the data stream to eliminate duplicate entries. All but one of any group of identical lines is removed by this program.

*Note: Running **uniq** on an unsorted list is likely to be of no use because identical lines must be adjacent to each other to be seen as duplicates.*

Let's take the previous example one step further by generating a word list for **wisdom.txt**. Send the file through the following pipeline to generate a list of unique words found in the file. This example illustrates an interesting point. The pipe symbol works as a line-continuation character because the shell sees an incomplete command and uses the secondary prompt (>) to let you know that more input is needed to complete it. You can carry this to as many lines as you need to write your command.

```
$ cat wisdom.txt | tr [A-Z] [a-z] | ↵
> tr -cs "[A-Z][a-z]" "[\012*]" | sort | uniq ↵
and
beginning
bertrand
conquer
cruelty
fear
is
main
of
one
russell
source
sources
superstition
the
to
wisdom
$
```

The first **tr** filter in the pipeline does the case conversions shown in the previous run, and the second substitutes a newline (shown as the octal code \012) for any nonalphabetic character. The -c option on **tr** causes the set of characters in the first string to be complemented, inverting the sense of the test. The strings are quoted to protect any special characters from processing by the shell. The notation [\012*] means "repeat the newline as many times as necessary to provide a corresponding one for every character in the first string."

Use the -c option with the **uniq** program to get a frequency of occurrence for each word. The command is the same as the one you just issued, plus the added option. It produces the following:

```
1 and
1 beginning
1 bertrand
1 conquer
1 cruelty
2 fear
2 is
2 main
4 of
1 one
1 russell
1 source
1 sources
1 superstition
3 the
1 to
1 wisdom
```

PIPEFITTING WITH THE *tee* PROGRAM

In the examples presented to this point, we have either viewed the output of a program on screen or sent it packing to a file by redirection. In a few cases, we have sent output to a printer. But what do you do if you want to see it *and* save it? Become a plumber.

The **tee** program duplicates a stream, creating two or more identical streams. The standard output can still be presented as input to other filters in a command pipeline, such as a pager program. The named file or files receive exactly the same data. The program effectively clones the data stream. You can use this to advantage to capture program output to create a permanent record of a session.

Figure 34.2 shows the effect of the following command, which captures the output of an **ls** command in a file called **ls.out** while displaying it on the screen:

```
$ ls | tee ls.out ↵
noble.txt
od.out
quote.txt
refer.txt
wisdom.txt
$ ▯
```

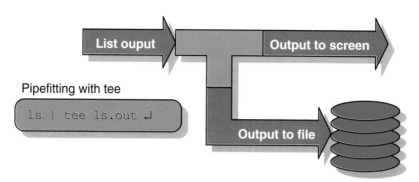

Figure 34.2 *The **tee** program is a cloning filter. It duplicates a stream, which lets you send the same output to your screen and to one or more files simultaneously.*

Let's be sure it worked:

```
$ cat ls.out ↵
noble.txt
od.out
quote.txt
refer.txt
wisdom.txt
$ ▯
```

Looks good. Don't get carried away with this program. Trying to capture an interactive editing session (**ed file | tee ed.out**, for example) will capture output messages issued by the editor, but not your keystrokes. Save it for use with data streams generated by non-interactive programs. Also, if you need to add to the contents of a capture file, use the **-a** option of **tee** to force output to be appended to the file.

WHAT YOU NEED TO KNOW

The UNIX pipe feature leads to some interesting data processing possibilities. This lesson shows you how filters work and how to apply the standard UNIX filters in command pipelines. The next lesson focuses on the **sed** program, which is used as a filter for editing text streams. Before discovering the joys of stream editing, review the following topics:

- ☑ A filter program reads from standard input and writes to standard output. Most filter programs apply a transformation of some kind to the data stream.

- ☑ Numerous standard UNIX filter programs give you a capable toolkit of canned solutions that can be easily combined to produce custom solutions.

- ☑ The **tee** program lets you duplicate a data stream, letting you view and capture the data at the same time.

Lesson 35

Finding Text and Files

"Where did I leave my keys? They'll probably be in the last place I look!" Sometimes it's like that with files, too. This lesson gives you the lowdown on two important sleuthing tools that help you quickly locate text and files. The topics covered are the following:

- The **grep** program for finding text in a file or a set of files
- The **find** program for locating files and directories in the directory hierarchy

THE grep UTILITY PROGRAM

In Lesson 18 we used **grep** to help identify a terminal type to use in setting the TERM variable. As you know, the program does a global search for a pattern specified by a regular expression and prints any lines that match the pattern. The program name is derived from the syntax of the **ed** editor's global search feature, which expresses a search as **g/**re**/p**.

The syntax of a **grep** command is **grep** [*options*] *re* [*file...*] where *re* is a limited regular expression. If the regular expression contains any special characters (the metacharacters $, *, [, ^, |, (,), or \), enclose the entire expression in single quotes to protect them from processing by the shell.

If you don't name any files, **grep** reads its input from standard input. The program is often used in command pipelines to filter data streams. This lesson shows examples of **grep** taking input from files and from pipelines.

PATTERN MATCHING

Figure 35.1 illustrates the search process at various stages. The process of pattern matching starts at the beginning of each line and stops at the terminating newline. Searches do not match text that spans line boundaries.

In the figure, **grep** attempts to find text that matches the pattern **ball**. The first attempt at a match fails immediately because the **b** in the pattern (shown in the yellow stripe) doesn't match the first character (**P**) of the line (shown in the green stripe). The second try starts at the next position in the line (on the **u** in this example). That fails too.

The ninth try looks promising, but it also fails. There is a match on the letter **b** in the line and the pattern, but the next letter in the pattern fails to match the corresponding character in the line. The fourteenth try is the charm. All four characters in the pattern match corresponding characters in the line. At this point, **grep** prints the "matched" line and moves to the next line in the file or data stream to continue the search.

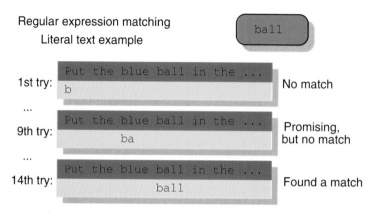

Figure 35.1 *A search for a string of literal characters (each stands for itself) begins at the left end of the line. If no match is found, the starting point is advanced one character position. This search yields a match on try 14.*

You can instruct **grep** to invert the sense of its basic operation by using the **-v** option. This option tells **grep** to print only lines that are *not* matched by the pattern. You typically use the inverted sense option when it's easier to write a pattern to match lines you don't want in the output.

For example, you want to create a list of job candidates who are certified in any one of several specialties. The applicant data file—let's call it **candidate.dat**— contains records having several data fields. One field identifies a "primary certification" and uses the default value of **none**. The easiest way to list certified candidates is to invert the print condition:

```
$ grep -v none candidate.dat > certified.dat ↵
$ □
```

This simple-minded approach works only if there is no other field that can have a value of **none**.

If **grep** is getting its input from a pipeline or a single file, it prints only the text of each matching line. In the following example, the **cat** program generates a stream of text that is filtered by **grep**. The **grep** program finds and prints a matching line without any indication of what file the line came from (**grep** doesn't have any way to know):

```
$ cat *.txt | grep penniless ↵
I'd rather be a penniless writer than a wealthy politician.
$ □
```

If the source of data is a set of named files, each matched line is printed with the name of the file as a prefix. You can suppress this behavior by using the -h option. If a named file cannot be found or is not readable, **grep** normally prints an error message. You can suppress error messages about missing or unreadable files by using the -s option.

*Note: A second version of the **grep** program called **fgrep** does a fixed-string search and can search for multiple strings in parallel (use the -f option with a file that contains search patterns, one per line). It can run faster than **grep** in most cases because it doesn't have to interpret metacharacters and uses a more efficient search technique than **grep**.*

ESSENTIAL GREP FEATURES AND SYNTAX

The **grep** program is a specialized tool that searches globally (**g**) in a file or data stream for lines that are matched by a pattern (regular expression, or **re**). Each matched line is printed (**p**), or displayed if you prefer. The program is based on the **ed** editor's search feature and its name reflects that fact. The program can read input from a named file or obtain it from redirection or a command pipeline.

The only required argument in a **grep** command is the regular expression that specifies the pattern. Matched lines are passed in their entirety to standard output unless the command line contains the -v option, which inverts the sense of the command (print lines *not* matched by the pattern). Other options control the printing of error messages (-s) and file prefixes during multifile processing (-h).

USING METACHARACTERS IN PATTERNS

If the pattern you specify for a search contains metacharacters, **grep** modifies its matching process a bit. For example, the ^ metacharacter matches the initial (leftmost) line segment and $ matches the ending line segment. The search pattern **^printer** matches the word "printer" only if it occurs at the beginning of a line, and **printer$** matches it only at the end of a line. The expression . matches any single character.

The character class, [*str*], matches any one of the characters in *str*. The pattern [**bhs**]**it**, for example, matches **bit**, **hit**, and **sit**, but not **fit** or **wit**. (To match all of those and any other three-character strings that end in **it**, use .**it** as a pattern.)

You can match a character from a range by specifying the end points separated by a dash ([**a-z**] to match a lowercase letter, for example). [**0-9**] matches any digit. To match any nondigit character, use the character class [**^0-9**]. The ^ at the beginning negates the class. To match the ^ itself, place it anywhere after the first position in the class ([**abc^**]).

Review the material on regular expressions in Lesson 22 if you are uncertain about how regular expressions work and how to apply them.

CLOSURES

The * metacharacter is called a *closure operator*. It repeats to the greatest extent possible the effect of the preceding character or metacharacter, including the character class. The character **t**, for example, matches itself as you would expect. The expression **t*** matches the longest possible sequence of **t**s. Therefore, the expression **.*** matches any sequence of characters, including none, up to the next new-line character. To find at least one, double the character. For example, **aa*** matches at least one **a** and any longer sequence of **a**s up to the end of the line.

Two other closure operators can be used with the program **egrep** (expression **grep**), which is a third version of **grep** that handles essentially full regular expression syntax and allows you to specify combinations of patterns. Table 35.1 summarizes the closure operators.

Operator	Closure Description
*	Match zero or more occurrences of the preceding character or metacharacter
+	Match one or more occurrences of the preceding character or metacharacter (**egrep**)
?	Match zero or one occurrences of the preceding character or metacharacter (**egrep**)

Table 35.1 The closure operators give you the tools need to write regular expressions that match repeated sequences of characters and strings.

Learn to apply the closure operators to enhance your string-matching prowess. The example in Figure 35.2 shows how a closure can match a sequence of characters between specified end points. The first pattern expands to match the longest possible sequence of single characters between the **c** and the **er**. The search finds a **c** eventually, sees a series of matches to the **.*** closure (any repetition of single characters), and stops when the **er** pattern is matched.

Regular expression matching
Metacharacter example

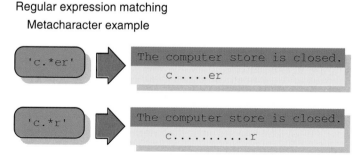

```
'c.*er'  ⇨  The computer store is closed.
                     c.....er
```

```
'c.*r'  ⇨  The computer store is closed.
                   c..........r
```

Figure 35.2 A pattern that contains a closure attempt to match the longest sequence of characters possible (but not past a new-line character).

If you specify the pattern less precisely, look what happens. The second pattern, **c.*r**, matches not only the word **computer**, but also the rest of the line up to the next **r** found in the word **store**. To paraphrase the Rolling Stones, "You can't always get what you want, but if you try sometime, you just might find that you get what you ask for." Write your search patterns with care.

The search pattern **^$** matches empty lines—those having a beginning and an end, but no middle (nothing between the previous new-line character and the one that ends the line being searched). To locate lines that appear to be empty, but really are not (they contain some combination of spaces and tabs), use the search pattern **^[→][→]*$**. The → symbol represents the Tab character. If your terminal doesn't have one, use CTRL-I (or buy a terminal that wasn't manufactured before the last ice age).

USING METACHARACTERS IN REGULAR EXPRESSIONS

Use metacharacters in patterns to match sets of strings. These special characters give you various ways to select lines for printing. You can anchor searches at the beginning (**^**) and end (**$**) of a line. Match text strings that meet certain criteria by using various individual metacharacters and combinations of them. Use **.** to match any single character, and the closure **.*** to match the longest possible sequence of single characters (***** means zero or more occurrences of).

The character class construct, [*str*], lets you match one of a set of characters specified as either collections of individual characters or as ranges. The special character **^** used to invert the class loses its special meaning when not in the first position. Similarly, the range character **-** is not special at the beginning or end of a character class.

Additional closure characters **+** and **?** work only with the **egrep** (expression **grep**) program. The **+** closure character means one or more occurrences of the preceding expression and **?** means zero or one occurrences.

FILTERING DATA

While it is no replacement for a full-featured database management system, UNIX tools such as a text editor (choose among several), **grep**, and other utility programs give you what you need to handle simple data-management tasks. We'll use **grep** and a file containing sample data from a computer software company to illustrate how you can find information you need quickly.

The file **sales.dat** contains sales data for a mythical software company:

```
$ cat sales.dat ↵
wp:east:1q93:300:37500
wp:west:1q93:520:65000
```

```
wp:east:2q93:421:52625
wp:west:2q93:604:75500
wp:east:3q93:357:44625
wp:west:3q93:511:63875
wp:east:4q93:421:52625
wp:west:4q93:604:75500
ss:east:1q93:185:37000
ss:west:1q93:266:53200
ss:east:2q93:200:40000
ss:west:2q93:350:70000
ss:east:3q93:432:86400
ss:west:3q93:333:66600
ss:east:4q93:400:80000
ss:west:4q93:338:67600
$ ▢
```

The following command finds all records (lines) that contain the word "east" and prints them. It is not necessary to match an entire line. If any portion of a line matches the search pattern, the entire line is printed:

```
$ grep east sales.dat ↵
wp:east:1q93:300:37500
wp:east:2q93:421:52625
wp:east:3q93:357:44625
wp:east:4q93:421:52625
ss:east:1q93:185:37000
ss:east:2q93:200:40000
ss:east:3q93:432:86400
ss:east:4q93:400:80000
$ ▢
```

Another example, based on the same file finds all records in the data file that contain information about spreadsheet (ss) sales. Any line that contains the string "ss "anywhere in the line is matched and printed:

```
$ grep ss sales.dat ↵
ss:east:1q93:185:37000
ss:west:1q93:266:53200
ss:east:2q93:200:40000
ss:west:2q93:350:70000
ss:east:3q93:432:86400
ss:west:3q93:333:66600
ss:east:4q93:400:80000
ss:west:4q93:338:67600
$ ▢
```

Although this approach works with this simple data file, there is a potential problem. A matching pattern in some other field might cause irrelevant lines (records) to be matching, producing erroneous reports. Be sure to choose carefully the names you use for key field values. Better yet, use another UNIX tool, **awk**, which allows you to specify the fields and provides many convenient data-manipulation features. The **awk** program uses C-like syntax and is a full application program. It is not covered in this introductory book.

FINDING FILES

You can find files by two different means. The first identifies files that contain specified strings. The second searches the directory hierarchy to find files based on information about them.

LOCATE FILES BASED ON CONTENT

You can use **grep** with a search pattern in combination with ambiguous names to find files in a directory, based on their contents. The shell expands the filename wildcard characters (?, *, and [*str*]) to a list of names that match the specified filename pattern, and **grep** peeks inside each of the files to find lines that contain strings that match the search pattern.

The following command example, run in a directory containing a book in preparation, identifies text files that contain references to IBM:

```
$ grep IBM chap??.txt ↵
chap01.txt:IBM and compatible PCs running UNIX are more common
chap11.txt:Microsoft and IBM versions of DOS.
$ ❑
```

Searches of this type make sense for text files only. Groping through binary files with **grep** is likely to produce unseemly results and will probably put your terminal or modem into orbit.

USING *find* TO LOCATE FILES

Our focus changes now to finding files based on their names and other external attributes. A program called **find** lets you scan the directory hierarchy from a specified starting directory looking for files that meet certain criteria. Figure 35.3 shows a search for files named **outline**. The search starts in Rocky's home directory and works its way to the end of every possible branch of the hierarchy below that point. In the figure, two files that match the search pattern are found.

The **find** program is one that violates every sacred tenet of good program design. Its options are full text words, not single letters. The options can not be combined under a single option flag (-).

In addition, certain combinations of options require critical ordering of the options. However, this is an essential tool that you should learn to use.

The -**name** option takes a filename or directory name argument, which specifies the item being sought. The -**print** option causes the current pathname to be printed (relative to the starting location). In combination, the two options locate and identify files that match the pattern. You can use shell filename metacharacters in the name pattern, but you should protect them with quotes if **find** is issued from the shell command line.

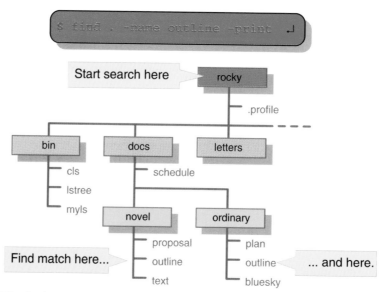

Figure 35.3 The **find** *program searches from the specified starting point to the end of every branch of the directory hierarchy below it. This example starts* **find** *running at the current directory (.) looking for files named* **outline**. *Each match prints the pathname of the found file.*

The example looks like this on screen:

```
$ find . -name outline -print ↵
./docs/novel/outline
./docs/ordinary/outline
$ ▯
```

The **find** program can also be used in conjunction with other programs to list files that haven't been accessed for a specified period of time, to automatically remove files that meet specified criteria, and to archive files for off-line storage.

Finding Files

Use **grep** to identify files in a directory, based on the contents of the files. Given a directory full of files, you can easily lose track of which files contain certain information. By using **grep** with a regular expression to specify a text search and shell wildcard characters to ambiguously name the files to examine, Ollie North could quickly have found and purged all references to Iran-Contra, for example. (But he couldn't get at the system backups!)

Use **find** to locate files anywhere in the directory hierarchy, based on external attributes of the files. The **find** program lets you search for files from a specified starting point to the extremes of every branch below it. You can list the full pathnames of all files located by **find**, execute commands on those files, and a variety of other actions. It is frequently used to purge old files from a system by removing them or archiving them, and for preparing collections of files to be copied to users on the same UNIX system or remote systems.

What You Need to Know

The programs described in this lesson help you to locate text and files in various ways. In addition, they give you the means to manipulate text and files for reporting, analysis, archiving, and other common tasks. The next lesson introduces you to the **sed** stream editing program, which is a more general-purpose test-manipulation tool than **grep**. Check your understanding of these points before moving on to Lesson 36:

☑ Use the **grep** program to finding text in files. The program prints all lines that are matched (or not matched) by a pattern. Also use **grep** with multiple filename arguments to identify files that contain common text.

☑ Filter data streams by using **grep** to select lines based on pattern matches.

☑ Locate files in the directory hierarchy by using the **find** command. The program locates files based on their external attributes.

Lesson 36

Stream Editing

In Lesson 35 you learned how to use **grep**, a specialized utility program, to locate text in files and to filter a data stream to select only records (lines) that match specified patterns. This lesson shows you how to use **sed**, a general-purpose stream-editing program. It encompasses the capabilities of **grep** and much more. The topics covered in this lesson include the following:

- Stream-editing principles and techniques

- The **sed** program

- Inline scripts

- Script files

- Stream editing examples

STREAM-EDITING BASICS

The **sed** program is a direct descendant of the **ed** editor program, so most of what you know about **ed** is applicable to **sed**. The fundamental difference between the programs is that **ed** is interactive and **sed** is not. It operates on named files or on a data stream obtained from input redirection or a command pipeline.

Most interactive editors place limits on the length of a line and the number of lines that can be edited. The limits vary from system to system, and they're usually quite large, but if you exceed them you're out of luck and have to resort to splitting the file and working on pieces. An advantage of stream editing is that you can edit files of any size.

> ### UNDERSTANDING STREAMS
>
> Recall that a stream is a visualization of a sequence of bytes as a flowing entity, like a stream of water. We have used the concept of a stream and its application in input and output service in discussions of the standard I/O streams and in the command pipeline discussions. Review Lesson 17 for the details of standard files and streams. Also, review the discussions of streams in Lesson 34 as they relate to filter programs—the **sed** stream editor is the quintessential filter program.

OVERLAP WITH THE *grep* PROGRAM

The **grep** program does one specialized part of the work that **sed** can do, so technically there is no need for **grep**. However, **grep** is a bit easier to use for the intended purpose of finding and substituting text strings. In addition, it is built into many shell programs that would have to be rewritten if it went away.

After you gain familiarity with the use of **sed**, you might find it instructive to convert some **grep** and **sed** commands to the alternative form. Such practice shores up your knowledge of syntax details and occasionally produces solutions that are easier to understand and use.

SYNTAX AND OPERATION

Let's get the formal stuff out of the way first. These next few paragraphs describe the command-line syntax of **sed** commands and the mechanics of its operation. Read this once to get familiar with the terminology and return to it after trying the examples presented in this lesson. Learning to use tools like this is similar to learning to play a musical instrument: it requires study and practice.

The general form of a **sed** command is

```
sed [-n] [-e script] [-f script-file] [file ...]
```

where the brackets indicate optional components. You instruct **sed** to edit lines read from a file or a list of files (named on the command line) or from a stream (obtained via some form of redirection). The original files are not modified in any way. The output of **sed** goes to your screen by default. You can capture that output to a file via output redirection and later copy the file back onto the original file(s) to effect permanent changes. The output of **sed** can also be sent to a command pipeline for further processing.

*Note: Do not use output redirection from **sed** to any file it is using for input: **sed** script filename > filename or **sed** script < filename > filename. In such cases, **sed** will overwrite the contents of its input file, causing the data the file contains to be lost. (The file is truncated to zero bytes before it is read.)*

The overall operation of **sed** is cyclical. The following sequence is repeated for each line of input:

1. Read a line of input into a *pattern space* (a buffer where the editing commands are applied to the text).

2. Apply all editing commands that select the pattern space (selection is based on addresses associated with commands).

3. Copy the edited pattern space to standard output and delete the pattern space.

Alterations to the sequence defined above occur in certain situations. For example, lines are not copied to standard output automatically if the -n option is specified on the command line. Also, certain commands, not described in this introductory treatment, copy the pattern space to a *hold space* and the reverse, and perform other advanced editing actions.

Editing scripts presented in the **sed** command line are called *inline scripts*. You can also package scripts into a file and tell **sed** to read the file by using the -f option. If you use only one inline script and no script files, the -e option is not needed.

When you experiment with simple stream-editing tasks, you are likely to use **sed** in shell command lines. Once you have a working script that is apt to be used repeatedly, you can package it in a shell script file (see Lessons 37 and 38) to make it easier to use. This lesson deals with **sed** only as a command typed interactively, although we use the -f option to read scripts from files in some examples.

Scripts for **sed** are composed of editing commands that have the following general form:

```
[addr [addr]] [!] action [arguments]
```

Each address is expressed in one of the following ways:

- A decimal line number (lines are numbered consecutively starting at 1 and accumulate across file boundaries)

- A symbolic reference to the last line (**$**)

- A context using **ed**-style regular expression notation (*/re/*)

Commands containing no addresses effectively select every pattern space. You can limit the effects of editing commands by specifying line ranges (**4,7***cmd*, for example) or specific lines (**3d**).

INLINE SCRIPTS

Given an empty editing script, **sed** simply passes lines of input through to the output without change. Use single quotes with nothing between them to specify an empty script. The following command works like a **cat** command. It reads from the named file and prints each line.

```
$ sed '' wisdom.txt ↵
Fear is the main source of superstition,
and one of the main sources of cruelty.
To conquer fear is the beginning of wisdom.

                    Bertrand Russell
$ ❏
```

You won't use **sed** this way, but it shows the essential behavior of copying input lines to standard output. Now let's apply a simple demonstration editing script that actually does something.

Using the same input file as in the previous example, the following command replaces the word "main" with "primary":

```
$ sed 's/main/primary/' wisdom.txt ↵
Fear is the primary source of superstition,
and one of the primary sources of cruelty.
To conquer fear is the beginning of wisdom.

                    Bertrand Russell
$ □
```

The script in this command performs a simple text substitution. When a line containing a match for the literal pattern "main" is found, the substitution is made. The default behavior of **sed** is to print all lines, whether substitutions are made or not, so you do not need to append a **p** command to force printing.

Figure 36.1 shows the same text file being processed to eliminate blanks line from the output. The figure depicts the way **sed** reads a line into the pattern space, edits it according to the script, and sends it in modified form to standard output. The script **/^$/d** matches lines that contain no text at all (matches initial and ending lines segments with nothing in between) and deletes any matching lines from the output stream.

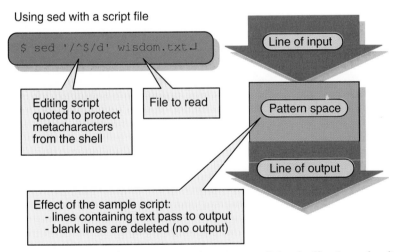

Figure 36.1 *The stream editor* **sed** *uses a pattern space as an editing buffer. It reads a line of input into the pattern space, performs any requested editing actions that affect the line, and sends the edited pattern space to standard output. This sample script deletes blank lines.*

The script is quoted to protect the metacharacters from processing by the shell. (To the shell, ^ is an old form of |, the pipe symbol, and $ retrieves the value of a variable.) By placing the metacharacters within quotes, the shell passes the characters exactly as they appear to **sed**.

The script has a flaw that might cause seemingly blank lines to escape deletion. Any space or tab in the line would cause /^$/d to fail because **sed** would not see the line as empty. Modify the pattern to /^[→]*$/d to solve the problem. The character class contains a space and a tab and combined with the closure operator *, matches any sequence of spaces and tabs, including none.

UNDERSTANDING THE SED PROGRAM

The **sed** program is a programmable filter. It is a general-purpose program based on the **ed** editor. Although a bit more difficult to use than **grep**, which does one specialized task— global search and replace, **sed** is a broad-based and powerful text manipulation tool.

The **sed** program takes a script or a set of scripts, each preceded by a -e option. The inline scripts presented to this point are single editing actions specified by using the standard editing commands together with literal text and regular expressions to form search patterns.

All lines read in by **sed** from a file or stream are edited according to the script(s) and sent to standard output unless a command such as **d** (for delete) removes them from the output stream.

SCRIPT FILES

If you have two or more editing actions to perform, use either multiple inline scripts (each preceded by a -e option flag). The following command gathers keyboard input and converts the strings "brn" and "brown" to the string "BROWN".

```
$ sed -e 's/brn/BROWN/' -e 's/brown/BROWN/' ↵
The quick brn fox ran into the brown house. ↵
The quick BROWN fox ran into the BROWN house.
$ ▢
```

You can also package editing scripts in a script file and tell **sed** to read the scripts by using a -f option. Figure 36.2 shows a **sed** command that reads lines from the file **story** and edits the lines according to the commands in the script file **convert**. The script contains the editing command **s/usa/USA/g**, which changes all occurrences of "usa" to "USA". It could contain other editing commands (represented by the ellipsis in the figure).

Specify your substitutions carefully. A problem with the sample script is that a word that contains the string of characters "usa" is also converted. Thus, the word "refusal" is converted to "refUSAl"— not good. Using the command

```
s/ usa/ USA/
```

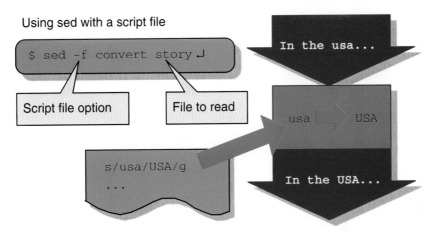

Using sed with a script file

$ sed -f convert story ↵

Script file option

File to read

s/usa/USA/g
...

In the usa...

usa → USA

In the USA...

Figure 36.2 The **-f** *option tells* **sed** *to read editing commands from a script file. The script file can contain comments (lines starting with* **#***), but it must contain at least one editing command.*

is an improvement, but not enough. A word like "usable" not at the beginning of a line or sentence is converted, so there's still more work to do.

What we really need is a way to match the pattern only if it stands as an isolated word. Recent versions of **ed** and **sed** and most versions of the **ex/vi** editor use the syntax \<*string*\> to do just that. Write the command as

```
s/\<usa\>/USA/g
```

to avoid unwanted conversions.

TURNING OFF AUTOMATIC PRINTING

The default behavior of **sed** is to print all lines that are not deleted from pattern spaces. This is effectively a **1,$p**, an **ed**-style action that prints the entire editing buffer.

At times, you may want to take complete control of the printing of lines to standard output. To do this, use the **-n** option on the **sed** command line. The following example shows how to extract lines containing the pattern **main** from the file **wisdom.txt** without automatically printing all lines:

```
$ sed -n '/main/p' wisdom.txt ↵
Fear is the main source of superstition,
and one of the main sources of cruelty.
$ □
```

Using sed with Redirection

If you run **sed** without naming a file or a set of files, it reads standard input, which is your keyboard unless input is obtained from some form of redirection. Here is an example of **sed** in a command pipeline. It receives the output of an **ls** command and prints the five lines at the head of the list. (When the output of **ls** is redirected, it is one entry per line, even if the default format is columnar.):

```
/usr/augie/test: ls | sed '5q ↵
LOST
callsign.1st
callsign.out
convert
f1
$ ▯
```

This example uses a **sed** command script that makes no sense in the **ed** editor, but it is perfectly acceptable for **sed**. The filter resulting from this use of the quit command when a particular line is reached provides this ability to glance at the first few lines of a file or stream.

When something like this is done often enough by enough users, you can be sure someone will make a standard program out of it. Just as there is a **tail** program for viewing the last few lines of a file or stream (we used it in examples in several earlier lessons), there is also a **head** program for viewing the first few lines of a file or stream (ten lines by default). The **head** program is coded in C and compiled, but the essence of the program is shown in the simple **sed** command pipeline you just read.

In the following example, **sed** edits text from the file **refer.txt** received by input redirection. The script matches every ending line segment, represented by the $ anchoring metacharacter, and inserts a newline character into the output stream.

```
$ sed 's/$/\↵
/' < refer.txt ↵

Overheard at a job interview:

...
touching, indeed, but do you have

anything else we could look at?

$ ▯
```

Figure 36.3 might help you visualize the process.

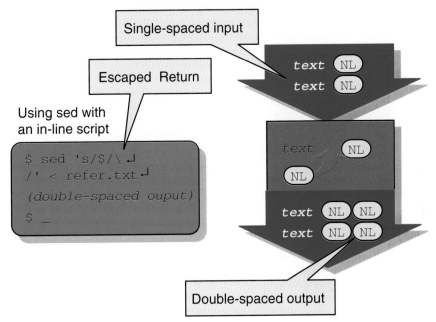

Figure 36.3 *The newline character is allowed in the replacement string of a substitution command, but it must be escaped to prevent ending the command early. In this example,* **sed** *matches the end of each line and inserts a newline character, effectively double-spacing the output.*

This is a little bit trickier than it looks. A regular expression never matches a newline character itself. Rather, it matches an ending line segment. Because no other characters are specified in the pattern, the substitution does not remove anything. It simply adds the newline character, which leads to another explanation.

The script uses an escaped Return to specify the replacement text. The command spans two physical lines, but it is logically a single line that contains an embedded newline character.

```
$ sed 's/$/\↵
> /' < refer.txt ↵
...
$ ▢
```

Why newline and not carriage return? When you press RETURN, the terminal device sends two characters: the carriage return (ASCII code 13 or CR), followed by a line feed (ASCII code 10 or LF). UNIX says "why use two when one will do?" and, on input, converts these pairs to the alternative ASCII definition of code 10, the newline or NL. On output to your screen or other device, UNIX translates NL to the equivalent CR/LF pair required by most physical devices.

Understanding Escaped Returns

As you learned in lessons throughout this book, the UNIX system buffers commands into lines. Nothing happens until you press RETURN. But if you need to insert a Return into the command, as in the previous example, you have to do something to prevent the Return from executing the command before it's completely keyed in.

One of the quoting mechanisms described in Lesson 15 is the use of single quotes surrounding the command-line items needing protection. The single quotes assure us that the entire script is passed to the program. Within the protected script passed to the **sed** program, if a Return is needed in the replacement text of a substitution command, it needs to be protected yet another time to prevent it from ending the command prematurely. The easiest way to do this is to use a \ ahead of the Return. The resulting command spans two physical lines, but it is logically a one-line command.

What You Need to Know

This lesson gets you started using **sed**. It is stream-editing program that is based on **ed** and encompasses the capabilities of **grep**. You will find that **sed** commands, especially those with complicated scripts, are usually best packaged in shell command files.

The next lesson introduces you to the joys of programming the UNIX shell, giving you the opportunity to extend your knowledge and use of **sed** and other UNIX utility programs. Check your understanding of the following topics before taking the plunge:

☑ The **sed** program is a non-interactive (batch) utility used for stream editing. It uses editing scripts to edit text streams on the fly. The original files are not altered.

☑ Inline editing scripts come from the UNIX command line. Protect special characters from the shell by enclosing inline scripts in single quotes. Use the -e option for each script if you use more than one or if a -f option is used.

☑ Scripts can also come from files. Use comments (leading #) to describe what the script does. Script files must contain at least one editing command.

☑ Stream editing scripts conform closely to the **ed** form with minor variations. The **sed** program uses the same regular expression syntax as **ed**.

Lesson 37

Shell Programming Basics

This lesson shows you how to write *command files*. Such files are often called *shell scripts* or *shell programs*. Don't let the terminology scare you off. The process of creating command files is not difficult, and developing the ability to create such files can greatly improve your productivity. The following topics are covered in this lesson:

- Installing your own command directory

- Updating your PATH variable to include your command directory and the current directory

- Creating your own command files and making them executable

- Running your command files

ADDING A PERSONAL COMMAND DIRECTORY

As you become familiar with how UNIX works, you will begin using more complex commands. As you will learn, typing long, involved command lines is a tedious chore, and you might yearn for shortcuts. In addition, you might find that you run certain combinations of commands repeatedly. At this point, you probably need to write your own *command files* to automate these repetitive tasks.

All of the commands you have run so far have executed programs from one of the system directories identified by your PATH variable. The default command directories are protected system resources. You are not allowed to put your own programs in them, yet you want the convenience of being able to run a program by typing only its name, regardless of what your current directory is. Otherwise, each time you run the command, you must type the command's full pathname.

Note: Unlike DOS, which always searches the current directory first (even if you don't want it to), UNIX searches only what you tell it to search.

To do this you need to set up your own command directory and add its pathname to your PATH variable. Your system administrator may have already done this for you, so check with him or her first. Use **ls** to see if there is a **bin**, **cmd**, **pgm**, **util**, or similarly named directory under your home directory. If so, see whether the needed pathname is part of the PATH string by using **echo $PATH**.

Here is an example taken from a new user's account, where such a directory has not been set up:

```
$ ls ↵
$ echo $PATH ↵
/bin:/usr/bin:/usr/ldbin
$ ▢
```

This account is pristine. No directories. No files. PATH shows only standard system directories for a pre-SVR4 UNIX system. The components of a PATH string are directory pathnames separated by colons. This account does not search a personal command directory. It doesn't search the current directory either. If you have a command directory and a pointer to it in PATH, you're ready to roll. Otherwise, use the following procedure to set up your log-in account:

1. Type **cd** to be sure you are in the home directory.
2. Use **mkdir** to create a **bin** directory and **chmod 755** to make it available to you for full access and provide read and execute access for everyone else:

```
$ mkdir bin ↵
$ chmod 755 bin ↵
$ ▢
```

3. Edit your configuration file (**.profile**, **.login**, for example) to add the pathname to PATH. If it contains a PATH assignment, add the required pathname to it. If there is no PATH entry, add one of the following form: **PATH=$PATH:$HOME/bin**.
4. Log off and log back on again.

Figure 37.1 shows a partial directory hierarchy that includes a **bin** directory. This directory becomes a repository for your own commands. You are not limited to one personal command directory. Set up several if you need special project command directories, but put them in the PATH after the system directories for security and performance reasons.

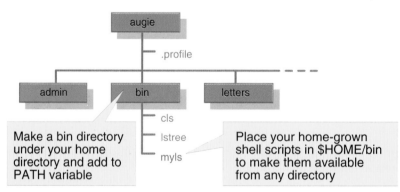

***Figure 37.1** Create a directory for commands under your home directory. The name **bin** (for <u>bin</u>ary) is traditional, but **cmd**, **pgm**, and **util** are also popular choices. In addition to creating the directory, you need to add its pathname to your PATH variable.*

CREATING YOUR OWN COMMAND FILES

With the preliminaries out of the way, it's time to get down to business. Think about the commands you type when you **cd** to a different directory. A **pwd**, perhaps, to be sure you know where you are. Then maybe an **ls** to see which files and directories are there. Just for the heck of it, you could also run the **du** command to see the amount of disk use in this branch of the directory tree.

You could issue these three commands separately, as shown here:

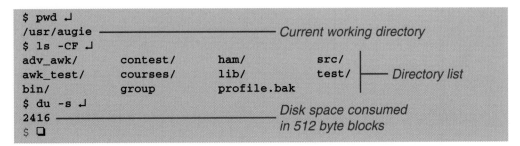

Notice how the commands and output are interleaved (command, output, command, output, ...). The options on **ls** produce a columnar listing (**C**) and file-type information (**F**). The file types and indicators are

- Ordinary file (none)
- Executable file (*)
- Directory (/)
- Symbolic link (@ on SVR4 and later)

The **du** program displays disk use in terms of 512-byte blocks (without regard to the actual block size on your disk). The **-s** option tells **du** to print only the summary (total blocks) for the named directory (. by default).

You have learned that you can write the commands all on one line if you separate them with semicolons. This produces a block of output without intervening commands, but you still have to type the three commands each time you want to use them:

```
$ pwd: ls -CF; du -s ↵          Three commands
/usr/augie ──────────────────── Current working directory
adv_awk/        contest/     ham/        src/
awk_test/       courses/     lib/        test/──── Directory list
bin/            group        profile.bak
2416 ──────────────────────────── Disk space consumed
$ ▫                              in 512 byte blocks
```

Packaging Commands in Files

Now let's make a shortcut command, your first shell script. (In the listings that follow, substitute your login name and chosen directory name for mine.) First you need to create a file that contains the commands to be executed, and then you need to mark it executable so it can run:

```
$ cat > myls ↵
pwd
ls -CF
du -s
(CTRL-D pressed here)
$ ▢
```

When the prompt returns, use **chmod** to set the required permissions (+x sets execute permission for all users). The surrounding directory listings show the effect of the mode change:

```
$ ls -l myls ↵ ──────────────────────────── View current permissions
-rw-r-----   1 augie     group        19 Jan 08 19:39 myls
$ chmod +x myls ↵ ──────────────────────── Make file executable
$ ls -l myls ↵ ──────────────────────────── View updated permissions
-rwxr-x--x   1 augie     group        19 Jan 08 19:39 myls
$ ▢
```

Now you're ready to test this shell script:

```
$ myls ↵
myls:  not found
$ ▢
```

What gives? The listing shows that the program is in the current directory, but it's not found. Why? Recall the earlier discussion of PATH variable and the need to specify the current directory in PATH. You'll need to add . to the PATH statement in your configuration file. (Append the characters :. to the end of the PATH statement, save, and restart to make the change take effect.) For now, just specify where the shell should find the program by using ./ before the program name:

```
                                    ── Current directory reference
                                    ── Command name
$ ./myls ↵
/usr/augie
adv_awk/        contest/       ham/            src/
awk_test/       courses/       lib/            test/
bin/            group          profile.bak
2416      .
$ ▢
```

Terrific. That's a lot easier to type than a string of commands, so you'll be more likely to use it. But there is one more step. The command needs to be in your command directory to be accessible to you at all times. Use the **mv** command to put the command in its new home:

```
$ mv myls $HOME/bin ⏎
$ □
```

UNDERSTANDING SHELL SCRIPTS

When you find yourself running a sequence of commands regularly, make a shell script to automate the process. If you haven't already set up your personal command directory, do so now using the procedure described earlier in this lesson. Then follow these steps to create a working shell script file:

1. Create the file of commands using an editor or by other means.

2. Set the mode of the file to executable (**chmod 755** *cmd_file*).

3. Move or copy the shell script file into your personal command directory.

After you have created the shell script and put it in the command directory, you can execute the file from anywhere in the directory hierarchy.

WHAT YOU NEED TO KNOW

A shell script is a file that contains the names of one or more commands. (DOS batch files are a limited form of UNIX shell scripts.) When you execute the shell script file (by typing the script filename), UNIX will execute each command the file contains. With one shell script under your belt, you'll find it easier to write other scripts. As you work, monitor the kinds of commands you run and think about ways to package sequences of commands that you run regularly. Write scripts and put them in your command directory for ready access.

The next two lessons wrap up this introduction to UNIX by showing you how to use the shell language and supporting features to your advantage. Review these topics before tackling the next level:

☑ Set up a personal command directory to provide a central repository for your command files (shell scripts).

☑ Edit the PATH variable in your configuration file to include your command directory (**$HOME/dirname**) and the current directory (.)

☑ Create command files, make them executable, and place them in your command directory for easy access by you and your associates (they need to add your command directory path to their PATH variables).

☑ Run your command files from anywhere in the file system simply by typing their names.

Lesson 38

Batch Processing with Shell Scripts

This lesson and the next show you the power and scope of the UNIX shell as a programming language. This lesson describes some of the important mechanisms of the shell that make it a powerful programming environment.

An exhaustive treatment of programming is beyond the scope of this book. The material presented here is intended to highlight important language features and entice you to investigate them on your own. The topics covered include the following:

- Shell programming language features
- Command substitution
- Parameter substitution
- Command exit status
- Command lists

THE SHELL PROGRAMMING LANGUAGE

The primary purpose of a user-interface shell is to act as an interpreter of your commands. The UNIX shells do that job well, sporting a wide range of features and capabilities that have been described elsewhere in this book. Thus far we have used the shell only in its limited capacity of a command interpreter. It's time to unleash the power hidden behind the calm exterior represented by the $ (%, #, or other) prompt.

Built into the shell is a full-fledged programming language. All of the tools you need to write programs are supported. The shell programming language includes the major components described in this lesson. For a formal description of the language, refer to the manual pages in the user documentation (command reference) for the shell you are using.

COMMAND SUBSTITUTION

Command substitution is an important feature of the shell. Commands inside of back quotes (grave accents as in `command`) are interpreted by the shell, and the standard output of the commands can then be used as all or a part of a word in other shell language constructs. Effectively, standard output of *command* replaces the quoted command string.

Note: *Be sure to use back quotes, not ordinary single quotes.*

The following example shows how the command substitution feature can be used to add variable information to messages. The basic command is an echo that prints a message containing the current pathname:

```
$ echo "Listing for `pwd`:"; ls -1 ↵
Listing for /usr/augie/test:
total 108
-rw-r-----   1 augie    group     15026 Jan 16 13:48 LOST
-rw-r-----   1 augie    group        49 Jan 11 17:22 callsign.1st
-rw-r-----   1 augie    group        44 Jan 11 17:23 callsign.out
-rwxr-xr-x   1 augie    group       127 Feb 02 05:12 chkargs
-rw-r-----   1 augie    group        16 Jan 29 12:55 convert
...
$ ▢
```

This example is typed on the command line, but scripts like this are usually packaged into shell script files. Take a look at the **myls** shell script in the previous lesson and see how you can modify it to use command substitution in a message, rather than the standard **pwd** invocation that it currently uses.

SHELL PARAMETERS AND SUBSTITUTION

A *parameter* is a storage location with an associated name. It stores a value that can be read and modified as a program executes. The shell maintains a set of parameters that are available for you to read and use in your programs. The shell supports two kinds of parameters:

- *Positional parameters* (the digits 0–9)
- *Keyword parameters* (also called a variables)

Generally, the value of a parameter is obtained by ${*parameter*}. The braces around the parameter name are needed only if the name is part of a larger sequence of characters in which the next character is a letter, digit, or underscore that is not intended to be part of the parameter name.

Other parameter substitution forms let you assign default values, based on whether a parameter is defined (exists and has a value). For example, ${*parameter:-altvalue*} uses the *parameter* value if it exists and is not null. Otherwise *altvalue* is used.

POSITIONAL PARAMETERS

The positional parameters that you can access directly are numbered 0 through 9. The values of command-line arguments are stored in positional parameters. Parameter 0 is set to the currently running program name when a shell starts.

To see the value stored in a positional parameter, use the **echo** command. (If you are using the KornShell, you can use the **print** command instead of **echo**.) To check the name of your login shell, for example, type this command:

```
$ echo $0 ↵
-sh
$ ▢
```

A preceding dash before the name of your shell (such as **sh**) indicates that it is an interactive shell. Any subshell that you start, either deliberately or as a side effect of something else you do, typically shows up as simply **sh** (or **ksh**, **csh**, and so on) indicating that it is a non-interactive shell.

You can use the **set** command to store values in the current shell environment. In the following example, **set** takes values from the output of the **date** command (**Fri Feb 04 12:00:00 PST 1994** in this example) and places the first entry (word) into $1, the second into $2, and so on, until it runs out of values to store. The two grave accents surrounding the **date** command obtain the program's standard output by command substitution. That output is used to form the argument list of the **set** command:

```
$ set `date` ↵
$ ▢
```

To see the effect of the command, use **echo**:

```
$ echo $1 ↵
Fri
$ echo $2 ↵
Feb
$ ▢
```

Positional parameters beyond 9 are available, but they can only be accessed by first shifting them into one of the numbered positions. The **shift** statement does that job. The **shift** statement moves positional parameters one position leftward. Positional parameter 0 (the program name) is not affected by **shift**.

To see the effect of **shift**, try this sequence of commands (using the same set of parameters obtained by the **set** command shown above):

```
$ echo $1 ↵
Wed
$ shift ↵
$ echo $1 ↵
Feb
$ ▢
```

Each shift overwrites the previous value of parameter 1 with what was in 2, 2 is overwritten by 3, and so on. If you keep shifting, eventually, all parameters except 0 are effectively shifted out of existence.

KEYWORD PARAMETERS

The environment variables, such as HOME and PATH (see Lessons 16 and 18) are *keyword parameters* that are used by the shell. The values of those variables are set by inheritance and by your configuration files(s).

You are free to name and use other keyword parameters, as long as you choose names that are not in conflict with any of the reserved names. Check your system documentation for a complete summary of the standard names and check local customs for names that may be reserved for specific uses related to your work.

Create your own keyword parameters by using an assignment statement of the form

name=value

where *name* is any identifier that is not reserved or already claimed for another purpose. This is the same method used to define any keyword parameter, such as the environment variables.

The one-character names listed in Table 38.1 are keyword parameters that are automatically set by the shell.

Parameter	Description
#	The number of command-line arguments (does not count the program name).
*	A list of all arguments to the shell (the program name is $0). "$*" looks like a single word with embedded blanks.
@	The same as $* except when quoted. "$@" expands to the list of supplied arguments, each as a separate field.

Table 38.1 These built-in shell parameters (also called variables) provide important data that your shell programs can use. (continued on next page)

Parameter	Description
-	Options supplied to the shell.
?	The exit status of the most recent synchronously executed command.
$	The process ID of the current shell.
!	The process ID of the most recently run background command (started with **&**).

Table 38.1 These built-in shell parameters (also called variables) provide important data that your shell programs can use. (continued from previous page)

The variables listed in the table are meaningful to standard UNIX programs and to your own programs. The shell modifies some of the values as it runs. Within a shell script, the values of these parameters can be used to check command-line syntax to be sure the user specified it correctly, to gather values from command-line arguments and use the program name in messages.

You can also use keyword parameters in command lines to add to or override the environment of a command. The **vip** program (**vi** with modified **p**rompting) is a useful example. If you use the visual editor, **vi**, you probably know that you can escape to a "permanent" subshell by issuing the :sh↵ command. This features lets you work on a possibly unrelated task, such as handling mail, and then return to the previous editing context.

This is a handy feature indeed, but there are potential problems. UNIX systems usually accept CTRL-D as way of terminating all programs, including the login shell. (Some UNIX shells have an **ignoreeof** or equivalent feature that prevents you from logging off accidentally.) You can't always tell by looking whether you are in your login shell or in a subshell. Pressing CTRL-D in a login shell logs you out, but in a subshell, it takes you back to your previous editing context..

Here is the **vip** program, which you might want to place in your own **bin** directory as an executable shell script:

```
$ cat vip ↵
: vip

env PS1="SUB> " vi $@
$ ▯
```

The script illustrates some useful points. The first line contains a : as the first character. To a standard UNIX shell, this is the null command, which doesn't do anything. The text that follows is the command's argument list, which is evaluated by the shell. In this usage, it is effectively just a comment telling readers the program name. However, it instructs the C shell to run the script as a standard shell script by invoking **sh** instead of **csh**. Doing so guarantees that the program will be understood by the shell.

The second line is blank. Use blank lines in your scripts to separate parts of your program. This tactic improves readability and costs only one character per line. Get into the habit of writing programs that are readable. You will save yourself and others a lot of trouble when it comes time to understand and possibly modify the program.

The third line of the script is the one that does the work. It consists of a parameter declaration that modifies the environment of an invocation of the **vi** editor. The parameter assignment **PS1="SUB> "** establishes the prompt that is to be used for each invocation of a subshell from within the editor. That gives you the information you need to know whether you are going to be logged off or returned to your editing session when you press CTRL-D.

The $@ following the **vi** command name is a means of passing all of the positional parameters presented to **vip** on to the **vi** program. This will result in any optional and filename arguments being passed to **vi** without processing by the shell script. You invoke **vip** just as you would invoke **vi** itself:

```
$ vip file ↵
(visual editing session starts)
```

COMMAND EXIT STATUS

Program exit codes, usually 0 for successful operation and nonzero to indicate a failure of some kind, are important to the shell. The exit code or *exit status* is used by the shell to implement the control features of the language.

The shell saves the exit status of the most recent synchronously run command in the ? variable. The value is available to you and to interested programs by using the $? notation. Programs that run other programs, such as the program development tools, accounting packages, and many others depend on this exit status to determine whether to continue processing or halt.

To see the effect, try this. Type a command that runs correctly, such as **date**, and then examine its exit status with **echo**:

```
$ date ↵
Tue Feb 01 22:05:07 MST 1994
$ echo $? ↵
0
$ ▫
```

The command ran successfully and the exit code of 0 reflects this fact. Now type a deliberately bad option and test again:

```
$ date blah blah ↵
date: bad conversion
Usage: date [ MMddhhmm[yy] ] [ +format ]
$ echo $? ↵
2
$ □
```

The program reports the problem to you in reasonable detail, and sends back an exit code of 2, which indicates an abnormal exit of a particular kind (bad conversion). The date program tried to convert the silly arguments into a date-and-time string and intelligently refused, after finding it unsuitable.

This discussion is intended primarily to show you the importance of providing valid exit codes in your programs. Adding the statement **exit 0** at the end of a script file returns a meaningful success value to the calling program (your shell for example). Any other value is taken to mean a processing error has occurred, as in the date program example.

COMMAND LISTS

A *command list* is a sequence of simple commands or command pipelines that are separated from each other by special list-separator symbols. Table 38.2 lists the command list separators and describes their effects.

Separator	Description
;	Execute the preceding pipeline sequentially (synchronous execution).
&	Execute the preceding pipeline in the background (asynchronous execution).
&&	Conditionally execute the following command list (success).
||	Conditionally execute the following command list (failure).

Table 38.2 Use these separators in a command list to define the relationships among the commands in the list.

The ; separator is described in Lesson 15, and the & symbol is described in Lesson 20. Two additional separators provide conditional execution of commands.

The **&&** separator causes the list that follows it to be executed only if the preceding pipeline has an exit status of 0 (success). The || separator inverts the sense of the test, so that the command list is executed only if the preceding pipeline fails (yields a non-zero exit status). Figure 38.1 illustrates these actions.

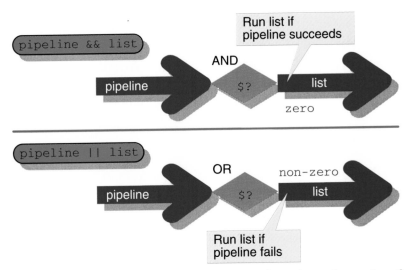

Figure 38.1. The && (AND) and || (OR) separators provide conditional execution of a list based on the success or failure of the preceding pipeline.

WHAT YOU NEED TO KNOW

This lesson describes and illustrates the primary features of the shell programming language, except for the control mechanisms (branching and iteration) and functions, which are described in the next lesson. Review these topics before moving on to Lesson 39:

- ☑ The UNIX shell is a complete and capable programming language. It has all of the need control features and attributes of an interpreted programming language.

- ☑ Command substitution provides a convenient means of extracting output from a command and using the output via substitution as part of other commands.

- ☑ Parameter substitution is the process by which values are extracted from parameters. Values can be modified automatically in various ways based on their initial values or the lack of values.

- ☑ Command lists are the primary means of expressing the actions of a shell script, and their exit status values control the flow of program execution.

- ☑ Program exit status provides an indication of the success or failure of programs.

Lesson 39

Using the UNIX Shell Programming Language

By now, you should have a pretty good feel for the shell programming tools at your disposal. The next step is to learn about the control features of the shell.

This lesson also describes a technique for programming that is widely used and generally applicable. In addition, examples of the program-development process are presented to give you more concrete demonstrations of it use. The topics covered in this lesson include the following:

- The control structures of the shell (selection and iteration)
- What programming is and how to go about doing it
- Techniques for developing and testing programs

CONTROL STATEMENTS

The normal flow of control through a program is sequential. A program consists of statements that normally execute one after another until none remain. A *statement* in shell language terminology is a command. The commands you can use include standard UNIX programs, your own shell scripts, and special commands that are built into the shell.

The sequential flow of program execution can be altered by selection statements, iteration statements, and by calls to subroutines (other programs or built-in functions).

Iteration statements include **while**, **until**, and **for** loops. Jumping backward to earlier commands creates a loop. Statements within the loop are run repeatedly, as long as a certain condition persists.

SELECTION STATEMENTS

Selection statements include several forms of **if** statements and a one-out-of-many branch statement called the **case** statement. Jumping forward in a shell script to bypass commands creates a branch—in effect, a fork in the road.

The flow chart, a convenient graphical tool for showing the steps of a process of any kind, is used in the figures in this lesson. The arrows show the direction of flow of control through a program or process. Each box represents a step to be performed. The diamond-shaped element represents a test that can have one of two or more outcomes.

The form of a simple **if** statement is presented in Figure 39.1, which shows the **if** statement in a script and illustrates the behavior by using a flow chart. The first list represents a simple command or a pipeline that produces an exit status. If the value of the exist status is 0 (logically true), the list of commands in the **then** clause is executed. Any other exit status causes the **then** clause to be bypassed. The list of commands is not executed.

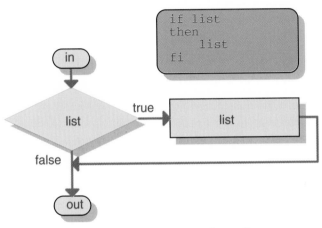

```
if list
then
        list
fi
```

Figure 39.1 *The simple **if** statement provides a way to conditionally execute a command list. If the first list yields a true (0) exit status, the list after **then** in the loop body is executed. Otherwise the list is skipped.*

An **if** statement must be closed by using the keyword **fi**, which is **if** spelled backwards. Visualize these keywords as bookends, holding the elements of the enclosed script together. Leaving out any of the keywords in the construct elicits an error message from the shell.

Notice the use of indentation that shows that the second list statement is subordinate to the **if** statement. Although indentation is not required by the language, you should use indentation to make your programs readable. If every line is jammed against the left margin, the program looks very dense and is difficult to read. Use the examples in this lesson as a guide to one style of indentation. Other styles are possible, of course. Choose one style and use it consistently.

Shell scripts often begin with an **if** statement that checks for errors on the command line and conditionally bails out if errors are found. The **test** command works in conjunction with **if**. The **test** command has many options that let you test for a variety of conditions. For example, this shell script fragment checks to be sure that the command received exactly two arguments (in addition to the program name):

```
# check command-line syntax
if test $# -ne 2
then
        # report failure
        echo Usage: $0 arg1 arg2
        exit 1
fi

# other code goes here

# report success
exit 0
```

The **test** feature (implemented as a separate program on some systems and as a built-in shell command on others) uses operators to specify the kind of comparison to be done. The **-ne** operator means "not equal." Other operators include **-eq** for equal, **-lt** for less than, **-z** for zero length string, and so on. Read the formal description of **test** in your command reference manual.

Each piece of the shell script is commented to describe its purpose. The shell accepts the # anywhere in a line to start a comment. A comment ends automatically at the end of the line it starts on. In the shell script, a comment describes the line or block of lines below it. In addition, you can use inline comments to put notes on individual lines if the code needs explaining, as it often does, because shell language constructs can be quite cryptic.

Put the script just shown into a file called **chk2**, mark it executable, and run it. Without arguments it produces the following output:

```
$ chk2 ↵
Usage: chk2 arg1 arg2
$ echo $? ↵
1
$ ▢
```

The message issued is helpful. If it had just said "wrong argument count," the user would be left to figure it out by trying various combinations of command and arguments. The usage message tells the user what program name to use and the number of arguments expected. It could be even more elaborate, specifying such things as minimum and maximum values for each argument, and other details.

The program also provides a nonzero exit status to the shell. This value can be used by the shell or other programs to control their actions. If **chk2** receives the expected number of arguments, it does nothing except return a successful exit status:

```
$ chk2 1 2 ↵
$ echo $? ↵
0
$ ▢
```

An optional third list, which provides an alternative command list for execution, can be placed in an **else** clause. This form of the **if** statement provides an either/or behavior, shown in Figure 39.2.

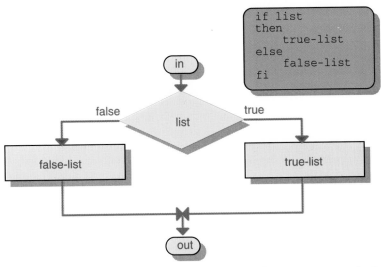

Figure 39.2 *Adding an **else** clause to a simple **if** statement produces a two-way selection between alternative command lists.*

You can put **if** statements inside of other **if** statements. This practice is called *nesting*. When an **if** statement is nested in the **else** clause of another **if**, you use the keyword **elif**, which combines **else** and **if** keywords. This leads to the general form of an **if** statement (items inside square brackets are optional):

```
if list then list
[ elif list then list ]
...
[ else list ]
fi
```

An **if** statement with multiple **elif** clauses produces a cascading effect much like a waterfall. This is a multi-way branch mechanism that selects one out of many possible paths. Control flows to only one of the clauses of the **if** statement and then passes to whatever follows the **if** statement in the script.

THE CASE STATEMENT (MULTI-WAY BRANCH)

Another decision-making tool, the **case** statement also provides a multi-way branch, but usually more efficiently than the cascading **if** statement. The form of a **case** statement is

```
case word in
pattern) list ;;
...
esac
```

in which the **word** is evaluated and compared to the pattern(s) associated with the lists. Control passes to first pattern that matches **word**, and the **list** is executed. The construct ends with **esac**, which is **case** spelled backward (another bookend pairing).

A catch-all case of * matches any pattern not matched by any other pattern ahead of it in the list of patterns. For this to work, therefore, the *) label must be last.

The following program fragment shows how a **case** statement can check command-line syntax within a program. If the user specifies an argument that is recognized, the **case** statement selects an appropriate response. Otherwise it issues a usage message:

```
: message.sh
# check command-line syntax
case $1 in
"hello")
        echo Hello, World!
        ;;
"goodbye" | "bye")
        echo "Goodbye, cruel world!"
        ;;
*)
        echo Usage: $0 [ hello | goodbye | bye ]
        exit 1
        ;;
esac

exit 0
```

The **$1** reference gets the value of the first command-line argument after the program name, and the **case** statement compares the value to its user-specified labels. The first match found causes the associated command list to be executed. Control then passes to the statement following the entire case construct.

Note: *The usage message gets the program name from $0 so that it always uses the name the program is called by even if someone has changed the name of the program.*

The "goodbye" case label contains an alternative pattern ("bye"). Use the vertical bar to separate alternative labels in a case label. A match to any one of the patterns causes that branch to be taken. The following example shows a hit and a miss:

```
$ message.sh bye ↵
Goodbye, cruel world!
$ mess*.sh ↵
Usage: message.sh [ hello | goodbye | bye ]
$ ▯
```

THE WHILE AND UNTIL LOOPS

If, instead of jumping forward in the script, we jump backward, we form a loop. The **while** and **until** statements are two of the standard shell loop statements. A **while** loop executes the enclosed list of commands as long as the controlling list is true (yields a 0 exit status). An **until** loop runs until the exit status becomes true. Figure 39.3 depicts the operation of a **while** loop.

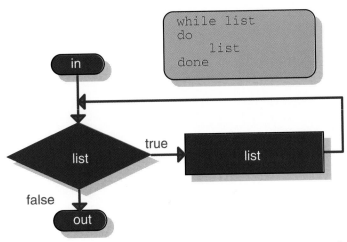

```
while list
do
        list
done
```

*Figure 39.3 A **while** loop executes the second list as long as the first (controlling) list yields an exit status of 0 or true.*

The **until** loop flow chart looks the same, except that the true and false labels on the decision box are reversed. The second command list is executed once for each iteration of the loop. If the first list is false immediately, the second list is not executed at all. The **toupper** program demonstrates the **while** loop. It reads text from the keyboard and converts all lessers to uppercase.

```
$ cat toupper ↵
: toupper
# Convert user input to uppercase text

while true
do
        echo "Input (No input means quit): \c"
        read text
        if test -z "$text"
        then
                break
        fi
        echo $text | tr [a-z] [A-Z]
done

exit 0
$ ▯
```

The word **true** in the statement **while true** is a standard UNIX command. It always returns 0. Another command, **false**, always returns a non-zero value.

THE FOR LOOP

The **for** loop has the form

```
for name [ in word ]
do
    list
done
```

The **for** loop executes the command list once for each name in **word**. The **name** variable is set in one of two ways. For each iteration of the loop, **name** is assigned the value of the next name in **word**. If no word is provided, values are obtained from the positional parameters (set from command-line arguments).

The following example shows a **for** loop that obtains its name values from command-line arguments. The program **linecount** uses **wc** to count the number of lines in each of the files named on the command line and reports the name and line count of each in a separate formatted message:

```
: linecount
# print the names and line counts for
# files named on the command line

for name
do
      count=`cat $name | wc -1`
      echo $name contains $count lines
done
```

The **name** value is used in two places in this script. The first use is in the assignment of a value to **count**. The second is in the message printed by **echo**.

By using command substitution, the count of lines is obtained and saved in **count**. The **wc** program with a -l option and a filename argument prints the number of lines and the filename. Without a filename argument, **wc** doesn't know the name, so it prints only the number of lines in the file. By piping the output of **cat** through **wc**, we get just the number of lines in the named file.

When this program runs with *.txt as a filename argument, it produces the following output on my system:

```
$ linecount *.txt ↵
indent.txt contains 4 lines
newfile.txt contains 5 lines
noble.txt contains 3 lines
...
words.txt contains 4 lines
$ ❑
```

As written, this program works correctly only with text files.

What Is Programming?

There is a technique to programming. Some programmers use it instinctively while most others have to work at it. The biggest problem for many programmers at all levels of experience is trying to write code (program statements) before they understand the problem and before they have a design for the solution. For simple programs, you may be able to do the planning in your head, but for programs of consequence, you need to be a bit more rigorous in your approach to programming.

The program-development process is succinctly described by the phrase *analyze-design-code-test* and depicted in Figure 39.4. All or part of the process is repeated based on test results until a working program pops out. Ignoring for the moment any possible shades of gray, the program either works or it doesn't. If it doesn't work, the reason could be a poor understanding of the problem or a misstep in design or coding. Jump back to the appropriate step and try again.

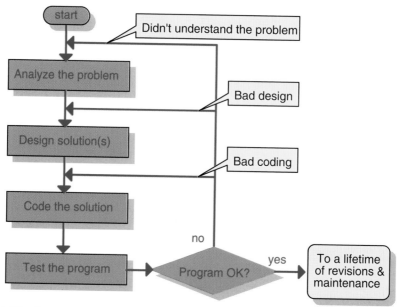

Figure 39.4 *The flow chart of the analyze-design-code-test cycle identifies the main steps in the program-development process. If the design phase produces a solution written in a high-level pseudo-code language, this method is suitable for coding a program in any computer language.*

Let's apply the methodology depicted by this flow chart to the design of a program that maintains a notes file. With such a loose description of the program, we need to sit down with potential users and shape a more precise description of what to build. Let's do that during the analysis step.

THE ANALYSIS STEP

Keep in mind that lurking behind every big problem are lots of little problems, many of which have already been solved by someone else. Don't be too proud to uses existing solutions to common problems. From the brief description, it would seem that editing might be necessary to allow for corrections to input errors. Here is the statement of the problem that might evolve from a discussion with users:

Write a program that does the following tasks:

1. Create and maintain one or more notes files. A global file in the user's home directory could be supplemented by named notes files in local directories. Use the global file unless another is named on the command line.

2. Put a date and time stamp ahead of each new note. Append notes to the end of the file.

3. Use the **vi** editor or the editor specifically named in the EDITOR environment variable. Someone might actually prefer to use **ed**.

THE DESIGN STEP

Designs are best described in *pseudocode*, a mixture of human and computer language constructs. It is a high-level language that hides details of any particular language, yet it clearly expresses what must be done in each step. Low-level languages deal with the gory details of how things are done, such as moving bytes into and out of memory. High-level languages deal with broader, more general themes, such as how to read a file, without getting the programmer involved with the details of how it is done. Use indentation to show *subordination* of statements or steps:

```
check number of command-line arguments
if none
    use the global notes file
else if one argument
    use named file
else too many args
    print error diagnostic and quit

if editor preference specified in a variable
    use preferred editor
else
    use the vi editor

append date/time stamp to the notes file
start editor at the end of the file

end program
```

This description mixes human and computer languages to describe the problem from a high-level point of view.

The Coding Step

Once you have a good description of a solution in pseudocode, the solution can be coded (programmed) in almost any computer language with relative ease (provided, of course, that you know how to "speak" the language). In this lesson, we use the standard UNIX shell programming language, the Bourne shell, **sh**, for the coding step.

The coding sample that follows introduces several features of the UNIX shell that are explored in detail elsewhere in this lesson. View this code as an example of what a shell program looks like and learn the details later. The KornShell (**ksh**) can run this shell program, too, but the C Shell (**csh**) uses a different vocabulary and syntax, so it cannot run the program as is.

Create a file called **notes.sh** with the following contents. This is one way to code the example from the description. You could use different programs and different statements to achieve each objective. A program that works correctly is a good one, just as any landing you can walk away from is a good one.

```
: notes.sh
# Use the vi editor or one specified by the EDITOR
# variable to update a notes file. Use the global
# notes.txt file under home unless an argument names
# another to use.

# check command-line syntax
case $# in
0) # use default notes file
        NOTESFILE=$HOME/notes.txt
        ;;
1) # use the specified name as a note repository
        NOTESFILE=$1
        ;;
*) # too many arguments
        echo Usage: $0 [ notesfile ]
        exit 1
        ;;
esac

# append a note to the file (default or named)
echo "\n----- `date` -----\n" >> $NOTESFILE
if test "$EDITOR" = "vi" -o -z "$EDITOR"
then
        # use vi at end of file
        vi + $NOTESFILE
```

```
else
        # accept default editor
        $EDITOR $NOTESFILE
fi

exit 0
```

The use of command substitution in the **echo** command conveniently inserts the date and time stamp into the middle of a line of dashes used as a banner. The **\n** sequences cause new-line characters to be printed before and after the banner line. The program user starts editing by issuing any command that enters text input mode.

In the test for an editor, the **-o** option means OR. The exit status of test seen by **if** is 0 (true) if the EDITOR variable is set to **vi** or is not set at all. In either case, the **vi** editor starts at the end of the file. If the test fails (non-zero exit status), EDITOR must be set to something other than **vi** and the starting position for editing and data is determined by the editor.

The purpose of the + option in the **then** clause is used by previous versions of **vi** and supported by the most recent releases for compatibility. The new practice is to use **-cG** instead of + for this purpose. The **-c** option runs a command, and the command **G** seeks the end of the file (**$G** or just **G** means goto last line).

THE TESTING STEP

To test the program, mark it executable and run it in the current directory. You may need to use **./** in front of the program name if you haven't added the current directory to your PATH. See Lesson 37 if you haven't attended to this detail. Given no arguments, **notes.sh** adds your note to the global notes file:

```
$ notes.sh ↵
(editing session runs)
$ □
```

After you leave the editor, you can view your notes with **cat**, **pg**, and so on:

```
$ cat $HOME/notes.txt ↵
----- Wed Feb 02 12:38:24 MST 1994 -----
This is the first of a series of brilliant notes about nothing.

----- Wed Feb 02 12:39:00 MST 1994 -----
And here's the second.

----- Wed Feb 02 12:40:18 MST 1994 -----
Last note. I'm putting me out of your misery.
$ □
```

You might not need encouragement to do this, but you should deliberately misspell commands, leave off comment delimiters, and introduce other errors into a program like this (relatively short and simple) to see what kind of error messages the shell issues. You will find that they're not always immediately helpful, but they usually point you in the right direction if you learn how to interpret them.

WHAT YOU NEED TO KNOW

Shell script writing is an excellent way to develop programs. The shell language is high-level and very compliant. UNIX developers often code prototypes of applications in shell scripts. Eventually (sometimes never), the program might be rewritten in a compilable language, such as C, to make it run faster or to protect its secrets from prying eyes. In this chapter, you have learned the following:

- ☑ Use the control statements (selection and iteration) to alter the normal sequential flow of control and statement execution in your shell scripts.

- ☑ Use any standard UNIX programs, your own shell scripts, and other programs as subroutines in your shell scripts.

- ☑ Learn and apply a technique for developing and testing programs that forces you to think before you code program statements.

Index

Q

R

S

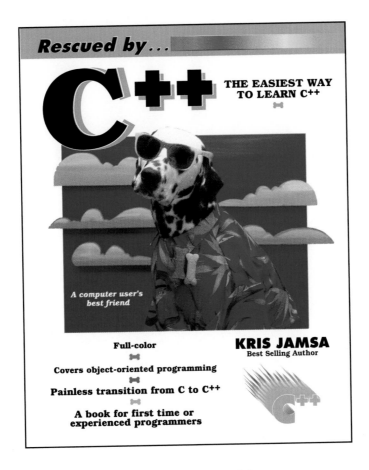